*Margins of Precision*

# Margins of Precision

## ESSAYS IN LOGIC AND LANGUAGE

### MAX BLACK

*Professor of Philosophy*
*Cornell University*

### Cornell University Press

#### ITHACA AND LONDON

*First published 1970*

International Standard Book Number 0-8014-0602-1
Library of Congress Catalog Card Number 75-128369

PRINTED IN THE UNITED STATES OF AMERICA
BY VAIL-BALLOU PRESS, INC.

*To Samuel, Christina,
and Matthew*

Dawle jyiduh joenchiueh de bianyuan,
yeujow faan'erl youyuh-chiilai le.
(At the margins of precision, the universe wavers.)
—*Hu Hsai*

# *Preface*

I HAVE here assembled about half of the essays I have published since the appearance of my last collection, *Models and Metaphors* (1962), choosing those that have aroused most controversy or those published in places sufficiently obscure to escape attention. The essay on Dewey was written earlier but, to judge from correspondence, still has some interest. As in the past, I have chosen topics where there is still work to be done. May others do better.

Permission to reprint has kindly been given by the editors of books and journals in which these essays first appeared. (Full details are contained in "Additional Notes and References" at the end of the book.) My thanks are due to Professor Y. R. Chao for translating the epigraph, and to Mr. Michael Whalley for valuable help in preparing the book for publication and making the index.

MAX BLACK

*Ithaca, New York*
*March 1970*

# Contents

# I

# *Reasoning with Loose Concepts*

A MAN whose height is four feet is short; adding one tenth of an inch to a short man's height leaves him short; therefore, a man whose height is four feet and one tenth of an inch is short. Now begin again and argue in the same pattern. A man whose height is four feet and one tenth of an inch is short; adding one tenth of an inch to a short man's height leaves him short; therefore, a man whose height is four feet and two tenths of an inch is short. In this way, it seems, we can reach the absurd result that a man whose height is four feet plus any number of tenths of an inch is short. For, if the first argument is sound, so is the second; and if the second, so is the third; and so on. There appears to be no good reason for stopping at any one point rather than at another; it is hard to see why the chain of arguments should ever be broken. But the conclusion is ridiculous; it is, for example, preposterous to say that a man whose height is seven feet is, nevertheless, short.

The argument I have presented is an example of an ancient type of sophism, sometimes known as the "heap" (*sōrites*) or the "bald man" (*falakros*). Although the sophism has been known for over two millennia, I have been unable to find an altogether satisfactory explanation of the fallacy committed.

Cicero's account of the *sōrites* runs as follows:

No faculty of knowing absolute limits has been bestowed upon us by the nature of things to enable us to fix exactly how far to go in any matter; and this is so not only in the case of a heap of wheat from which the name is derived, but in no matter whatsoever—if we are asked by gradual stages, is such and such a person a rich man or a poor man, famous or undistinguished, are yonder objects many or few, great or small, long or short, broad or narrow, we do not know at what point in the addition or subtraction to give a definite answer [*Academica* 93, H. Rackham, tr., *Loeb Library* (1951), p. 586].

On the authority of Diogenes Laertius (II, 108), the original form of the argument, ascribed to Eubulides, is said to have run as follows:

Isn't it true that two are few? and also three, and also four, and so on until ten? Two however are few. So also ten are few.

In the variation known as the *falakros* (*Hor. Ep.*, II, 1, 45) it seems to have taken the form, How many hairs must be torn from the head to produce a baldhead?

All these arguments depend upon gradual variation of some magnitude—the number of grains in a heap of corn, the number of hairs on a man's head, the length of a body, and so on—in a series of cases in which, as we commonly say, it seems hard to "draw a line." The fallacy dies hard. It is not uncommon to be faced with the peremptory demand, "Where do you draw a line?"; we are then confronted with the same sophism.

On being asked where he would draw the line, a judge is said to have replied, "Wherever I shall think it proper and fitting to draw such a line." But any arbitrary division between long and short, rich and poor, is bound to seem unsatisfactory to anybody who has felt the force of the gradual progression. According to Cicero, it was the policy of Chrysippus, when questioned step by step, "to come to rest," i.e., to make a halt at some point. Cicero represents Carneades as retorting, "So far as I am concerned, you may not only rest but even snore; but what's the good of that? for next comes somebody bent on rousing you from slumber and carrying on the cross-examination: 'If I add 1 to the number at which you became silent, will that make many?'—you will go forward again as far as you think fit." He continues: "Why say more?

[2]

for you admit my point, that you cannot specify in your answers either the place where 'a few' stops or that where 'many' begins; and this class of error spreads so widely that I don't know where it may not get to" (Cicero, *loc. cit.*). Cicero adds, "If you have a solution of the problem and won't reply, that is an arrogant way of acting, but if you haven't, you too don't *perceive* the matter" (Rackham tr., p. 587).

My aim is to "perceive the matter," to understand clearly what is wrong with the sophistical argument. I shall consider and criticize some of the solutions that have been offered and I shall outline what seems to me to be the correct answer.

It will be convenient to telescope the entire chain of arguments into a single argument, in the following way:

Every man whose height is four feet is short.

Adding one tenth of an inch to a short man's height leaves him short.

Every man who is shorter than some short man is short.

*Therefore,* every man is short.

Here, I have supplied the premise, "Every man who is shorter than some short man is short," in order to include the cases of men whose heights are not exact multiples of a tenth of an inch. For convenience of reference, I shall call this compressed form of the sophism the *sōrites* argument.

The choices of four feet to start with, and one tenth of an inch for the increment, are obviously immaterial: any initial height that is *clearly* short would serve, and any increment, no matter how small. We need a *small* increment, of course—the smaller the better—if the argument is to be persuasive. There is nothing startling in the idea that an increase in height of two feet might convert a short man into a tall one. But we can reach a cumulative increase of two feet (or any other amount) if we accumulate a sufficient number of minute increases.

The conclusion of the *sōrites* argument is false, so something must be wrong with the premises, or with the reasoning, or with both together. If not, it would be easy to generate a contradiction by producing a parallel argument. We might

[3]

start with the new premise, "Every man whose height is seven feet is tall," and then, by using the supplementary premise, "Subtracting one tenth of an inch from a tall man's height leaves him tall," obtain the conclusion, "Every man is tall." This second argument has the same form as the first; if either is sound, so is the other. But it is self-contradictory to affirm that every man is both short and tall.

We may as well begin our examination of the *sōrites* argument by conceding its *validity*. For the pattern of reasoning is the familiar and unimpeachable one known as "mathematical induction." *If* every man having a certain height is short, and *if* the height of a short man can always be increased by a tenth of an inch without his ceasing to be short (and *if* a man shorter than a short man is short)—if all of these are true, every man *must* be short. Now when we have a valid argument with a false conclusion, we know that at least one of its premises must be rejected.

Of the three premises used in the *sōrites,* the third, which I added as a supplement, "Every man who is shorter than some short man is short," is a necessary truth, and above suspicion. Again, it is pointless to challenge the first premise, "Every man whose height is four feet is short." Perhaps you think it not absolutely certain that a man whose height is four feet is short; but then you must admit that some man— a midget perhaps—is short, and if you do so, and also accept the remaining premises, you will be forced to admit that *every* man is short. The argument purports to show that if *any* man is short, *every* man is short; and the parallel argument purports, with equal plausibility, to show that if *any* man is tall, *every* man is tall.

We seem driven, therefore, to reject the remaining premise, i.e., to reject the assertion, "Adding one tenth of an inch to a short man's height always leaves him short." I shall call this the *inductive premise*. The negation of the inductive premise can be expressed as follows: 'There is a certain height, $h$, such that a man of that height is short, while a man

[4]

of height $h$ plus one tenth of an inch is not short." Let us now modify this last statement to read as follows: "There is a certain height, $h$, such that a man of that height is short, while a man of height $h + \delta$ is not short, no matter how small $\delta$ may be." This last statement is, of course, a generalization of the negation of the inductive premise. Were this generalization true, I would propose to say that the concept of being short is *sharply bounded* or, alternatively, that it has a *sharp boundary*. In general, to say that some concept, $C$, is sharply bounded will mean that some state of affairs is an instance of $C$, while another state of affairs, differing as little as we please from the first, is an instance of not-$C$. Any concept that is not sharply bounded I shall call a *loose* concept. A more common label, which I myself have used in the past, is "vague concept," but this may be misleading and has pejorative implications that I want to avoid.

My examination of the *sōrites* seems to have driven me to deny what I called the "inductive premise." And since the same result would have emerged from replacing the increment of a tenth of an inch by any other increment, no matter how small, I seem to have been driven to saying that the concept of being short is sharply bounded, i.e., that there is some critical height, $h$, such that a man of that height is short, while a man who is taller by even the slightest amount is not short.

I say I seem to have been "driven" to this position, because the result is quite absurd. We know enough about our uses of the word "short" to be certain that there is no critical value for its application. Any sensible person who was asked to specify the *precise* height at which a man ceased to be short would quite properly regard the task as impossible. And if we offered a number of persons some special inducement to draw a definite line between short men and others, at what seemed to them an appropriate place, it is quite certain that we should get conflicting answers. The "line" would be "drawn" in different places by different persons, all equally competent to judge, and even the same man would

[5]

draw the line in different places on different occasions. There is obviously no way of resolving these fluctuations of usage by appeal to a dictionary or to some other authority. A standard meter is still kept in Paris, but nowhere in the world shall we find a standard short man preserved in a Bureau of Standards. Our concept of being short is *intended* to be loose, is intended to have no sharp boundary. Anybody who thought it possible to *find out* the point of transition between short and not-short would be making a mistake about the present uses of the word "short." The question, "How short is short?" has *no* answer.

So I seem to have landed in the uncomfortable position of being unable to affirm the inductive premise (because that would commit me to holding that all men are short) and unable to deny it either (since that would imply that the concept of being short is sharply bounded). Must I then reject the venerable principle of excluded middle? It is important to notice that the difficulty is not confined to words such as "short," "tall," "bald," and "rich," which would generally be conceded to be fluctuating in their application and hence "vague" in some pejorative sense. The very same difficulty can be made to arise in connection with any concept used to make an empirical statement. We might call a concept *empirical* if the assertion that at least one instance of that concept exists is a contingent empirical statement. So far as I can see, all empirical concepts are "loose" in the sense which I have explained.

I shall now examine briefly some of the more plausible suggestions that have been made for disposing of the *sōrites* argument. Anybody confronted with the *sōrites* argument is apt to retort that the puzzle arises from deficiencies in the concept of being short. If we had worked instead with the comparative concept of being shorter, it might be said, the puzzle would not have arisen. But this is an evasion, not a solution. If we employed concepts other than those used in the argument I have presented, the paradoxical conclusion might not arise. But rejecting the argument in favor of some other

[6]

argument does not tell us what was wrong in the original argument. Nor would an argument using the comparative concept be exempt from similar difficulties. We would hardly be prepared to say that a man whose height was one hundredth of an inch less than that of another man was really shorter. And if so, a similar argument leading to a paradoxical conclusion could easily be constructed.

Perhaps the most radical solution is due to Russell, who once said, "All traditional logic habitually assumes that precise symbols are being employed. It is therefore not applicable to this terrestrial life, but only to an imagined celestial existence" ("Vagueness," *Australasian Journal of Philosophy,* 1 [1923], 88). Anybody who agreed with Russell would presumably argue as follows: The *sōrites* uses the imprecise word "short"; traditional logic is applicable only when precise words are used; hence, traditional logic does not apply to the *sōrites*. But notice that this very argument uses "imprecise words" and must therefore itself be exempted from the application of "traditional logic." Does this mean that *no* standards of logical appraisal are applicable? Does it mean that a conclusion contrary to Russell's would have been just as good from a logical point of view?

The allegation that traditional logic is "not applicable" to reasoning with loose concepts might mean that no question of logical validity can arise in connection with *any* such reasoning; or it might mean that reasoning with loose concepts, while sometimes correct, is not controlled by "traditional" logical principles.

Consider, first, the drastic proposal to exempt all reasoning with loose concepts from logical appraisal. The resulting policy is tantamount to *forbidding* such reasoning. For if any conclusion whatsoever can be drawn from given premises, there is no point in drawing *any* conclusion. Now if all empirical concepts are loose, as I think they are, the policy becomes one of abstention from *any* reasoning from empirical premises. If this is a cure, it is one that kills the patient. If it is always wrong to reason with loose concepts, it will, of

[7]

course, be wrong to derive any conclusion, paradoxical or not, from premises in which such concepts are used. But the price exacted is too stiff. We need to be able to draw recognizably valid inferences from empirical premises if the fact-stating uses of language are to be maintained. Otherwise, a man would be allowed to affirm a proposition and its negation in the same breath, without embarrassment or need for explanation. Plainly, this will not do. Unless we are entitled to infer from the truth of "Tom Thumb is short" to the falsity of "Tom Thumb is not short," both statements will lose their power to convey information. A policy of prohibiting reasoning with loose concepts would destroy ordinary language—and, for that matter, any improvement upon ordinary language that we can imagine.

But if Russell intended to condone the use of loose concepts in inference (which I rather doubt), he must have envisaged the applicability of *some* rules of logical appraisal, possibly unconventional. If "traditional logic" leaves us in the lurch, because it works only in heaven, we shall have to turn to some mundane code to help us. We shall still have to invoke some "terrestrial logic" to explain the fault in the *sōrites*. But "terrestrial logic" makes no more sense than "Rumanian mathematics," and is at best a picturesque label for an evasion. Yet even Frege seems not to have seen this when he said that "a concept that is not sharply defined is wrongly termed a concept." (P. Geach and M. Black, eds., *Translations from Frege* [1952], p. 159). Of such alleged concepts, which would be "loose" in my sense, Frege goes on to say that they "cannot be recognised as concepts by logic; it is impossible to lay down precise laws for them" (*ibid.*). Frege therefore apparently agrees with Russell, and the same objections can be leveled against both.

One might hope to escape the absurd consequences of the *sōrites* argument, without modifying "traditional logic," by recognizing a division of the class of men, with respect to the concept of being short, into three, rather than into two, sub-

[8]

classes. It is at least a plausible suggestion that we should distinguish between men who are clearly short, men who are clearly not short, and the remaining men who are neither clearly short nor clearly not short. The last of these subclasses is commonly said to consist of "borderline cases" which jointly occupy a "fringe" or "penumbra" or "no man's land." This way of looking at the relation of the concept to its instances is valuable in understanding the role of loose concepts. But it is easy to see that it does not disarm the *sōrites* sophism.

Let us call a man who is within the penumbra with respect to the concept of being short, i.e., a man who is neither clearly short nor clearly not short, a "middle-sized" man. It will be remembered that what I called the "inductive premise" runs: "Adding one tenth of an inch to a short man's height leaves him short." Now that we have divided men into those who are short, those who are middle-sized, and those who are not short, we must reject the inductive premise. For the addition of one tenth of an inch to *some* man's height will convert him from being short to being middle-sized, i.e., will change him from being a clear case of a short man to a borderline case. But, as before, the formal denial of the inductive premise will imply that there is some height, *h,* such that the slightest increase in height above *h* will convert a man from a clear case of being short to a borderline case. In other words, we shall be forced to recognize a sharp boundary between the clear cases and the penumbra. This is unacceptable for the reasons I gave earlier in this paper: it is a feature of our use of a loose concept, such as that of being short, that there is no determinate point at which a transition from a clear case to a borderline case occurs. Whether we call men on the far side of the line that the puzzle requires us to draw "not-short" or "middle-sized" makes no difference. The force of the sophism is that it half persuades us, against our better judgment, that we *must* draw a sharp line—though all the time we know it would be absurd to do so. Increasing

[9]

the number of "lines" from one to two—or, for that matter, to some larger number—will not help us to see how we can reasonably avoid drawing any line at all.

Now it might be said that the disagreeable consequences of the *sōrites* are brought about by our tacit or explicit adherence to the principle of excluded middle. Frege said: "The law of excluded middle is really just another form of the requirement that the concept should have a sharp boundary" (*loc. cit.*). We feel that on being asked of a given man whether he is short, we have no option except to say either "Yes" or "No." (I have tried to show that admission of borderline cases does not help.) But if the use of the principle of excluded middle leads to absurd consequences, perhaps we ought to contemplate modifying that principle. Instead of saying flatly, "Every man is either short or not-short," perhaps we ought to consider saying, "Every man is either short or not-short, unless he is a borderline case." Upon expansion, this becomes, "Every man is either short or not-short, unless he is neither clearly short nor clearly not short." There is some suspicion of circularity here. I am tempted to say that the *criterion* for a man's being a borderline case with respect to the concept of being short is that the law of excluded middle does not apply to him. If this is right, the amended form of the law reduces to the useless triviality, "Every man is either short or not short—unless he is neither the one thing nor the other." On the other hand, if there is an independent criterion for a man's being a borderline case with respect to the concept of being short, we shall be back to the case of a trichotomy (say into "short," "not-short," and "middle-sized").

I am inclined to think that any such attempt to modify "traditional logic" makes the mistake of confusing the unstated conditions for the application of a rule of logic with a supposed deficiency in the rule itself. Anybody who thought it was a rule of English spelling that *I* always comes before *E* would be making a mistake, because he had omitted the exceptions—the correct rule must run "*I* before *E* except after *C*." But the borderline cases do not constitute *exceptions* to the rule of excluded middle; they are simply *irrelevant* to it. Whenever the rule can be used, it requires us to choose between a statement and its negation; but like any other rule, it may simply fail to fit the case in hand. The rule of excluded middle is intended to apply to statements having one or other of two determinate truth-values, but the rule itself leaves the conditions for its proper application to the judgment of its users.

I am now tempted to say that the rules of logic *presuppose* application to clear cases, though without *mentioning* any such restriction. In learning how to use logical principles in connection with ordinary concepts, I suggest, we have to understand the general agreement that only *determinate* statements shall be held subject to the rules. (Similarly, the principles of geometry are intended to apply only to *rigid* bodies; precise concepts are to logic, one might say, as rigid bodies to geometry.) It follows that whenever we use logical principles in reasoning with loose concepts, we must be on the alert for gradual slides into indeterminacy.

Let us apply this idea to the *sōrites* argument. I must reject the inductive premise—not on the ground of its falsity, but rather on the ground that it illegitimately bundles together proper and improper instances for the concept of being short. Am I therefore bound to agree that there is some determinate height, *h,* such that the addition of even one tenth of an inch converts a man from being short to being not-short? I think not. If I am led step by step along the slippery slope of the argument, a point will eventually come at which I *judge* that I can no longer properly say either that the man is short or that he is not-short. (Not that any radical change has occurred in the situation I am talking about: all that distinguishes the borderline man from his neighbor is that he is a trifle shorter.) I stop whenever I judge that my words are ceasing to work properly, without supposing that this implies any discontinuity in what I am talking about. Just as the sharpest knife eventually fails to cut, so even the best-defined empirical concept eventually fails to

[11]

discriminate—and there is nothing surprising about that. I have to *decide* where to call a halt (influenced, of course, by the practical or theoretical interests at stake) just because there are not and cannot be any *rules* for stopping.

I believe this is the right line to take, but it still needs some modifications. To insist that logical principles shall never be used except in connection with clear cases seems to me too severe a limitation. If I tell you to hand a book to the short man, in a situation in which there are only two men, one five feet tall and the other six inches taller, it would be pedantic to retort that I was abusing language. Here, the use of the concept elicits a definite response with respect to an instance that would elsewhere be judged "borderline." Sometimes, again, variations in the boundary of a loose concept are immaterial to the truth of a statement. If I say, "Short men usually marry short women" you may agree in the light of the evidence, even though you might draw the line more tightly than I do. For the principle might remain true, no matter where the line was drawn.

The correct view seems to be about as follows: In using a loose concept, I must know that there are instances that are indisputably "clear" and must be able to recognize such cases; and I must also be able to recognize "borderline cases." I must understand that the use of the customary logical principles presupposes an *ad hoc* demarcation, somewhere in the region of cases that are not indisputably clear; and, finally, I must understand that there are no rules for drawing such lines. Provided I understand all this, I may properly use a loose concept and reason with it, even at times about cases which are not indisputably clear.

The view I have been sketching requires us to reject both the inductive premise and its negation as illegitimate. Indeed, the demand that we choose between the two is already improper, because it treats the situation as if it were one in which the rules of the language enforced such a choice. When I play chess with a child, we may allow one another to "take back" bad moves. If we used the privilege too often, the game would be impossible to play; but if we retract a move only occasionally, the whole affair is quite feasible. Suppose an onlooker insisted that there must be some exact number of moves which was the most that either of us was entitled to take back. He would be wrong. The game we were actually playing allowed us to take back *any* number—provided they were not *too many* in number—and the looseness of the understanding was part of the game. To insist that we *must* specify the number is to try to make us play some other game. Now the same can be said about the *sōrites* argument. The man who presents it to us is trying to get us to use loose concepts as if they were strict; and our answer must be that we do not use our concepts in that way.

It follows from what I have been saying that reasoning with loose concepts will often demand judgment and vigilance. We run the risk of using the rules of logic *blindly,* assuming too easily that we are in sufficient accord with our hearers. If the presumption proves mistaken, we must blame not formal logic, but ourselves. To argue that the *sōrites* shows that something is wrong with logic would be like maintaining that the coalescence of raindrops reveals an imperfection of simple arithmetic.

# II

# *The Justification of Logical Axioms*

WHEN somebody asks us to justify the use of a rule of inference, the demand is sometimes intelligible and readily satisfied. I shall be contrasting such straightforward requests for justification with the more puzzling one in which, for instance, a philosopher asks for a justification of *modus ponens.*

A lecturer makes a statement of the form

(1)                    If $p$ then (if $q$ then $r$)

and immediately transforms it into the corresponding statement of the form

(2)                    If $q$ then (if $p$ then $r$).

He is then challenged by a member of his audience to justify his use of the rule employed. This is a clear case of a legitimate request for justification of a rule of inference.

Strictly speaking, we should always speak of justifying the *use* of a rule or a principle: considered by itself, a rule of inference is either correct or not, and from this standpoint all correct logical rules are equal. A question of justification arises when we want to know why somebody or anybody is entitled to *use* the rule. For the sake of brevity, however, I shall sometimes speak in the usual way of justifying the rule itself. My remarks can easily be adapted to fit the justification of principles, though I shall not discuss them explicitly.

Let the rule for transforming 1 into 2 be called $R$. When asked to justify my use of $R$, I need to know the point of the request, for unless I know where the shoe pinches I can do nothing. Without further specification, a call for justification is no better than a demand for *some* kind of defense,

[14]

and might plausibly be met by any number of responses.

When the questioner has not previously met the rule $R$, he may simply doubt whether it does invariably transform true statements into true ones. So he may be asking only to have this doubt dispelled. One way of doing so would be to appeal to authority. I might argue as follows:

All competent logicians use $R$.

Rules of inference used by all competent logicians are correct.

*Therefore, R* is correct.

While this might in fact dispel a doubt about $R$'s correctness, there would be something unsatisfactory about the response. Were I myself to accept the rule only on the authority of competent logicians, I would indeed have justified the rule to the best of my ability. But since the premises of the syllogism do not express my own reasons for trusting the rule, there would be a kind of deception or evasion in offering the syllogism as an answer.

I can do better than appeal to authority. By reminding the questioner of the truth-tables for material implication and by actually computing the truth-values for expressions of the forms 1 and 2, I can show directly, without appeal to extraneous authority, that the rule is correct. I have then offered my own reasons for accepting the rule, and there is no deception. Here is a clear case of the justification of a rule of inference.

The second procedure may be held to show *why* the rule is correct in a way in which the first procedure did not. It can therefore be used when the questioner, while not doubting that the rule is correct, because he trusts the lecturer perhaps, still wishes to understand why it is so.

In such clear cases, the justification is an argument, and so itself involves the use of rules of inference. Let us call it a *deductive justification.* A deductive justification would be pointless if the premises, definitions, and rules it employs were not acceptable to the questioner to whom it is addressed. So, a necessary condition for a deductive justification to work is the existence of a certain fund of premises, definitions, and rules of inference, equally acceptable to both questioner and answerer. The questioner's fund consists of items that he treats as unproblematic, i.e., as needing no justification in the given context, though he may wish to demand their justification on another occasion. Given a knowledge of my questioner's fund, my task of deductive justification is the determinate one of producing a proof from given premises by means of given rules of inference. Though I know no mechanical procedure for solution, I know in advance what counts as success. I know what I am seeking, even if I fail to find it.

Imagine now a justification seeker who announces that he will refuse to allow the use of any rules of inference whatever. It would be preposterous for him to pretend that he in fact accepts no logical rules at all, so he must be willfully refusing his interlocutor to employ rules that are unproblematic for both parties. In the face of such a demand, it would be folly to offer a deductive justification. To do so would be as absurd as proposing to play chess with an opponent who refuses to allow the pieces to be placed on the chessboard. Now it sometimes looks as if a philosopher who asks for a justification of *modus ponens* were setting this absurd task.

But are there no cases where we are justified in saying or doing something in the absence of any possible proof that what we are saying or doing is right? It seems that there are. I might say, for instance, "There's a rainbow over there!" and if you objected, reply, "Look for yourself." Here, I rely upon a fact, not an argument from true premises, and I might be said to have been justified in what I originally said, to have had a valid title, as it were, solely because the fact obtained. Similar considerations apply to so-called sense-datum reports. Asked to report what I see (in a familiar restricted sense of "see"), I may reply, "A red patch on a white background" (call this statement S). In the sense of justification first considered in this paper, it is impossible for me to justify my saying *S*. An argument from my veracity and intention to speak the truth would be as irrelevant as the argument from authority previously considered. I feel I ought to cite a certain fact as my title for saying *S*, only the peculiarity of the case is that I cannot communicate the title to another. If I say, "The reason why I said I saw a red patch on a white ground was that I really did see it at the time," I am merely repeating myself and not improving my case. Since I was supposed to be making a sense-datum avowal, any elaboration is pointless. I propose to say that a man who truthfully produces a sense-datum report has a *warrant* for what he says.

There is an impressive philosophical tradition, extending from Aristotle to Franz Brentano and beyond, that claims the possibility, indeed the necessity, of providing a warrant for logical and mathematical truths. The position is dominated by a supposed analogy between vision and an alleged process of "mental insight," characteristically expressed in a metaphorical terminology of "evidence," "intuition" (Latin: *intuere*, to look), "the light of reason," "clarity," "distinctness," and so on. So it is that Locke, to take but a single example, can say that "intuitive knowledge" is "irresistible, and, like bright sunshine, forces itself immediately to be perceived, as soon as ever the mind turns its view that way; and leaves no room for hesitation, doubt, or examination, but the mind is presently filled with the clear light of it" (*Essays*, Bk. 4, Chap. 1, Sec. 1).

Here Locke is conceiving of the certification of a simple necessary truth, such as that one and two make three (one of his own examples), as a kind of *perception*, or at least as something sufficiently akin to perception for the language of vision to be appropriate. The mind "perceives the truth" of the simple arithmetical proposition, he says, "as the eye doth light, only by being directed towards it." Let us recall our former example of the man seeing a red patch. There we had the speaker making a sense-datum report *because* a certain sense-datum fact obtained. And now, when somebody affirms that one and two make three, not mechanically, but in full awareness of what he is saying, there is supposed to be a strict analogy. There is supposed to be an event, metaphorically described as "perception" of the truth of the arithmetical proposition, which is the thinker's ground or reason or warrant for holding that one and two make three. On this view, anybody who affirms that one and two make three is justified by a certain mental fact, although he cannot use that fact to convey an intelligible justification to another person. Here, as in the sense-datum case, there is nothing better to do than to "look for oneself."

The supposed analogy between vision and "mental insight" must be rejected. When a proposition is called "self-evident," the intended meaning is that the proposition in question shall contain its own truth-ground. (The old sense of "evidence" that is relevant is approximately "that which makes the proposition true," and the later sense in which "evidence" is always evidence *for* something is not in point; no rationalist has wanted to subscribe to the absurd view that any proposition can be evidence *for* itself.) A self-evident proposition is self-certifying, has its warrant engraved upon its own face, as it were. It follows that to understand a proposition of this sort is already to be in possession of all that is relevant to its truth. Thomas Reid said self-evident propositions "are no sooner understood than believed" (*Essays,* Woozley, ed., p. 358), but the correct formula is, rather, that understanding a self-evident proposition necessarily includes *knowing* the proposition to be true. There are not two things, first understanding the proposition and then seeing it to be true by the "light of reason"; *in* understanding it, we necessarily know it to be true, and if we have any doubt we could not have understood what we thought we were doubting. There can be no suspension of belief about a self-evident proposition.

Now we can see why the supposed analogy between vision and "mental insight" or intuition breaks down. When a man claims a private title for his perceptual report, there is a logical gap between a certain perceptual fact and another

[18]

fact consisting of his saying that he has the perception in question: he could see the red patch without saying that he saw it. And unless there were such a gap, there would be no sense in his claiming to have a title or ground for his assertion. The implied existence of a distinct truth-ground is essential to the whole conception. But precisely this feature of vision proper is intended to be absent in the case of "mental vision." Since the truth-ground of a self-evident proposition is intended to be included in that very proposition, understanding and verifying here collapse into one and the same thing, and it no longer makes sense to speak of having even a private justification or title.

Having now eliminated any possibility of justifying such a rule as *modus ponens,* which I shall continue to use as an example, it seems that the correct verdict must be that it makes no sense to ask for a justification in such cases. But what is to be done if somebody asks for such a justification apparently in good faith? Certainly it might look as if a genuine question was being asked and that something better than a refusal to answer was demanded.

Various cases deserve to be distinguished. In one type, the questioner's own practice in drawing inferences would show that he does not conform to the rule in question. Presented with concrete arguments with premises of the forms $p$ and *If p then q* respectively, he either refuses to draw the conclusion, $q$, or insists on drawing some contrary conclusion. This would be decisive evidence that he does not use the expression "if . . . then" in our way. For we have no better way of determining whether a man understands the expression in the usual way than by observing how he uses it in inference. Should this type of case arise, the correct answer to a request for justification of *modus ponens* would be to inform the questioner that he does not use "if . . . then" in the standard way. And should he then ask. "Well, *how* is it used?" the best we can do is to provide clear cases of our usage. "You see that $p$ is true and *If p then q* is true. Therefore, $q$ is true. *That* is how we use 'if . . . then.' " In teaching, the practice provides no

[19]

*reason* for using "if . . . then" in the standard way, and so provides no justification. In using the rule, I do not do so *because* the rule is used in that way—I simply use it, without a reason or justification. So, our production of typical uses of the rule should be regarded as indoctrination, rather than as argument. I *teach* the other man to follow the rule, and my end is achieved if he comes to accept it in his practice. And if he doesn't after all, there is nothing more to be done.

I have been arguing that use of *modus ponens* in standard ways is a criterion for understanding the standard use of the expression, "if . . . then." The point may be reinforced by considering how we would determine, in the case of some connective in a foreign language, whether it was to be taken as synonymous with "if . . . then." A decisive way of settling the matter would be to determine whether the users of a language did in fact unhesitatingly make the transition from premises of the form $p$ and $pXq$ (where $X$ is the expression whose synonymity with "if . . . then" is being tested) to $q$. If we found that they failed to make the transition from $p$ and $pXq$ to $q$, or sometimes made the transition to something incompatible with $q$, we would have conclusive evidence that it would be wrong to translate $X$ by "if . . . then."

The second type of case is one where the questioner does use the rule in his practice, but declines to affirm it. (Perhaps he wishes to be cautious and thinks he is not entitled to affirm the rule as being correct in *all* cases.) There seems to be nothing to do but to remind him, by appeal to his practice, that he *does* accept it and might as well recognize that he does.

We can imagine him saying, "I know that $p$ is true, and I know that *If $p$ then $q$* is true; but why *must* I say that $q$ is true?" The proper answer is that there is no "must" about the case. I have assumed that he understands the use of "if . . . then" and hence *does* make the transition to the appropriate conclusion without hesitation. The correct reply is, "If you consider what you do, you will recognize that you *do* draw the conclusion. There is no interval between considering and understanding the premises and wondering whether you have to accept the conclusion. *In* affirming the premises, you thereby affirm the conclusion." The language of necessity here is as inappropriate as it would be in the absurd question, "Why must I write the initial letter 'a' when I write the word 'apple'?" In writing the word, I do write its initial letter; or to put the matter in another way, the expression "writing a word without writing its initial letter" stands for nothing that could occur. So the idea that we might have had a choice of doing something else but for some restraint is an illusion. Similarly, the form of words, "Understanding and accepting premises of the form $p$ and *If $p$ then $q$*, but not accepting the corresponding proposition of the form $q$" describes nothing at all. And again, the idea that there might have been something else to be done, which the reasoner is prevented from doing, is an illusion.

Finally, consider the case in which a *philosophical* question about the justification of *modus ponens* is raised. After hearing all that I have now said, a philosopher is apt to feel that the processes of inference admittedly in use have been made to appear arbitrary or even irrational. He may agree that I have correctly described our practice (indeed there can hardly be any serious question about *that*) and still feel that unless some philosophical support for the practice can be provided, there will be no reason for priding ourselves upon our rationality. And the chances are that he will label the view I have been defending as an extreme form of "conventionalism." It would take me too far afield to defend myself against this charge. Perhaps it may be sufficient to say here that a capacity to adhere to simple patterns of inference such as *modus ponens* is one of our criteria of rationality. If a man affirms $p$ and also *If $p$ then $q$* (and so, according to my view, thereby affirms $q$) but proceeds as if $q$ were false, and perhaps even persists in so doing after we have drawn attention to his reasoning, we rightly treat him as irrational. But it would be an extraordinary use of language if we said that a man who used *modus ponens* without any reasons was behaving irrationally. For if there are not and cannot be any reasons, it would be irrational to seek them. The charge of irrationality is better leveled against those who persist in demanding reasons, of a sort they cannot specify, in cases where there is good reason to hold that there cannot be any reasons.

As to a possible charge of conventionalism, I may point out that it is no part of the view I am presenting that *modus ponens* is "true by convention" or something of that sort. For if there can be no question of *choosing* to adopt the rule, as I have been contending, there can be no question either of adopting a convention or coming to an agreement that the rule shall hold. If conventionalism means to imply such a choice, or agreement, or convention, its very formulation involves a logical absurdity. Far from advocating a form of conventionalism, then, I am denying that any form of conventionalism can make sense.

To sum up: I have been arguing that an apparent request for justification of *modus ponens* has to be met, not by an answer, but by a demonstration that the question is illegitimate. The question has to be *dismissed,* and if possible in such a way as to convince the man who raised it in good faith that it is proper to dismiss it. To the man who has not mastered the use of "if . . . then," we try to teach that use by example; to the man who expresses absurd scruples about affirming the rule, even though he is in fact committed to using it, we try to show that these scruples are absurd, by showing that the counter-instances it envisages (*p* and *If p then q,* but possibly *not-q*) cannot be expressed without absurdity; and as for the philosopher who still demands some ultimate ground or justification for logic, we must try to persuade him that not everything needs or can need justification, and that to recognize the application of this truism to certain simple logical rules or principles does not commit us to any form of dogmatism, or conventionalism.

[22]

# III

# *The Gap between "Is" and "Should"*

IT HAS often been held that ethical statements cannot follow from premises consisting exclusively of statements of fact. Thus Karl Popper once said:

Perhaps the simplest and most important point about ethics is purely logical. I mean the impossibility to derive [*sic*] nontautological ethical rules—imperatives; principles of policy; aims; or however we may describe them—from statements of facts. Only if this fundamental logical position is realized can we begin to formulate the real problems of moral philosophy, and to appreciate their difficulty.[1]

Popper would presumably wish to make a similar claim about all nonfactual statements: like many other philosophers, he believes that only statements of fact can follow from statements of fact. This is the contention that I wish to examine in what follows. I shall try to show that there is a good sense in which some statements about what should be done do follow from factual premises.

Contemporary writers, such as R. M. Hare [2] and P. H. Nowell-Smith,[3] who agree with Popper, usually quote a fa-

[1] *Aristotelian Society Proceedings,* supp. vol. 22 (1948), p. 154.

[2] Hare says: "Popper rightly refers to the rule as 'perhaps the simplest and most important point about ethics'" (*The Language of Morals* [Oxford, 1952], p. 31). In Hare's treatment, the autonomy principle takes the special form that no imperative conclusions can be validly drawn from premises that do not contain at least one imperative (p. 28).

[3] Nowell-Smith says that an argument from factual premises to an ethical conclusion "must be illegitimate reasoning, since the conclusion of an argument can contain nothing which is not in the premises, and there are no 'oughts' in the premises" (*Ethics* [London, 1954], p. 37).

mous passage from Hume's *Treatise*.[4] Hume maintains that
all the moralists he knows make an imperceptible transition
from observations about human affairs or assertions about
the existence of God, all expressed with "the usual copula-
tions of propositions, *is* and is *not*," to normative conclusions
"connected with an *ought* or *ought not*." He says that this
transition is "of the last consequence" and needs to be explained: "it is necessary . . . that a reason should be given
for what seems altogether inconceivable, how this new relation can be a deduction from others, which are entirely
different from it."

As a tribute to the remarkable influence this passage has
exerted, I propose to assign to the principle that only factual
statements can follow from exclusively factual statements the
title "Hume's Guillotine." By "factual statements" here and
throughout, I mean such as can be expressed by sentences
whose copula is "is" or "is not" but cannot be expressed by
sentences containing "should," "must," "ought," and so forth.

It is not clear whether Hume is intending to offer an argument or is merely insinuating skeptical doubts.[5] Considered
as argument, what he says is singularly unconvincing. He implies that it is fallacious reasoning to introduce into a conclusion "some new relation or affirmation," expressed by
"ought" or "ought not," that is "entirely different" from the
relations or affirmations occurring in the premises. The
strength of his position depends upon the interpretation that
is given to the expression "entirely different"; "ought" is
different from "is," of course, but if Hume thought this was

---

[4] *A Treatise of Human Nature*, Bk. 3, Pt. 1, Sec. 1.

[5] In his paper "Hume on 'Is' and 'Ought,' " *Philosophical Review*, 68
(1959), 451–468, A. C. MacIntyre argues against the customary interpretation of Hume's remarks. He contends that Hume was only raising
a *question* about the derivation of an "ought" from an "is," which is
subsequently answered affirmatively in Hume's own ethical theory. I
side with MacIntyre's critics in holding this reading to be unsound in
spite of its ingenuity. See R. F. Atkinson and M. J. Scott-Taggart in
*Philosophical Review*, 70 (1961), 231–244; also Antony Flew and Geof-
frey Hunter in *Philosophy*, 38 (1963), 178–184.

sufficient to disqualify the "ought"-conclusion, he himself was committing an error of reasoning. The sense of "entirely different" that Hume needs is one in which $A$ counts as entirely different from $B$ when and only when a statement containing $A$ cannot be logically derived from premises containing $B$, but not $A$. Now whether "ought" is entirely different from "is" in this sense is the very question at issue. Hume, if taken to be offering an argument, is assuming what needs to be established, namely, that an "ought" can never be derived from an "is."

Why are modern readers predisposed to endorse Hume's Guillotine? One reason may be the widespread but mistaken view that no term may occur in the conclusion of a valid argument unless it occurs, or can be made to occur by suitable definitions, somewhere in the premises. If "valid argument" meant the same as "valid syllogism," the view would be correct—but it is easily shown not to be so in general. Consider, for instance, the following simple argument. A citizen is a person; therefore a married citizen is a married person. Here the word "married" occurs for the first time in the conclusion, yet the argument is valid as it stands, without benefit of suppressed premises. One obstacle to the recognition of this elementary point is an unfortunate but popular metaphor of the conclusion being "contained" in the premises.[6] But there is no useful sense in which the conclusion of a valid argument can be said to be "contained" in the premises; that is merely a misleading way of saying that the conclusion really does follow from the given premises, without the addition of supplementary assumptions.

It is in fact quite easy to show that some kinds of "ought"-statements, *pace* Hume, really do follow from "is"-premises. Consider, for instance, the following valid argument:

[6] It is interesting to find G. E. Moore in his *Commonplace Book* (London, 1962) taking "$p$ contains $q$" to mean that $p$ is a conjunction having $q$ as one of its conjuncts (p. 342). Upon this literal construction of the metaphor of "containing," it is not surprising that Moore speedily concludes that $p$ can entail $q$ without containing it.

Vivisection causes gratuitous suffering to animals.

Nothing that causes gratuitous suffering ought to be done.

*Therefore,* vivisection ought not to be done.

From this argument, we can easily derive another valid argument proceeding from "is" to "ought":

Vivisection causes gratuitous suffering to animals.

*Therefore,* if nothing that causes gratuitous suffering ought to be done, vivisection ought not to be done.

And in general, "If $A$ then $B$" entails "If $B$ ought not to be done, $A$ ought not to be done." [7]

Although this example may serve to discredit the dogma that an "ought" is never derivable from an "is," I do not attach much importance to it and shall not rely upon it in my argument. For when "If $B$ ought not to be done, $A$ ought not to be done" is entailed by "If $A$ then $B$," the former statement will serve no useful purpose in an ethical argument. Our only reason for asserting it will be our knowledge of the truth of the factual statement "If $A$ then $B$" from which we can derive any consequences that follow from the trivial ethical statement that it entails.[8] (Contrast a nontrivial ethical hypothetical such as "If something ought to be done, one ought not to boast of having done it," whose truth is not guaranteed by a corresponding factual hypothetical.) I shall say nothing more about cases in which the "ought"-conclusion is complex, because I want to discuss the more fundamental case in which the normative conclusion is free from sentential connectives.

A second reason that may predispose modern philosophers to accept Hume's Guillotine is the view, more popular in our own time than in his, that "ought"-statements make no truth claims at all and are therefore disqualified to serve either as premises or as conclusions. I take it as certain, however, that

[7] For further examples of this sort, see A. N. Prior, "The Autonomy of Ethics," *Australasian Journal of Philosophy,* 38 (1960), 199–206.

[8] I owe this point to J. M. Shorter. See his article, "Professor Prior on the Autonomy of Ethics," *Australasian Journal of Philosophy,* 39 (1961), 286–287.

we can reason, for example, from expressed to unstated orders, which I choose as undoubtedly having a primary function other than that of making a truth claim. From the orders "Answer questions on every page" and "Initial page on which questions are answered," I can infer the unstated order "Initial every page." The conjunction of the first two orders logically implies the third, in the sense that it would be impossible to obey the first two orders and not to behave *as if* one were obeying the third, unstated, order.[9] We can exhibit logical relations between orders—or, for that matter, between promises, resolutions, and so forth—which are the same as, or at least closely analogous to, the familiar relations of implication, equivalence, compatibility, and the like, that are involved in all arguments.

With these preliminaries out of the way, we should now be able to take a fresh and unprejudiced look at Hume's Guillotine.

To those who claim the existence of an unbridgeable logical gap between "ought" and "is," I offer for consideration the following counterexample:

Fischer wants to mate Botwinnik.[10]

The one and only way to mate Botwinnik is for Fischer to move the Queen.

*Therefore,* Fischer should move the Queen.

I am assuming that these statements refer to some game in progress.

Here, it seems to me, both premises state matters of fact, while the conclusion is a nonfactual "should"-statement. (An "ought"-statement might have been used instead, the differences between "should" and "ought" being immaterial here.)

---

[9] Of course, there is more to *obeying* an order than performing the action prescribed by it. Cf. the recent discussion, "Imperative Inference" by B. A. O. Williams and P. T. Geach, *Analysis*, 23 (supp., 1963), 30–42.

[10] One might wish to qualify the premise to read "Fischer wants to mate Botwinnik, *if that is possible,*" but there is no point in the addition and the subsequent discussion is in any case unaffected.

I hope it will be agreed that the first premise, "Fischer wants to mate Botwinnik," is factual. The relevant sense of "what" is that of actively wanting, as it were—being in a state of already taking or being set to take the necessary steps to achieve the end in question—not a free-floating desire, wish, or aspiration.[11] Were Fischer himself to make the corresponding first-person utterance, "I want to mate Botwinnik," he might perhaps be taken to be expressing only a resolution to achieve the end and so to be making no truth claim. But the third-person statement used as a premise in the example is a straightforward statement of fact about Fischer, supported by the usual sort of evidence about human behavior.

Anybody wishing to deny that the example discredits Hume's Guillotine will probably contend that the correct conclusion is really factual. He might say that the proper conclusion should run "Fischer's best move is the Queen move" or, perhaps, "The one and only way in which Fischer can win is by moving the Queen," both of which statements are "factual" in the broad sense in which that term is here being used. The objection might run that the conclusion of my counterexample really follows from the premises only if that conclusion is itself given a factual interpretation.

For example, Professor Von Wright, in his recent paper on "Practical Inference," [12] argues in just this way. He considers the following "practical" argument:

*A* wants to make the hut habitable.

Unless *A* heats the hut it will not become habitable.

*Therefore*, *A* must heat the hut.

He asks whether the argument is "valid," even though *A* may be unaware of the practical necessity of the action to be performed. Von Wright replies:

[11] Cf. G. E. M. Anscombe: "The wanting that interests us, however, is neither wishing nor hoping nor the feeling of desire, and cannot be said to exist in a man who does nothing towards getting what he wants" (*Intention* [Oxford, 1957], p. 67).

[12] *Philosophical Review*, 72 (1963), 159–179.

The answer depends upon how we interpret the "must." If we understand the phrase *"A* must heat the hut" *to mean the same as* "unless *A* heats the hut, he will fail to attain some end of his action" or to mean the same as "there is something *A* wants but will not get, unless he heats the hut," then the answer is affirmative [p. 164, italics added].

Thus Von Wright manages to certify his practical inference as valid only by interpreting its conclusion as factual. I agree that if we are asked what we mean by saying that so-and-so "must" do such and such, or "should" do such and such (the differences between the meanings of the two words being unimportant here) we should sometimes answer in the way that Von Wright has claimed. But I disagree with his implication, if it is intended, that in so doing we should be giving *the meaning* of our "must"-statement.

If I say to someone, "Do your best," he might ask me whether I meant "Work as hard as you can, without worrying about success," and I might reasonably agree that I did mean that—but the alternative forms of words do not mean the same. To say what the speaker meant may be only to specify the implications of his utterance in a given context. Now, "must," "should," and similar words used with normative force in practical inferences are highly schematic and admit of various specifications in alternative contexts; but to admit this is not to concede that the "must"-statements are synonymous with their appropriate specifications—nor is it to concede that the meaning of "must" varies from context to context.

I wish to argue that the "should"-conclusion of the counter-example is not intended to be merely another way of saying that the best move is such and such or that the only way the player can achieve his end is by making that move. My object is to stress the distinctively performative aspect of the utterance "Fischer should move the Queen," while trying to show that the "should"-statement, so understood, without reduction to its factual implications in context, still follows from the premises.

[29]

In saying that there is a performative aspect to saying "Fischer should move the Queen," I mean that a speaker who uses this form of words counts as doing something more than, or something other than, saying something having truth value.[13] He is not just saying something that is true or false, but is doing, and counts as doing, something more than that. But what does such a speaker count as doing when he makes a "should"-statement? An adequate account of the linguistic act in question, involving an examination of the various interrelated functions of "should" (in the special kinds of contexts relevant here), would make for too lengthy a digression.

The beginnings of an answer might, however, be obtained by taking the second-person use, *"You* should do such and such," as primary, in the hope of explaining the first- and third-person uses in terms of their relations to that second-person use. It is plausible to hold that the prime function of the second-person formula is to urge the hearer to adopt a course of action selected by the speaker as preferable, optimal, or correct. That the implied valuation of the courses of action available to the hearer is subordinate to the urging function can be seen in the following way. The speaker's evaluation of a selected action as preferable or obligatory gives him a reason for urging his hearer to perform that action. Now, contrary to what is sometimes said, there seems to be no linguistic violation in urging a man to do something, even when the speaker has no reason with which to back the recommendation.[14] There is no linguistic or conceptual impropriety about saying, "I feel you should do *A*, though I can't give you any reason why you should." It might be said that the use of the second-person "should"-formula normally arouses a presumption that the speaker has reasons for saying

---

[13] I am drawing here on Austin's discussion of performatives. See Chapter 10.

[14] Thus Charles E. Caton says, " 'ought'-judgments are logically a kind of statement which must be supportable by reasons . . . if he [the speaker] cannot give reasons, he should hesitate to reiterate his assertion or should retract it" (*Philosophical Quarterly,* 13 [1963], 150).

what he does, but since the same might be said about any kind of statement whatever, this cannot be a distinctive peculiarity of the meaning or function of "should." A further presumption is that the speaker normally wants his hearer to do what he says that he should do, but this presumption, like the one concerning the existence of supporting reasons, can be defeated in special circumstances. If I have bet heavily on your losing the game of chess in which you are engaged, I shall not want you to win, but if you ask my advice and I see that you can win by moving the Queen, I am still required to say, "You should move the Queen."

Consider the following sequence of possible utterances:

"The one and only way in which you can mate is by moving the Queen."

"Your best move is the Queen move."

"You should move the Queen."

"Move the Queen."

The first of these is a neutral, nonperformative comment on the situation, while the last is a straightforward imperative—a forthright verbal push: the "should"-utterance stands between these, as a sort of hybrid, implying an evaluation based upon matters of fact, but partaking also of the imperative force of the bare incitement to action. According to circumstances, the use of the "should"-utterance would count as advising, inciting, admonishing, urging, suggesting, and so on. Although we have no single word to cover all such activities, I think we can see that there is something common to all of them: in default of a better word, I shall use "advising," in an extended sense, to cover everything we do in telling another what he should do. I want to emphasize that "should," in second-person uses, has the practical function of "advising" (prodding, or whatever you may choose to call it), the same in all such uses. I shall not say anything here about the interestingly different third- and first-person uses of "should."

In order to render prominent the "performative" aspect of the conclusion of my counterexample, I shall now switch

[31]

to a second-person variant. Consider, therefore, any argument of the following form:

You want to achieve *E*.

Doing *M* is the one and only way to achieve *E*.

*Therefore,* you should do *M*.

Here the conclusion is intended to express "advice," and not to be merely another way of restating the factual conditions expressed by the premises. With this understanding, can we properly say that the conclusion follows by logical necessity from the premises?

It is often said that any argument of the above form is really an enthymeme with an unstated premise, possibly of the form:

Everybody should do anything which is the one and only way to achieve anything that he wants to achieve.

Since this general premise is held to be "normative" or "practical," its addition is held to convert the original inference into a formally correct one still conforming to Hume's Guillotine. My answer is that the proposed additional premise must be held to be analytic, in the sense of being guaranteed correct by virtue of the meanings or functions of the terms it contains. If so, its presence is unnecessary, as in the parallel case of an argument from contingent premises to a contingent conclusion. (If such an argument is valid when an analytical premise is imported, it remains so when that premise is removed.) I need not insist upon this, however. For if somebody still wishes to insert that additional general premise, I would urge upon him that the very reasons making him reluctant to agree that nonfactual conclusions might follow from exclusively factual premises ought to make him reject the idea of a necessarily true conditional having a factual antecedent but a nonfactual consequent. Hume's Guillotine applies to such a conditional statement just as plausibly as it does to an argument. Indeed, by rendering the original argument formally valid, we are simply smuggling in the principle of inference as an extra premise and are leaving all the substantial questions of validity unsettled. (We may here recall similar moves in connection with questions about the validity of inductive inferences. Those who say that such inferences are enthymematic and insist upon adding a general premise merely shift the question of validity to that of the validity of the imported premise.)

Another misconception, traceable to Kant, consists in thinking of the conclusion of any "practical" argument as "hypothetical." This may be intended to mean that the only correct conclusion from the given premises must have the conditional form "*If* you want to achieve $E$, you should do $M$." But how can we stop there? Given, as we are, the premise that "you" do want to achieve $E$, *modus ponens* requires us to go all the way to the "categorical" conclusion "You *should* do $M$." Unless we did intend to "go all the way," there would be no point in invoking the first premise; for the genuinely hypothetical or conditional statement "If you want to achieve $E$, you should do $M$" follows from the second premise alone. (And of course such a conditional statement, made in ignorance of the other's actual end, has none, or almost none, of the "prodding" force that I have ascribed to the categorical "should"-statement.)

Equally untenable is the more drastic view that "should," as used in the contexts here considered, has a variable condition as part of its meaning. On this view, "You should do $M$" is elliptical and really means the same as "If you want to achieve $E$, you should do $M$." But then what does the "should" in the expanded sentence mean? It would be absurd to repeat the maneuver by arguing that what is really meant is "If you want to achieve $E$, you should, if you want to achieve $E$, do $M$." For this way lies an infinite regress. On the other hand, there is no good reason to suppose that "should" means two different things in "You should do $M$" and "You should do $M$, if you want to achieve $E$," respectively. A good reason against supposing this is that, were it true, arguments by *modus ponens* in which the categorical and the hypothetical statements occur together would have

[33]

to count as invalid. If we want to use the traditional terminology, we must say that the conclusion of my counterexample
is categorical: a man who, knowing his hearer's end, says
"You should do $M$," is advising him unconditionally, without
qualifications or reservations. Those who resist this conclusion usually have in mind what might be called a "terminating" or "definitive" use of "should," in which the speaker
advises an action only after considering the case in the broad-
est possible perspective, including any moral considerations
arising. But this kind of case is exceptional.

Those who insist on the so-called "hypothetical" nature of
the "should"-conclusion have seen an important point, nevertheless. Consider the following case: $A$, playing chess with $B$,
asks me for advice. I see that the one and only way to check-
mate is to move the Queen and say "You should move the
Queen." A bystander, $C$, however, who has overheard this,
objects that $B$ is in such precarious health that the shock of
being suddenly mated by an inferior player might induce a
stroke and kill him. $C$, therefore, says to $A$: "You should not
move the Queen—perhaps you ought to break off the game."
Is $C$'s advice or admonition in conflict with mine? If it is, I
cannot properly argue that my advice follows from the two
factual premises about $A$'s purpose and the necessary and
sufficient condition for achieving it. For the addition of
further premises—for example, about $B$'s state of health and
the probable consequences to him of defeat—would produce
a conclusion contrary to mine.

It seems to me that $C$'s comment involves a change of subject. When $A$ asked me for advice, I rightly supposed he was
consulting me as a chess player and answered accordingly. It
would have been an objection to my remark to point out
some other mating move, or to argue that the move I recommended would not have the desired effect. But to introduce
moral considerations is to change the topic. $A$ asks, "What
shall I do *in this game*?" but $C$ replies, in effect, "Don't play
the game at all!" Of course, I am not suggesting that moral
considerations are subordinate to those of chess strategy; nor

[34]

am I implying that it was wrong for $C$ to answer as he did because he was not asked for moral advice. It may be morally right to answer irrelevantly—as when asked for technical advice on firearms by a would-be murderer.

The truth behind the view that the conclusions of "practical" arguments are hypothetical seems to be about as follows. The use of "should" and its normative cognates in such contexts is specified in a certain way, usually made plain by the nature of the context. "You should do $M$" has the force of "You should do $M$—given that you are playing chess and that the question is about *that*." One might say it is a presupposition that the advice, according to circumstances, is restricted to answering a question about game strategy, a legal question, a prudential one, and so on. (It is no doubt an important point about moral injunctions that they cannot be restricted or limited in a parallel fashion. It is normally absurd to say, "It is your duty to do $M$—given. . . ." Given *what*? Nothing seems to fit except "given that you are a moral agent" and even that imposes no restriction analogous to those I have mentioned.) Henry Sidgwick stated the point accurately when he said of Kant's so-called hypothetical imperatives that "they are not *addressed* to anyone who has not accepted the end." [15]

I turn now to my main question. Given that you want to achieve $E$ and that doing $M$ is the one and only way of achieving $E$, does it follow as a logical necessity that you should do $M$? It is obvious that the truth of the factual premises provides at least a good reason for saying "You should do $M$." Indeed, the truth of the premises constitutes a conclusive reason for saying, in the given context, "You should do $M$." Given that my interlocutor is playing chess and solicits advice about the game, the fact, if it is a fact, that he can mate the opponent only by moving the Queen provides me with a *conclusive* reason for urging him to do that rather than anything else. It would be absurd to say "The

---

15 *The Methods of Ethics*, 4th ed. (London, 1890), p. 6 (italics added).

one and only way you can mate the opponent is by moving your Queen—and that's why I say you should not move the Queen!" If we heard someone say this, apparently in earnest, we should reasonably suppose him to have made a slip of the tongue, to be joking, transmitting a code message, making some esoteric allusion, or otherwise using his words in some unusual way. Were all other suppositions to fail, we might even conclude that he did not understand what he was saying. But no sense could be made of the supposition that he did understand what he said, spoke literally, and still meant what he seemed to be saying. The test I have been applying here parallels a test we might apply to an argument with factual premises and a factual conclusion. Given a simple argument patently invalid, say of the form "$P$, if $P$ then $Q$, therefore not-$Q$," we could make no sense of the supposition that somebody might utter it, understand what he was saying, and mean what he seemed to be saying. If this test does not fully express what we mean by saying that the factual premises entail the factual conclusion, it at least constitutes a strong criterion of entailment.[16]

There is one important difference between the case I have just cited and that of a practical inference from "is" to "should." When a man thinks that $P$ and also that if $P$ then $Q$, it is logically impossible for him not to think also that $Q$: he may of course assert the premises explicitly without uttering the conclusion, but it is impossible that he should fail to think $Q$—say it "in his heart" as it were. To assert the premise in question while showing signs of doubting or wondering about the conclusion would be an indication of stupidity, failure to understand, or some other cognitive deficiency. (This case needs to be distinguished from that previously discussed, in which the speaker seems to be assert-

[16] R. M. Hare *defines* entailment as follows: "A sentence $P$ entails a sentence $Q$ if and only if the fact that a person assents to $P$ but dissents from $Q$ is a sufficient criterion for saying that he has misunderstood one or other of the sentences" (*op. cit.*, p. 25). This is unsatisfactory, for fairly obvious reasons.

ing not-*Q*.) But a man might refuse to say "You should do *M*," even though he had affirmed the factual premises whose truth constituted a conclusive reason for making the "should"-statement: having conscientious scruples about giving advice in such cases, he might have trained himself so well to abstain from giving it that he did not even think "You should do *M*" in his heart. We could not properly call such a man irrational or ignorant of the language. Because giving advice is performing a voluntary action, a man may in general abstain from the activity without incurring a charge of irrationality. Giving advice by means of "should"-formulas is a linguistic practice just as much as the making of promises is; and just as a man may have reasons so good for making a certain promise that it would be irrational for him to give a contrary promise but might choose not to make a promise at all, so also in the case of "advice."

This important point of difference between the two cases may help to explain the common insistence that moral conclusions cannot follow from factual premises. Suppose for the sake of argument that a moral injunction of the form "I ought to do such and such" might be related to nonmoral premises in a manner analogous to the relation I have claimed to obtain between the conclusion and the premises of my counterexample: then a man accepting the nonmoral premises would not, as a matter of logical necessity, have to accept the moral conclusion and so be required to think it. For he might in such cases refrain from drawing the moral implications from the facts: this would not be an indication of incapacity to reason or failure to understand the meaning of "ought" but might be a sign of moral deficiency. (One can sometimes blamelessly abstain from nonmoral practices, but nobody has the right in general to neglect relevant moral considerations.)

Too much must not be made of this admission. If a moral conclusion is ever related to nonmoral premises in the fashion I have imagined, then, given that a moral conclusion is to be drawn, we have no choice as to which conclusion it shall be.

[37]

Or, to return to my original example, given that the speaker is committed to offering some advice or other, the only advice that he can rationally offer is "You should do *M*." That is why, upon being asked to consider the complex conditional question "Given that *A* wants to achieve *E* and that *M* is the one and only way for him to achieve that end, should he do *M*?" we feel the compulsion to answer, "Of course!" Courtesy, if nothing else, obliges us to consider the question raised and so to adopt the posture of a judge. It would have to be a very exceptional kind of person who could evade the question by saying, "I never pass judgment."

For the reasons now before us, I am reluctant to say that the practical "should"-conclusion is entailed by its factual premises: the important contrast with straightforward cases of entailment might indeed be marked by using some such label as *"latent* necessity" or *"virtual* necessity." On my view, the practical conclusion is "hypothetical" in quite another way from that in which Kant thought of the matter: between the factual premises and the practical conclusion there is a sort of gap, bridgeable only by an agent's willingness to engage in the relevant activity or practice. The truth of the premises restricts the performance, whether that of "advising" or something else, to a single possibility, but there will be no performance at all unless the agent chooses to follow the path.

Given the truth of the factual premises concerning a man's end and the necessary and sufficient condition for attaining that end, and given that one is to make some second-person "should"-statement, one must say, "You should do *M*"—and nothing else will do. What kind of a "must" is this? It seems to mean here precisely what "must" means when we say that anybody affirming the premises of a valid deductive argument must also affirm that argument's conclusion. Choice of the given "should"-statement is enforced by the rules, understandings, or conventions governing the correct uses of "should" and the other words occurring in the argument: nobody who understands the premises of the practical argument and knows the rules for the proper use of "should" can honestly offer any other "should"-conclusion. In this respect, the parallel with "theoretical" arguments is strong. Accordingly, no special "practical" logic is needed in such cases: the relevant principles are the familiar ones employed throughout deductive reasoning.

The general pattern for other cases of the relation between a practical or performative utterance and factual reasons for making that utterance may be explained as follows. In the case of some performatives, though not in all, some of the conventions governing the correct use of the performatives prescribe that if certain factual conditions obtain, only a determinate, specifiable performative of the type in question may properly be used.[17] If we form a practical argument, whose premises state the factual conditions in question while its conclusion expresses the relevant performative, we shall then have a case analogous to those I have been discussing. For instance, the following seems to me a "strict" practical argument:

Unless I do something about it, you will take action $A$.

If you take action $A$, you will be killed.

*Therefore,* I warn you not to take action $A$.

If I am to warn you at all—which is not necessary, except possibly on moral grounds—I must use the negative warning formula, on pain of misusing language. Indeed, the case is very close to the earlier ones discussed in this paper, since one way of giving the warning would be to say "You should not do $A$."

[17] In terms of Austin's analysis of the "infelicities" of performatives in his *How to Do Things with Words,* J. O. Urmson, ed. (Oxford, 1962), pp. 14–15, what I am calling "factual conditions" fall under what he calls the "circumstances . . . [which] . . . must be appropriate for the invocation of the particular procedure invoked" (p. 15). Austin would count the use of the wrong performative in the circumstances I envisage as a "misinvocation" (p. 18) of the special sort that he calls a "misapplication" (*ibid.*). It is an understatement to say, as Austin does, that the act is then "disallowed" (*ibid.*). I am urging that logic requires the act to be rejected as improper.

My conclusion, therefore, comes to this: some nonfactual conclusions do follow and can be shown to follow from factual premises, even when proper allowance has been made for the "performative" aspects of such conclusions.

Very little might be held to have been accomplished by making such trivial arguments as I have considered logically respectable. But once Hume's Guillotine has been discredited, we may hope to find more important arguments containing valid transitions from "is" to "should" or from "is" to "ought." If I am not mistaken, the following argument from factual premises to a moral conclusion is valid:

Doing $A$ will produce pain.

Apart from producing the pain resulting from $A$, doing $A$ will have the same consequences that not doing $A$ would have had.

*Therefore, A* ought not to be done.

In other words, if the consequences of doing some action differ from those of abstaining from that action only by producing avoidable pain, that action ought not to be done. If I am to be shown mistaken in this claim, somebody will have to demonstrate that a person ready to make a moral judgment and accepting the premises could decline to make the moral judgment expressed by the conclusion, without thereby convicting himself of failure to understand the terms used, or some other cognitive defect. A detailed demonstration is required—not an appeal to a dogma which ought by now to have been finally exploded.

# IV

## *Rules and Routines*

I TAKE it for granted that education consists in large part of a sustained effort to generate capacities for skillful performance. Even "theoretical knowledge" of facts and principles, if it is to be of any value, must be manifested in certain modes of activity. All education aims, in the first instance, at "know-how."

Two distinct ideals of intelligent and skillful performance have an immediate appeal. The first is of graceful, free-flowing, action unimpeded by self-conscious reference to instructions. One thinks immediately of the natural movements of animals—but also of certain exercises of high skill: Menuhin's playing the violin as if it were as easy as breathing. Action of this kind gives an impression of freedom from conscious effort or calculation: the musician "loses himself in the music," though with intense control and awareness. A contrasting ideal is of deliberate calculating action according to an articulated program. An example might be a mathematician expounding a formal proof in public, with each step explicitly defended by cited reasons. Absence of ease and grace in such a performance is compensated by a high degree of "rationality." "Free-flowing" activity, at its best, looks like a dance: "rational" activity, at its worst, like drill.[1]

The antithesis between "dance" and "drill," between free-

---

[1] But consider the following description: "A moment before they had been swaying drunk. The touch of arms sobered them: they went through the manual from A to Z before us perfectly. More than mechanically perfect it was: a living, intelligent pattern and poem of movement" (T. E. Lawrence, *The Mint* [Jonathan Cape, 1955], p. 186). Drill *can* have the aesthetic grace of a "dance."

flowing and calculated action is too vague to have much value as a guide to education. Instead of pursuing it, I shall try to take a hard look at a particular type of "calculated action," characterized by the presence of governing *rules*. My object is to become somewhat clearer than I now am about the nature and the educational significance of such "rule-governed action."

1

Consider the differences between two familiar activities: doodling (*D*) and completing an income tax form (*F*). Both may be intentional and voluntary, but seem to have almost nothing else in common. About *F*, we can say the following things, none of which are true of *D*:

(1) It makes sense to say of one of the steps taken in *F* that it was a *mistake,* or that it was *wrong.*

(2) Nobody can be regarded as doing *F* unless he would treat certain entries as mistakes, and would try to *correct* them.

(3) Each step in *F* has an *intrinsic reason,*[2] which can be offered as an explanation, clarification, or defense of what he is doing.

(4) Nobody can count as doing *F* unless he treats as obvious reasons that justify what he is doing.

(5) It makes sense of a particular instance of *F* to say that it is *unfinished* or incomplete.

(6) In order to be doing *F,* the agent must have the completion of the task as an end in view.

(7) Anybody doing *F* must know *how to do it,* which implies that he could do *F* on other occasions and could show another person how to do it.

---

[2] I shall not try to define this. If asked why I am entering my age on the form, I should be giving an intrinsic reason if I said "Because the instruction asks for it." An extrinsic reason would be: "Because I am afraid of the penalty for omission."

(8) To do *F* is to make repeated reference to the *instructions* for doing *F,* each of them being treated as an injunction to be followed, "obeyed."

Now it would be absurd to say of a doodler, that he had made a wrong stroke, was trying to correct it, had a good or bad reason for doing it that way, had left the doodle unfinished, knew how to teach doodling, or was following instructions for doodling.[3] To doodle is to do as one pleases, in the spirit of the Abbey of Theleme, under the sole sway of pleasure; but to follow instructions, as in *F*, is to enter the realm of right-and-wrong, justification by reasons, standards of completeness, and built-in generality of procedure—in short, to behave rationally.

Completing an income tax form is a perspicuous instance of *rule-invoking* (or explicitly rule-governed) action. In the only sense that needs consideration here,[4] a rule is a *general instruction,* expressed in a formula that states *what is to be done* in order to achieve some stated or understood end in view. A standard formula for such a rule is: "In order to arrive at *E*, do *A*1, *A*2, . . . in such and such a sequence and in such and such combinations." A rule is a recipe for a designated achievement.

Of the eight features of rule-invoking action listed above, the last encompasses all the others. For instance, following the rule in question is necessarily being ready and able to treat some acts as mistaken (point 2): the rule defines classes of actions that are correct *according to the rule* and there is no logical gap between obeying the rule and obeying the rule correctly.[5] On the other hand, none of the first seven points

[3] This must not be taken too literally, of course. One can, more or less playfully, treat even doodling as a kind of task. But the artificiality is patent.

[4] Further discussion of the concept of a rule is to be found in Chapter VI of my *Models and Metaphors* (Ithaca, N.Y., 1962).

[5] This is an important reason why imputation of rule-governed behavior involves the presence of more than mere irregularity of be-

separately, nor all of them together, suffice to define rule-invoking action. A man may do something wrong because he fails to respond correctly to a specific command (*not* a rule!); my reason for drinking may be that I am thirsty, but it would be perverse to insist that I am following a rule, and so on. Even a man whose actions conform to all seven of the points, need not be regarded as rule-governed in his behavior.

What, then, is it to *obey* a rule explicitly invoked?

## 2

Of course, the rule must be understood and the agent must try to do as the rule prescribes. Is there anything more? Must we suppose some distinctive act of "obedience" intervening between understanding and acting? In general, not. Cases where an agent reads a recipe, hesitates, says aloud, "I'll use it," and then proceeds to do so might plausibly be regarded as including distinctive acts of "obedience." But this is unusual. Very likely, the cook reads the recipe and at once starts arranging the ingredients for a Dundee cake without any intervening act of recipe-adoption. *Obedience to the rule is shown by trying to do as instructed.* If this were not so, somebody could read the instructions, do exactly as he was told (with repeated reference to the explicit instructions) and still be able to claim that he "simply chose to do what the recipe required" without really obeying it. The claim would be absurd: here actions really do speak louder than words, and their force cannot be cancelled by a protest or a mental reservation.

Knowing how to respond to a rule *as a rule* is something

---

havior. Sometimes I push at a door marked "push," sometimes not; I may or may not take my walking stick when I go for a stroll. Both types of deviation from simple regularity might be predictable by some causal theory. What distinguishes the first from the second as "rule-governed" is the way in which the agent *treats* the deviation. If I curse when I realize I have left the stick behind, insist on going back for it, etc., that is *some* evidence that I am conforming to a rule.

that has to be learned: it is not a natural aptitude like breathing, but a distinctively human mode of behavior. The practice of giving and receiving rules involves a complex pattern of demands, objections, claims, and defenses that we overlook only because we were initiated into it so long ago. It is no more "natural" than the practice of playing games according to fixed rules. (We can easily imagine human beings unable to understand what it is to play conventional games; a human society lacking the "practice" of rule-giving admittedly strains the imagination.) This prior initiation and training, itself not induced by rule-invocation, makes it possible for an agent to *obey* a rule.[6] It is this earlier training, not some distinctive act of "obedience," that is essential for *following* a rule.[7]

This view of the matter has an important consequence. Participation in the rule-giving-and-receiving practice depends, as in all human institutions, upon a general presumption of *justifiable trust.* Unless rule-givers were usually trustworthy and rules for the most part "worked," there could be no viable institution of rule-using. (For the same reasons, if adults lied to their children, irresponsibly and unsystematically, most of the time, the children could never learn to talk.)

The general presumption of trust generates more specific

[6] If the reader thinks that reference to prior initiation into the "practice" shifts the burden of conceptual clarification without disposing of it, I would agree. Much more needs to be done by way of clarifying the nature of the practice.

[7] I have no space to discuss *disobedience* to rules (a mode of behavior of some interest to teachers). It may be enough to make the obvious point that disobedience or violation implies a kind of weak recognition of the rule: you cannot break a rule (in the primary sense of "break") without knowing what the rule is and understanding its pretensions to validity. The innocent can misbehave, but cannot break rules. It is tempting, but mistaken, to say that the violator stands the rule on its head, replacing it by an opposed rule, on the principle of "Your right shall be my wrong." But rule-breaking need not be done to rule (wrongdoing need not be principled): the rule can simply be ignored (suppressed, forgotten). Active and principled disobedience is a backhanded kind of tribute paid to the rule by the rule-breaker.

[45]

presumptions concerning presented rules. It is impossible (logically impossible, I think) for anybody to follow an instruction, qua rule of action, while thinking it detrimental to the end in view. If, so thinking, he performs the act prescribed, he is transforming the rule into a rule for another purpose— or into something other than a rule. Skeptical as I am about the accuracy of cook books, I can still *follow* a recipe for haggis for want of a better alternative. But if I think the printed recipe will produce only a nasty inedible mess, I cannot *accept* it as a rule for making haggis. (If I "go through the motions," my motive may be curiosity, the desire not to offend a Scotch friend, or something else; I am then "obeying" the rule only in some Pickwickian sense.) Obedience to a rule demands *some* confidence in the rule-giver.

No teacher needs to be told that the requisite confidence— the *consent of the taught,* as we might say—is often lacking: the child, acting under duress, does not really think that Teacher is usually right, or that the instructions thrust upon him really "work" (too often they don't!). The intended instructions are then responded to as *orders* or commands, to be obeyed (in another sense of that word). The task changes into that of "passing the test"—or, more generally, "satisfying Teacher." This, too, is education of a sort—education in how to coexist with arbitrary authority.

3

Rules, general instructions, purport to specify *good* ways to approach stated or assumed objectives (ends in view). A given rule may be defective in two distinct ways: by leading away from the end in view or by being unsuitable for use— roughly speaking, by being misdirected or by being inefficient. Similarly for other instruments: a hammer may be a poor one because it is too flimsy to drive nails home, or else because it is too heavy to be handled. The apocryphal rule for counting sheep by adding the number of feet and dividing by four is not misdirected, but is plainly inefficient. Let us call a rule that is not misdirected, that does prescribe actions conducive to the end in view, *right*; and a rule that is both right and efficient a *good* one. The goodness of rules is plainly a matter of degree.

Overlooking the vagueness in the notions of rules being "right" or "efficient," we can say that a question about the goodness of a given rule is determinable, in principle, by appeal to logic or to matters of fact. We can *prove* that hugging the wall of a maze will eventually lead to an exit; but it is a matter of experience that bread stays fresh in a refrigerator. Whether a rule is good is a cognitive issue, demanding knowledge, not decision or commitment. That is why rules can be freely adopted, when taken to be right and efficient, with no ultimate reliance upon authority. Given a chosen end in view and determinate skill, the rule's credentials are, in the end, rooted in the nature of the external world. Hence the step from a rule ("something to be done") to a corresponding principle ("the way things are") may need only a change of grammatical mood.

There is, to be sure, a certain duplicity in rules. The imperative mood in which they are naturally formulated suggests some external source whose special knowledge or expertise lends weight to the rule, giving it something of the force of recommendation, piece of advice, or even an order. ("Do such and such, because *I* say so, with proper authority.") Indeed, the practical point of obeying rules issuing from another is to relinquish initiative and responsibility for the time being. While I follow the recipe, my role as agent shrinks to the simpler and more passive one of *doing as I am told*—as if an experienced chef stood at my elbow. My interest shifts from the primary task of baking a cake to the secondary one of correctly following instructions, which is so much easier.[8] I act upon authority—and wish to. But such

---

[8] The consequent division and deflection of attention may have something to do with the jerky, angular or monotonous rhythm of *prescribed* behavior, that is so much despised by admirers of the free-flowing and spontaneous. Deflected attention has obvious dangers: it is all too easy to get too interested in the recipe and to forget about the cake. Any schoolroom can provide examples.

submission is, in the long run, wholesome only if eventually subjected to criticism. Sooner or later, provisional submission to the authority of rules must be tested by logic and against the facts. As justice must not only be done, but must be *seen* to be done, so also the goodness of rules (in any educational program aspiring to be rational) must in the end be *shown*—and not indefinitely assumed by an act of trust.

4

A man who deliberately obeys, "invokes," a rule can cite that rule as a *reason* for his action; one who blindly follows a routine, behaves regularly, cannot offer a reason of that kind—and may be able to offer no reasons at all. ("Why are you taking the walking stick?" "Because I want to!" That tells us nothing: we know that he was not taking it inadvertently.)

Reasons for actions are typically offered in order to defend or to justify the actions; to render them intelligible; or to amplify their descriptions, by reference to intention, motive, or purpose. In performing such meta-activities (as they might be called), the rule-invoking agent has intellectual resources unavailable to somebody performing superficially similar actions, routinely, blindly, "out of mere habit" or even "unaware." Let us say, for short, that rule-invoking action is potentially and distinctively *self-critical*. (By "self-criticism" I mean the processes of justification, explanation, and verbal elaboration already alluded to.) Paradoxically, the constraints imposed by adherence to a rule are balanced by greater scope and freedom to act at the "meta"-level. (This is why metamathematics demands *formalized* object-languages; and also why a sonnet in traditional form is easier to criticize than a piece of free verse.)

Reasons can render actions intelligible. When we say, of another's action, "We don't know what he is doing" or, sometimes, more explicitly, "We don't *understand* what he is doing," we can sometimes be enlightened by a statement of the agent's reasons and their supposed connection with his end in view. Given the rule invoked—if there is such a rule—we can make immediate sense of what is being done, whatever our ultimate reservations about the goodness of the rule employed. Conversely, where rule-connected reasons cannot be given, because the behavior in question is a blind routine, *this* mode of understanding is excluded—although causal explanation may still be available.[9]

Now apply this to a man's view of his own action. In invoking a rule, he understands up to a point precisely what he is doing—that is, treating the given rule as defining a good procedure for achieving an accepted end in view. But when a man's behavior is blind routine, there is an important sense in which he does not know *what* he is doing, or *why* he is doing it. This need not be discreditable if there is nothing to explain, nothing to understand; but is generally taken to be so, in moderation, where reasons might be given, by reference to an appropriate rule. A man unable to supply reasons when appropriate reasons are available falls short of acting with full rationality. The tie between rule-governed behavior and rationality goes far to explain and to justify educational emphasis upon such behavior.

## 5

I have been using the expression "rule-invoking action" to apply, in the first instance, to episodes in which attention is paid to printed or written instructions. It is natural to include under the same rubric the analogous cases in which the agent *recites* the rule to himself, aloud or "in his head." A rule thus recited may be remembered as issuing from some authority—or may simply have been discovered by the agent himself. These new cases are clearly "rule-governed."

Less clear, but in some ways more interesting, are actions satisfying most of the criteria for rule-invocation listed in

[9] Reasons may be given, sometimes, for intentional or purposive action that is not rule-governed. This is too large a topic to be pursued here.

Section 1 above, but in which there is no discernible explicit reference *to* any rule. A man who can still remember how to solve quadratic equations, as he was taught to do in school, does not perform the task with an open algebra book at his elbow, nor is he heard to mutter "Must do this; then do that. . . ." Indeed either of these would indicate imperfect mastery of the relevant rule of procedure, would be a sure sign that the rule had not fully entered into *his own possession*.

The well-taught solver of quadratic equations should have little trouble in formulating the controlling rule of procedure upon demand. But if he has trouble in describing his procedure, we may be able to do it for him. In either case, if all goes well, he will immediately *accept* the verbal formulation: he will say perhaps, "Yes—that is what I was doing all along!" Solving the equation is a very clear case of what I propose to call *rule-accepting* action. For paradigm instances of rule-acceptance, it is essential that the correct formulation of the rule seem obvious (and hence easy to find), and that once formulated it will be accepted unhesitatingly by the agent himself. The harder it is to formulate the rule, and the more reluctant the agent is to receive it, the less inclined we ought to be to treat the episode as a clear case of rule-acceptance.

There is a deliberate ambiguity in the label "rule-accepting," between "accepting the rule *all along*" and "accepting the rule *retroactively*." I think there is no harm in it. Some writers would speak of "implicitly rule-governed action" and of "subconscious" or even "unconscious" awareness of the rule. The accompanying imagery of the rule concealed in the wings, waiting to be brought before the footlights of consciousness—out of sight, but not out of mind, as it were—is admissible if not taken too seriously.[10] However we choose

---

[10] If the reader is strongly inclined to think that the conception of implicit or subconscious obedience *must* be right, let him consider the following. My regular practice of washing in the morning is *as if* I were *obeying a command*. Am I to be taken as obeying an implicit *command*?

to think about this, we shall need to grant the following points: (1) rule-accepting action, prior to its verbal articulation, already possesses most of the interesting features of rule-invoking action (correction of "mistakes," etc.); (2) it can readily be transformed [11] into potentially rule-invoking behavior by supplying the rule; (3) once this is done, the full resources of the self-critical "meta-activities" become available to the agent himself.

## 6

What shall we say, now, about actions manifesting many of the distinctive features of "rule-governed behavior" in which, however, the agent *cannot* formulate the rule and cannot or will not accept the verbal formula supplied by another? Take the case of a man riding a bicycle, without conscious effort or more than peripheral awareness of what he is doing. Professor Michael Polanyi has provided what he calls "the rule observed by the cyclist," [12] but his formulation occupies ten lines and contains reference to such technical notions as "angle of unbalance," "square of the speed," and "inverse proportionality." Obviously, the ordinary cyclist could not even understand the rule—and, if he did, would be unable to follow it (as Polanyi himself points out).

This type of case needs to be sharply distinguished from those already discussed. If we call such action *rule-covered,* as I would propose, we ought to take that to mean only that an outside analyst can give a certain kind of description of it—can view it *sub specie regulae,* as it were. This kind of verbal articulation is of no value, by way of "self-criticism," to the agent himself, although it may have considerable importance elsewhere. (If we want to simulate rule-covered action by machines, we need to formulate the rule, in order

[11] Verbal articulation will *change* the performance, in subtle or massive ways. Indeed its main point will often be to correct and to improve the performance.

[12] *Personal Knowledge* (London, 1958), p. 49.

to supply the machine with a program. In general, many logically equivalent programs could be contrived. If we thought of the human agent as *"really* following *one* of these programs,"* we would have the embarrassment of choosing among equivalent rules, none of which the agent himself would accept.)

7

Rule-covered behavior, as defined above, is easily confused with cases in which the agent's justified refusal to adopt a proposed "articulation" is due to inadequacy of the language of description.

Consider the following illustration. A beginner's book on chess might contain the rule: "A knight moves from one corner of a rectangle composed of three squares by two to the diagonally opposite corner, if that square is unoccupied, without regard for any other pieces in that rectangle." In moving a knight, a very slow witted learner might perhaps be heard reciting this clumsy formula; a somewhat brisker chap might be observed using a finger to trace out a 3 by 2 rectangle and checking that the diagonally opposite square is empty before moving. (In our terminology, the first action would be "rule-invoking," the second "rule-accepting.") But anybody who *had* to do either of these things would never make much of a chess player. If all goes well, a kind of *phenomenological compression* of the original formula occurs: a reduction to essentials, as it were. The player comes to *see* the target square as available for the knight—and, indeed, at the same time, to see the other available squares, arranged in a constellation of related positions. (The "assimilation" of the original formula demanded may require hard work and much practice, with varying degrees of success. Even with experienced players, "blindness" to possibilities is not uncommon.) The phenomenological prominence of the target square now functions as a criterion, and the criteria embodied in the original formula may be so effectively suppressed that "verbal articulation" may be disconcertingly difficult. (Consider how easy it may be to tie a reef knot—and how hard to say *what* one does.)

In such cases, the agent's resistance to a proposed articulation (which usually looks absurdly complex) may arise from his use of a private symbolism of visual cues, that has ousted the public and official terminology of the original instructions. Such symbolism is not "private" in the philosopher's technical sense of unintelligibility in principle to another. The structuring of a chess player's visual field, at which I have hinted, might be shown in a "public" diagram—for instance, in a film of a lone knight on a chessboard, upon which the "target squares" are suddenly made "prominent" (by being brought into relief by being outlined, changing colour, etc.). If such a nonverbal diagram were correctly understood, it would serve the function of the "verbal articulation" in rule-accepting behavior. I shall speak in such cases of *rule-guided action.*

Rule-guided action, that is appropriately articulated by nonverbal symbolism, and the intuitive transformation or "condensation" that makes it possible, seems to me of fundamental importance to educational method. (In spite of the efforts of Gestalt psychologists, it is still an unjustly neglected field of research.) It is connected in the most intimate way with the learner's necessary effort to impose a memorable order upon what looks initially like a chaos of unrelated items.[13] Whatever the topic—a mathematical proof, the conjugation of a verb, the salient features of the Industrial Revolution—the data must be "rendered down," simplified, structured, if they are to be assimilated, remembered, and properly used. Only in this way does *"the* rule" for achieving something become *"my* rule."

[13] See, for instance, Polanyi's discussion of "the kind of topographic knowledge which an experienced surgeon possesses of the regions on which he operates" (*ibid.,* p. 89). It seems to me unduly pessimistic to call such knowledge "ineffable."

8

Much of my discussion has turned, one way or another, upon the possibility of a verbal formulation of a rule. It may be as well, therefore, to consider certain fundamental limitations upon such "articulation." (I shall neglect some obvious practical limitations arising from lack of skill on the part of teacher or learner.)

The first limitation may be introduced by as trivial an example as that of somebody knitting a scarf. Whether or not the knitter resorts to printed instructions, *we* can certainly articulate a governing rule: say, "Knit plain and purl for a hundred stitches, then turn and continue" (call this formula *A*). Now the correct application of formula *A* is itself a rule-governed activity which might be articulated by another formula, *B* say, explaining how to make "plain" and "purl" stitches, and so on. (Cf. the "Instructions" sometimes appended to official forms, telling one how to do what one has been told to do!) Could one then not envisage a further formula, *C*, articulating the mode of application of *B*, and so on without end?

The infinite regress that threatens here is factitious. The chain of rules will quickly terminate, for want of an adequate vocabulary. The nearer we come to what is readily *seen* by an apt learner, the harder it becomes to articulate the governing rule, and a point is soon reached at which the effort of attending to the verbal formula positively interferes with the primary performance. (Try saying *what* you are doing while knitting—or while running downstairs.) Of course, sensible men soon abandon *saying* in favor of *showing*: however hard it may be to teach knitting by example, it is incomparably harder to do so by talking about it.

This point can be generalized: successful use of articulated rules presupposes mastery of skills (rule-governed performances) not controlled by *explicit* rules. Hence, "practice" must precede the critical activity of rule formulation. Only

[54]

in this way can the intellectual and educational values of rule-formulation be realized: without the prior foundation of more or less "blind" practice and experience, the rules degenerate into sterile verbalism.

## 9

I have tried to perform a preliminary survey—rough, but serviceable—of the complex notion of "rule-governed behavior." One moral I would like to draw is that the learner and the teacher are never faced with a stark choice between blind, unconscious, mastery ("rule-covered behavior" or the even more primitive outcome of "conditioning") and self-conscious adherence to explicitly formulated principles ("rule-invoking behavior"). Between these extremes, we have been able to discern types of intelligent and skillful performance ("rule-accepting" and "rule-guided" behavior), which combine the virtues of "free-flowing" and "prescribed" behavior. Here, ideally, there is no longer any conflict between the two ideals I invoked at the outset, and submission to the discipline of rules, freely adopted, becomes indistinguishable from the freedom of self-realization.

In working for this ideal harmony, a good teacher will be sensitively alert to the supreme importance of timing—the rhythm of alternation between the different modes of action. He will not shrink from brute conditioning, to lay a necessary foundation of primitive habits of response. But unless he wants his pupils to be no better than trained circus animals, he will try, at the right time, to change blind response into self-directed control by justified rules. He will be willing to break down primitive habits by analysis and criticism, if only for the sake of ultimately inducing higher levels of performance. (The ideal cycle, indefinitely repeated, will be from "rule-covering behavior" to "rule-invoking behavior" and then to "rule-accepting behavior" and "rule-guided behavior.")

There are, alas, no firm rules for what is "the right time."

Rules are defeasible, hedged about with *ceteribus paribus* clauses to be applied at the discretion of their users. But there are no useful rules for the application of discretion, tact, or judgment. A subtitle for this essay might have been "In Defense of Rules and Principles." I have hoped it might be read by those who will know that there is a time for throwing rule books away.

# V

# *Induction*

THE NAME "induction," derived from the Latin translation of Aristotle's *epagoge,* will be used here to cover all cases of nondemonstrative argument, in which the truth of the premises, while not entailing the truth of the conclusion, purports to be a good reason for belief in it. Such arguments may also be called "ampliative," as C. S. Peirce called them, because the conclusion may presuppose the existence of individuals whose existence is not presupposed by the premises.

Thus, the conclusion "All *A* are *B*" of an induction by simple enumeration may apply to *A*'s not already mentioned in the finite number of premises having the form "$A_i$ is *B*." Similarly, in eduction (or arguments from particulars to particulars) the conclusion "Any *A* is *B*" is intended to apply to any *A* not yet observed as being a *B*.

It would be convenient to have some such term as "adduction" to refer to the sense of induction here adopted, which is broader than the classical conception of induction as generalization from particular instances. Most philosophical issues concerning induction in the classical sense arise in connection with the more general case of nondemonstrative argument.

In what follows it will be convenient to use Jean Nicod's expression "primary inductions" to refer to those nondemonstrative arguments "whose premises do not derive their certainty or probability from any induction." Problems of philosophical justification are most acute in connection with such primary inductions.

It may be added that "mathematical induction" is a misnomer because the useful types of reasoning so labeled

[57]

are rigorously demonstrative. Given that the first integer has a certain property and also that if any integer $n$ has that property then so does $n + 1$, the next, it follows demonstratively that *all* the integers have the property in question. Inductive arguments, as here conceived, do not constitute mathematical or logical proofs; by definition induction is not a species of deduction.

### TYPES OF INDUCTIVE ARGUMENTS

In addition to the types of arguments already mentioned, the following are most frequently discussed:

(1) Elaborated induction (as it might be called) consists of more or less sophisticated variations of induction by simple enumeration, typically including supplementary information concerning the mode of selection of the individuals named in the premises and perhaps including reference to negative instances.

(2) Proportional induction is inference from the frequency of occurrence of some character in a sample to the frequency of occurrence of the same character in the parent population —that is, from "$m_1/n_1$ $A$'s selected by a stated procedure $P$ are $B$" to "$n_2/n_2$ $A$'s and $B$." Here the ratio stated in the conclusion may be other than the one stated in the premise; it is often advantageous to locate the final ratio within a certain designated interval.

(3) Proportional eduction is argument from sample to sample. From the same premises as in proportional induction a conclusion is drawn concerning approximate frequency of occurrence in a further sample obtained by the same procedure or by another one.

(4) Proportional deduction (commonly called "statistical syllogism") is inference from "$m/n$ $C$'s are $B$" (where $m/n$ is greater than $1/2$) and "$A$ is a $C$" to "$A$ is a $B$."

In all the above cases modern writers usually insist upon inserting some more or less precise indication of probability or likelihood, either within the conclusion itself or as an index of reliability attached to the mark of inference ("therefore," "hence," or the like). Careful attention to the probability or likelihood attributed to a given inductive conclusion is a distinct merit of modern treatments of the subject.

The foregoing list cannot claim to be exhaustive, nor are its items to be regarded as mutually irreducible. There is no general agreement concerning the basic forms of inductive argument, although many writers regard simple enumeration as in some sense the most fundamental.

HISTORY OF INDUCTIVE METHODS

Interest in the philosophy and methodology of induction was excited by the extraordinary successes of natural science, which tended to discredit the rationalistic conception of knowledge about matters of fact. The classical writers on the subject, from Francis Bacon on, have lamented the powerlessness of deduction to do more than render explicit the logical consequences of generalizations derived from some external source. If recourse to intellectual intuition or to self-evidence is repudiated as a source of factual knowledge, nothing better seems to remain than reliance upon the empiricist principle that all knowledge concerning matters of fact ultimately derives from experience. However, experience, whether conceived as sporadic and undirected observation or as the systematic search for specific answers extorted by planned experiment, seems to supply knowledge only of particular truths. Empiricists are therefore faced with the problem of accounting for the crucial step from knowledge of experiential particulars to reasoned acceptance of empirical generalizations sufficiently powerful to serve as the major premises of subsequent logical and mathematical deduction.

The aspiration of early writers was, characteristically, to demonstrate the conclusions of acceptable inductive arguments as true; not until the end of the nineteenth century did a more modest conception of inductive argument and scientific method, directed toward acquiring probability rather that certainty, begin to prevail.

[59]

## Problem of Induction

The celebrated problem of induction, which still lacks any generally accepted solution, includes under a single heading a variety of distinct, if related, problems. It is useful to distinguish the following:

(1) The general problem of justification: Why, if at all, is it reasonable to accept the conclusions of certain inductive arguments as true—or at least probably true? Why, if at all, is it reasonable to employ certain rules of inductive inference?

(2) The comparative problem: Why is one inductive conclusion preferable to another as better supported? Why is one rule of inductive inference preferable to another as more reliable or more deserving of rational trust?

(3) The analytical problem: What is it that renders some inductive arguments rationally acceptable? What are the criteria for deciding that one rule of inductive inference is superior to another?

These problems may be briefly labeled "justification," "differential appraisal," and "analysis." Many writers on induction have also occupied themselves with the task of codification, the formulation of a coherent, consistent, and comprehensive set of canons for the proper conduct of inductive inference. Important as it is, this task is not distinctively philosophical, except insofar as it requires in advance answers to the questions listed above.

In practice the three problems here distinguished cannot be pursued separately; a comprehensive general defense of inductive procedures involves specification, *inter alia,* of legitimate forms of inductive argument, and selection between alternative inductive rules or methods must rely, explicitly or not, upon determination of what, if anything, makes an inductive argument "sound." The *why* of inductive argument cannot profitably be isolated from the *how*.

It is characteristic of much recent investigation of the sub-

[60]

ject to concentrate on the last two of the problems listed, often in the hope of formulating precise canons of inductive inference (an inductive logic). These comparative and analytical versions of the problem of induction are thought worth pursuing even by writers who reject the general problem of justification as insoluble.

## HUME'S VIEW OF CAUSATION

For better or worse, all modern discussion of the philosophy of induction takes off from Hume's celebrated analysis of causation, whose connection with the philosophical problems of induction (a word that Hume never used) arises from his view that all reasoning concerning matters of fact is founded on the relation between cause and effect. Although Hume may be held to have given undue prominence to causation (his skeptical conclusions do, in fact, challenge every kind of nondemonstrative argument, whether or not grounded in causal imputation), it is easy to overlook and to be misled by the special form in which he conceived the problem of justification.

Hume, unlike such later writers as J. S. Mill, was not satisfied to analyze the notion of cause and effect into the notions of spatial contiguity, temporal succession, and joint occurrence; he fatefully added to these the criterion of "necessary connexion." That objects of certain kinds have been conjoined or associated in past experience might be no more than an extended coincidence. Something more is needed before one event can properly be recognized as the cause of the other; we must be able to pass from *post hoc* to *propter hoc*. In predicting a putative effect of a given event we can ensure contiguity and succession by choosing to look only for a spatiotemporally proximate event, and memory (if that can be relied on) will furnish knowledge of constant conjunction in the past. Whether we are truly justified in predicting the occurrence of the putative effect will therefore turn entirely upon whether there is good reason to assert that it is necessarily connected with its neighbor. Hume, in effect, chal-

[61]

lenged his reader to find anything in the observation of a single case of supposed causal action (for instance, in the favorite example of a collision between two billiard balls) that answers to the required "necessary connexion" between two events. No observation, however attentive, will discover more than contiguity and an internal habit of expecting association. Nor will examination of a series of cases, all exactly alike, help at all: a sum of zeroes is still zero.

But what did Hume mean by "necessary connexion"? Although he did not tell us in so many words, his main proof that we can "never demonstrate the necessity of a cause" rests simply upon the conceivability, and hence the logical possibility, of an event's being bereft of its putative cause. He seems, therefore, to have implied that our notion of a cause and its effect requires the existence of the one to be entailed by the existence of the other. If so, it does not need much argument to show that we can have no impression (direct sensory experience) of such entailment. Hume concluded that necessity cannot reside in the external world but must arise, as an idea, from an internal impression of the mind, a "determination to carry our thoughts from one object to another."

Repeated observation of the association of events leads us to the *habit* of expecting the association to continue "by means of an operation of the soul . . . as unavoidable as to feel the passion of love, when we receive the benefits" (*Enquiry Concerning the Human Understanding*, Sec. 5, Pt. 1). Our idea of necessary connection is nothing more than an internal response to the habit of expecting effects: "Upon the whole, necessity is something in the mind, not in objects." At this point skepticism is just around the corner; we are on the verge of such famous conclusions as that "all probable reasoning is nothing but a species of sensation" (*A Treatise of Human Nature*, Bk 1, Pt. 3, Sec. 8).

The reference to habit or custom explains nothing, of course, and is at best only a concise reference to the truism, which according to Hume's view simply has to be accepted,

[62]

that men do in fact expect events to be accompanied by effects. Without such habits of causal expectation men could hardly have survived—but this reflection, itself based on induction, cannot be a reason for belief in causation. For a philosopher so critical of such allegedly occult entities as power and energy, Hume was strangely carefree in his reliance upon habit or custom as a *vera causa*. In keeping with his own principles he ought to have turned as skeptical an eye on habit as on cause and ought to have concluded that our idea of habit is derived from nothing more than a habit of expecting that a man who acts in a certain way will continue to do so. But now the account looks circular. Have we any better reason to believe in the existence of habits—even if construed, in as reductionist a fashion as possible, as mere constant conjunctions—than we have to believe in causes? And would not everything that tended to show we have no sufficient basis in external experience for belief in the objective reality of causal connection also tend to show, by parity of reasoning, that we have no basis for believing in the existence of those habits that are invoked at least to explain, if not to justify, our ordinary causal beliefs?

It has seemed to nearly all of Hume's readers that his method must lead to a skepticism more sweeping than he himself was perhaps willing to recognize or to accept. If Hume had been correct about the origin of the idea of necessity, he would have been committed to a totally skeptical answer to the general problem of justification. Whether or not we can escape from the bondage of causal expectation, we are at any rate free to see that such a habit can provide no reason, in Hume's sense, for the belief in causal connection. And once we see this, wholesale skepticism concerning inductive inference seems inescapable.

Hume's skeptical conclusions cannot be dismissed on the ground that they originated in an oversimplified psychology of ideas and impressions, for his argument can, with little difficulty, be made independent of any psychological assumptions. Cause and effect are logically independent, not because repeated search fails to find any logical connection, as Hume's own account misleadingly suggests, but because it is a part of what we mean by cause and effect that the two shall be logically separable. It is tempting to say, then, that there is no reason why the separable consequent should follow its antecedent in any particular instance. We can very well imagine or conceive the cause's occurring without its usual consequent, and, in Hume's words, "nothing of which we can form a clear and distinct idea is absurd or impossible" (*ibid.,* Pt. 1, Sec. 7).

## NEO-HUMEAN ARGUMENTS

Even if Hume was wrong in including logical necessity in the idea of causal connection, a Neo-Humean can correct his argument without weakening its skeptical force. It is reasonable to say that what distinguishes a causal connection from a merely accidental association is that empirical rather than logical necessity obtains between the two events. This, in turn, may be rephrased by saying that the observed conjunction is a case of lawful and not merely accidental association. But then Hume's challenge to discover such lawfulness in experience remains as formidable as ever; no matter how many instances of joint occurrence we encounter, we will never observe more than the *de facto* association and will never have ultimate, noninductive grounds for believing in a *de jure* connection.

Thus, Hume's problem can be put into modern dress, without restriction to causal inference, as follows: An inductive inference from an observed association of attributes $(A_n - B_n)$ can justify inference to another case $(A_{n+1} - B_{n+1})$ or inference to the corresponding generalization ("All $A$ are $B$") only if the association is somehow known to be lawlike, not merely accidental. Yet how can this be known in primary inductions that do not themselves rest upon the assumed truth of other laws? Certainly not by immediate experience, nor *a priori,* nor, without begging the question, by appeal to induction.

[64]

The sharpest form of this version of the problem (called by its author the "new riddle of induction") is that of Nelson Goodman. Suppose all emeralds examined before a certain time $t$ have been green; use the label "grue" for the property of being green up to the time $t$ and being blue thereafter. Then all the evidence supports equally well the competing laws "All emeralds are green" and "All emeralds are grue." Here an instance of the comparative problem is raised in a particularly pointed and instructive way.

Goodman's challenge awaits an answer. Some writers have hoped to defend the received or standard modes of inductive argument by invoking criteria of relative simplicity. But apart from the yet unsolved problem of clarifying what simplicity is to mean in this connection, there seems no good reason why nature should obligingly make correct inference simple; often enough the best-confirmed law is less simple than others that would accord with the given evidence. Goodman's own suggestion to restrict defensible inductions to "entrenched" predicates (roughly speaking, those that have been frequently employed in previous inductive judgments) seems less than satisfying.

From the standpoint of the philosophy of induction the chief significance of Hume's memorable discussion (apart from its tonic effect in disturbing "dogmatic slumber") is that it brought into full daylight the problem of distinguishing between a merely accidental series of associations and the genuine laws that we seek by means of inductions.

### DEDUCTIVE STANDARD OF JUSTIFICATION

A demand that induction be justified arises, of course, from some supposed deficiency or imperfection. If all were obviously well with inductive argument, there would be no point in asking for any defense or justification. It is therefore of the first importance to be clear about the alleged weakness or precariousness of induction and the corresponding standard of justification to which appeal is covertly made. We need to know what is supposed to be the trouble with induction, for only when the disease is understood will the search for a remedy have much prospect of success.

The root of the trouble is plain enough in the writings of a hundred writers who have trodden in Hume's footsteps. All have been haunted by the supposedly superior certainty of demonstrative reasoning. If valid deduction from premises known to be true transmits certainty to the conclusion, even the best induction will seem inferior by comparison. (Locke said that induction from experience "may provide us convenience, not science"—*Essay Concerning Human Understanding*, Bk. 4, Chap. 12, Sec. 10.) The nagging conviction that induction somehow falls short of the ideals of rationality perfectly exemplified in valid deductive argument has made the problem of induction needlessly intractable.

If Hume, for instance, did not require that induction be shown as somehow satisfying the criteria of valid deduction, an answer to his question about how "children and peasants" learn from experience would be easy. The method employed, as he himself stated, is that of arguing from similarity of causes to similarity of effects. However, such an answer would obviously not have satisfied him, because this method will not guarantee the truth of the conclusion drawn; that is, it is not the kind of method that would be acceptable as justifying a valid deduction. Hume would have liked an inductive conclusion to follow from (be entailed by) premises known to be true, for anything less would not have seemed genuinely reasonable. Having shown, in effect, that no reason of this kind can be produced for primary inductions, he was forced to regard the question of justification as demonstrably insoluble. This conclusion has the notable inconvenience of leaving the comparative problem also insoluble (while the analytical task vanishes for lack of an object).

Hume's conclusion must be granted if his is the only sense of "reason" in point. If we never have a reason for an inductive conclusion unless we know the conclusion to follow strictly from premises known to be true, then we can have no reason for believing in primary inductive conclusions; it

[66]

is as reasonable to expect that thistles will bear figs, or something equally absurd, as it is to expect anything else extending beyond past experience. (Whether we can in fact bring ourselves to believe anything so absurd is beside the point.) Only in recent times have serious efforts been made to escape from the spell of the deductive model, used by Hume and his innumerable followers, by inquiring whether there may not be other proper and relevant senses of "reasonable." It will be argued later that belief in induction is reasonable in principle and that belief in one kind of inductive conclusion is more reasonable than belief in another.

The lasting attraction of the deductive model is not hard to understand. The *raison d'être* of deductive argument seems enticingly plain: valid deductions are truth-transmitting and truth-preserving—which, given an interest in obtaining novel truth, seems enough to show the point of deductive reasoning. (That this cannot be the whole story is obvious from the uses of deductive reasoning in exhibiting the consequences of propositions hypothetically entertained—not to mention *reductio* arguments and other uses.) By contrast the *raison d'être* of induction seems unclear and mysterious. It would be easy, although unsatisfying to the genuinely perplexed, to say that sound inductive arguments are "likelihood-transmitting," for likelihood is as unclear a concept as inductive correctness. Thus, it is natural to ask for and to expect a detailed answer to the question "Why should a reasonable man rely upon likelihood in default of truth?" Even if the power of sound induction to confer likelihood upon conclusions is regarded as sufficient to make inductive argument reasonable beyond further cavil, the question how such likelihood is conferred will remain. Attention thus shifts to the analytical task.

It may be added that an enduring source of disquiet concerning inductive argument is its disorderliness and formlessness by contrast with deductive argument. In deductive argument we flatter ourselves upon readily perceiving the underlying principles and their necessary connection with logical

[67]

form. By contrast with such classic simplicity and order the realm of inductive argument seems disconcertingly complex, confused, and debatable: an inductive argument accepted by one judge may be rejected, on good grounds, by another, equally competent judge; supposedly sound arguments from different sets of true premises may yield opposed conclusions; the very soundness of induction seems not to be clear-cut but to admit of gradations of relative strength and reliability. Given all this, it is not surprising that although many students have labored to introduce order into the field, others, abandoning any hope of so doing, have turned away from induction as a tissue of confusions.

## Types of Solution

The answers given in the literature to Hume's problem can be briefly summarized as follows:

(1) Hume's challenge cannot be met; consequently, induction is indefensible and ought to be expunged from any reasoning purporting to be rational.

(2) In the light of Hume's criticisms, inductive arguments as normally presented need improvement, either (*a*) by adding further premises or (*b*) by changing the conclusions into statements of probability. In either case a conclusion's validity is expected to follow demonstratively from the premises, and inductive logic will be reconstructed as a branch of applied deductive logic.

(3) Although inductive argument cannot be justified as satisfying deductive standards of correctness, it may be proved that inductive policies (rather than rules or principles) are, in a novel sense to be explained later, reasonable. Induction can be vindicated if not validated.

(4) Hume's problem is generated by conceptual and linguistic confusions; it must therefore be dissolved, rather than solved, by exposing these confusions and their roots.

These approaches are not all mutually exclusive. Thus (3), the pragmatic approach, is usually combined with (1),

[68]

repudiation of induction as an acceptable mode of *reasoning*. Apart from (4) all the approaches accept or make substantial concessions to Hume's major assumption—namely, that the only wholly acceptable mode of reasoning is deductive. This is true even of those who hold (3), the "practicalists," who might be supposed, at first glance, to be relaxing the criteria of rationality.

## REJECTION OF INDUCTION

The rejection of induction as a proper mode of scientific reasoning is sometimes found in the guise of advocacy of the so-called hypothetico-deductive method. According to such a view, the essence of genuinely scientific reasoning about matters of fact is the framing of hypotheses not established by given empirical data but merely suggested by them. Inference enters only in the control of hypotheses by the verification of their observable consequences: negative instances strictly falsify a hypothesis, whereas positive instances permit its use, pending further experimental tests, as a plausible, if unproved, conjecture. Science, as well as all reasoning about matters of fact aspiring to the reliability of scientific method, needs only the kind of reasoning to be found in deductive logic and in mathematics. Some such position was already adumbrated in the writings of William Whewell. It has at least the merit of drawing attention to the role of hypotheses in scientific method, a welcome corrective to the excessive claims of early partisans of inductive logic.

The most influential, and possibly the most extreme, of contemporary writers following this line is Karl Popper, who has often maintained that what is called induction is a myth, inasmuch as what passes under that title "is always invalid and therefore clearly not justifiable." In his own conception of scientific method such repudiation of induction is linked with the thesis that the purpose of scientific theorizing is falsification (demonstration of error) rather than verification or confirmation (provisional support of an approximation to the truth). Those who agree would rewrite putatively inductive

[69]

inferences to make them appear explicitly as hypothetical explanations of given facts. (Thus, instead of inferring "All $A$ are $B$" from premises of the form "$A_n$ is $B$," the first statement is offered as a more or less plausible explanation of why all the $A_n$ should have been found to be $B$.)

In spite of its enthusiastic advocacy, it is hard to see where this proposal accomplishes more than a superficial change in the form in which inductive arguments are written and a corresponding alteration in the metalanguage in which they are appraised. Any hypothetical explanation of given empirical data is intended to reach beyond them by having empirical consequences amenable to subsequent tests. If all explanations consonant with the known facts (always an infinite set) were treated as equally unjustified by the evidence, Hume's problem would certainly be set aside, but only at the cost of ignoring what provoked it—namely, the apparent existence of rationally acceptable nondemonstrative arguments. It can hardly be denied that there are nondemonstrative arguments lending reasonable support to their conclusions; otherwise it would be as reasonable to expect manna from heaven as rain from a cloud. Anti-inductivists have seldom been hardy enough to brand all inductive arguments as equally invalid, but as soon as they discriminate between alternative hypotheses as more or less corroborated, more or less in accord with available facts, they are faced, in a new terminology, with substantially the original problems of justification and differential appraisal.

INDUCTIVE SUPPORT FOR INDUCTION

To the layman the most natural way of defending belief in induction is that it has worked in the past. Concealed in this reply, of course, is the assumption that what has already worked will continue to do so, an assumption that has seemed objectionably circular to nearly all philosophers of induction. A stubborn minority (including R. B. Braithwaite and Max Black), however, insists that the appearance of circularity arises only from overhasty application of criteria applicable to deduction. Even in the limiting case, where the rule governing the supporting argument from previous efficacy is the very rule that is to be defended, it can be plausibly argued that no formal circularity is present. Nor is there the more subtle circularity that would obtain if knowledge of the conclusion's truth were needed to justify use of the self-supporting argument. In spite of spirited objections, this line of reasoning has not yet, in the writer's opinion, been shown to be mistaken.

The point that inductive support of induction is not necessarily circular has some importance as illustrating the interesting self-applying and self-correcting features of inductive rules; in virtue of these features, scrutiny of the consequences of the adoption of such rules can, in favorable cases, be used to refine the proper scope of inductive rules and the appropriate judgments of their strength.

A more serious weakness of this kind of defense, if it deserves to be called that, is lack of clarity about what counts as success in using the rule, which is connected in turn with the insufficiently discussed question of the *raison d'être* of induction considered as an autonomous mode of reasoning.

But even if this controversial type of inductive support of inductive rules ultimately survives criticism, it will not dispose of the metaphysical problems of induction. Those satisfied with Hume's conception of the problem are at bottom objecting to any use of inductive concepts and of the language in which they are expressed unless there is deductive justification for such use. They will therefore reject any reliance upon induction by way of defense, however free from formal defect, as essentially irrelevant to the primary task of philosophical justification. It must be admitted that inductive support of induction, however congenial to the layman, does not go to the roots of the philosophical perplexity.

## A PRIORI DEFENSES

A few modern writers (notably D. C. Williams and R. F. Harrod) have maintained that certain inductive arguments, unimproved by the addition of supplementary premises or by modification of the form of the conclusion, can be *proved* to be valid. Williams has argued, with surprising plausibility, that the probable truth of the conclusion of a statistical syllogism can be shown to be necessitated by the truth of the premises, solely by reference to accredited principles of the mathematical theory of chances. While admiring the ingenuity displayed in this approach, critics have generally agreed in finding it fallacious. That some modes of inductive argument are certified as sound or acceptable on broadly *a priori* (perhaps ultimately linguistic) grounds is, however, a contention of some versions of the linguistic approach.

### DEDUCTIVE RECONSTRUCTION

The effort to provide justification for induction through a reconstruction of inductive arguments so as to make them deductively valid has chiefly taken two forms.

*Search for Supreme Inductive Principles.* If a given nondemonstrative argument, say from the amalgamated premise $P$ to a conclusion $K$ (where $K$, for the present, is regarded as a categorical statement of fact containing no reference to probability), is looked at through deductive spectacles, it is bound to seem invalid and so to be regarded as at best an enthymeme, needing extra premises to become respectable. It is easy, of course, to render the original argument deductively valid by supplying the additional premise "If $P$ then $K$" (this premise will be called $Q$). In order for induction to be defended in the classical way, however, the premises have to be true and known to be true. Since $P$ was supposed not to entail $K$, the new premise, $Q$, will be a contingent statement of fact, knowledge of whose truth is presumably to be derived either by deduction from more general principles or by induction from empirical data. In either case, if the deductive standard of justification is to be respected, the process must continue until we obtain general factual principles, neither capable of further empirical support nor needing such support.

[72]

The line of thought is the following: Since $K$ does not follow strictly from $P$, the fact that the truth of propositions resembling $P$ in assignable ways is regularly associated with the truth of propositions resembling $K$ is a contingent fact about the actual universe. Looked at in another way, if events occurred purely at random, it would be impossible to make successful inductions; conversely, if inductions of a certain sort do systematically produce true conclusions, there must be a contingent regularity in the universe that should be capable of expression in the form of supreme principles or postulates of induction. Only if such postulates are true can inductions be sound; they must therefore be the assumed but unexpressed premises of all sound inductive arguments.

Favored candidates for the role of such enabling postulates have been the principle that the future resembles the past (Hume), a general principle of causation to the effect that every event has a sufficient cause (Mill), a principle of spatiotemporal homogeneity, which makes locations and dates causally irrelevant (Mill again), and a principle of limited independent variety ensuring that the attributes of individuals cluster together in a finite number of groups (J. M. Keynes, C. D. Broad; Keynes's principle, however, was intended to ensure only the probability of inductive conclusions). Any of these, if true, records the presence in the universe of a certain global regularity or order which permits inductive procedures to produce the desired true conclusions. For example, if we somehow knew in advance that a given attribute $C$ of an observed event must have some other attribute invariably associated with it, and if we further knew that the associated attribute must be included in a finite list of known attributes, say $E_1, E_2, \ldots, E_n$, then there would be a good prospect that repeated observations of similar events would eliminate all but one of the possible associations, $E_1 - E_i$. Refinements aside, this is how Mill, for instance, conceived of inductive method; his celebrated "methods" (which have received attention out of all proportion to their merits) reduce, in the end, to deductive pro-

[73]

cedures for eliminating unfit candidates for the title of necessary or sufficient conditions. (Later attempts to develop eliminative induction follow substantially the same path.)

It is clear that the whole interest of this program rests upon the considerations that can be advanced in favor of the supreme premises. If the supreme premises can be known to be true, the remaining processes of inference become trivial (so that there is no need for an autonomous logic of induction); if not, the entire project floats in the void.

The task of formulating plausible principles of the sort envisaged by this program has proved harder than Mill supposed. However, it may be argued that the search for them is pointless and misguided. For one thing, they would accomplish too much: if known to be true, they would allow the conclusions of selected primary inductions to be demonstrated as true, which is too much to expect. It is generally agreed (and rightly so) that the conclusion of even the best inductive argument may without contradiction turn out to be false—if only through bad luck.

Still more serious is the problem of how, from the standpoint of this program, the desired supreme premises could ever be known to be true. Since appeal to induction is excluded at this point on the score of circularity, and since the principles themselves cannot be analytic if they are to serve their desired purpose, there seems no recourse at all. At this point those who search for supreme inductive principles find themselves with empty hands. Mill, for instance, was compelled to let his whole program rest upon the supposed reliability of simple enumeration (the method he regarded as the weakest), in whose defense he had nothing better to say than that it is "universally applicable" (which, on his principles, delightfully begs the question); Keynes, forsaking his empiricist principles for a half-hearted flirtation with Kant, could do no better than to suggest that the ultimate principles rest upon "some direct synthetic knowledge" of the general regularity of the universe. Induction may indeed beg to be spared such defenders as these; better the robust

[74]

skepticism of Hume or Popper than the lame evasions of Mill or Keynes.

The conclusion seems inescapable that any attempt to show (as Bacon and many others have hoped) that there are general ontological guarantees for induction is doomed to failure from the outset.

*Recourse to Probability.* A more promising way, at least at first sight, of hewing to the deductive line is to modify the conclusion of an inductive argument by including some explicit reference to probability. This approach, influential since Keynes's spirited exposition of it, still has many adherents. If there is no prospect of plugging the deductive gap between $P$ and $K$ by adding further premises known to be true, then perhaps the same end can be achieved by weakening the conclusion. If $K$ does not follow from $P$, why not be satisfied with a more modest conclusion of the form "Probably, $K$" or perhaps "$K$ has such and such a probability relative to $P$"?

The most impressive projects of this sort so far available have encountered severe technical difficulties. It is essential to Keynes's program, for instance, that the probability of a generalization relative to an unbroken series of confirmatory instances steadily approach unity. The conditions necessary for this to be possible in his program are at least that the generalization have an initial nonzero probability and that infinitely many of the confirmatory instances be independent, in the sense of having less than maximal probability of occurrence given the already accumulated evidence. The supreme ontological principles to which Keynes was ultimately driven to appeal (see the preceding section) hardly suffice to satisfy these conditions; subsequent criticism—for example, by Nicod and G. H. von Wright—has shown that even more rigorous conditions are needed. (Von Wright has argued that the desired asymptotic convergence will result only if in the long run every instance of the generalization is scrutinized— which would certainly render the theory somewhat less than useful in practical application.) For all his importance as a founder of confirmation theory, the theory advocated by Keynes must be judged a failure.

*Carnap's Construction.* The merits of Carnap's impressively sustained construction of inductive logic, following in the tradition of Laplace and Keynes but surpassing the work of both in elaboration and sophistication, are still in dispute. Taking probability to express a logical relation between propositions, Carnap has shown how, in certain simplified languages, it is possible to define the breadth or logical width of a given proposition. (Roughly speaking, the degree of confirmation given by a proposition $x$ to a proposition $y$ is the ratio of the width of $x. y$ to the width of $x$.) The definition of logical width depends on the class of possible universes expressible in the language in question. In order to assign a definite measure of logical width it is necessary to adopt some method of weighting the various possible universes ("state descriptions," in Carnap's terminology) compatible with a given proposition. One of the merits of Carnap's analysis is to have shown that there is an entire continuum of alternative weighting procedures and associated inductive methods, each of which is internally coherent. The arbitrariness thereby recognized in inductive procedure has worried even the most sympathetic of Carnap's readers; still more disturbing is the emergence of what might be called the paradox of the unconfirmable generalization—the impossibility of ensuring, by Carnap's principles, that an unbroken series of positive instances will raise the probability of a generalization above zero. (Carnap retorts that an instance confirmation—that is, the conclusion of an eduction—does acquire progressively increasing probability, but this is insufficient to satisfy those critics who still hope to find a place for authentic generalization within inductive method.) It is too soon to decide whether such problems as these are more than the teething pains of a new subject. The ingenious modifications of Carnap's program suggested by, among others, J. G. Kemeny and Jaakko Hintikka offer some hope for their elimination.

More serious is the fundamental difficulty that flows from

Carnap's conception of confirmation statements as analytic. If it is a truth of logic (broadly speaking) that given the selected definition of confirmation, presented evidence confirms a given hypothesis to such and such a degree, then how could such an *a priori* truth justify any rational belief in the hypothesis? Or, again, if someone were to adopt a different definition of confirmation and thereby be led to a contrary belief, then how could he be shown to be in error? Carnap's answer is based on the notion that the bridge between confirmation, as defined by him, and rational belief is to be found in some principle for the maximization of expected utility (due allowance being made, however—in his sophisticated rendering of that principle—for subjective estimates of probabilities and utilities). Yet it seems that because considerations of probability also enter into the calculation of probabilities and expected utilities, a logical circle is involved here. Since Carnap's discussions of this fundamental point are still comparatively rough and provisional, it would be premature to reach any final judgment on the success that he and those who agree with him are likely to achieve in coping with this basic difficulty. (It might be said that difficulty with the connection between probability judgments and practice is not peculiar to Carnap's work, since it arises in one form or another for all theorists of induction who take the trouble to work out in detail the consequences of their principles and assumptions.) It may be held, however, that Carnap's relatively cursory judgments about the justification of induction belong to the least satisfactory parts of his work on inductive logic.

How much the recourse to probability will accomplish depends, of course, upon how the reference to probability is construed. With empirical interpretations of probability, such as those favored by "frequentists" (see Chapter VI), the probability conclusion still extends beyond the premises by covert reference to finite or infinite sets of events not covered by the given premises. The inductive leap remaining in the reconstructed argument will thus still leave the problem of induction unsolved. If, however, probability is construed in some logical way (as by Keynes or Carnap), the amended conclusion will say less than the premises and will therefore be untouched by subsequent empirical test; the deductive validity of the reconstructed argument will be saved only at the cost of rendering problematic its relevance to prediction and empirical control. In converting a purportedly inductive argument into a valid deductive one, the very point of the original argument—that is, to risk a prediction concerning the yet unknown—seems to be destroyed.

### PRAGMATIC DEFENSES

Answers of the pragmatic type, originally offered by Peirce but independently elaborated with great resourcefulness by Hans Reichenbach, are among the most original modern contributions to the subject. To many they still offer the best hope of avoiding what seems to be the inevitable failure of the attempts so far discussed. The germ of the pragmatic strategy is the reflection that in ordinary life, situations sometimes arise where, in default of reliable knowledge of consequences, problematic choices can still be justified by a "nothing to lose" argument. Faced with a choice between an operation for cancer and a sure death, a patient may choose surgery, not because of any assurance of cure but on the rational ground that nothing is lost by taking the chance.

*Reichenbach's "Vindication."* According to Reichenbach, the case is similar in what he takes to be the paradigmatic inductive situation. Given an antecedent interest in determining the probability of occurrence of a designated character (construed, by him, as the limit, in an infinitely long run of events, of the relative frequency of occurrence of that character), Reichenbach argues that the only rationally defensible policy is to use the already ascertained relative frequency of occurrence as a provisional estimate of the ultimate limiting value. A man who proceeds in this way can have no guarantee or assurance that his estimates, constantly revised as information about the series gradually accumulates, will bring him into the neighborhood of a limiting value of the frequency, for the provisional values of the relative frequencies may, in fact, diverge. In that case no predictive policy at all will work, and successful induction is impossible. However, if this should not be the case and the series really does have a limiting value for the relative frequency in question, we can know in advance, and with certainty, that the policy is bound eventually to lead the reasoner to estimates that will remain as close to the limit as desired. There is therefore nothing to lose by adopting the inductive policy: if the series of events under scrutiny is sufficiently regular to make induction possible, the recommended policy is bound to yield the desired result ultimately (and we know before we start that it will do so), whereas if the series is irregular enough to defeat the standard inductive policy, nothing will avail, and we are no worse off than if a contrary decision had been made.

This type of justification is often called "vindication," as Herbert Feigl termed it. It is claimed that in a sense the type of vindication sketched above resolves Hume's problem by bypassing it. We know for certain that what Hume desired— namely, certification of the soundness of inductive argument by the standard of demonstrative reasoning—cannot be supplied. But it would be fainthearted to leave the matter there. By conceiving the practice of induction as the adoption of certain policies, applied in stoic acceptance of the impossibility of assured success in obtaining reliable knowledge concerning matters of fact, we are able to see that such policies are, in a clear sense, preferable to any of their competitors. Standard induction is preferable to soothsaying because we know that it will work (will approach limiting values in the long run) if *anything* will.

To these plausible claims it has been objected that the analogy with genuinely practical decisions to act upon insufficient evidence is misconceived, for in the state of perfect ignorance postulated by defenders of the pragmatic approach no method at all can be regarded as superior to any other. Vindicationists have been relatively undisturbed by such general criticism; they have, however, felt obliged to

[79]

seek remedies for a grave technical flaw that threatens to wreck their entire program. Given the assumption that the best to be achieved by an inductive policy is asymptotic convergence to a limiting relative frequency, it is obvious that no policy for inductive estimation in the short run is excluded as unreasonable. Thus, from the standpoint of pragmatic vindication an unbroken run of $A$'s found to be $B$ would not make it unreasonable to predict the subsequent occurrence *in the short run* of $A$'s that are not $B$, provided only that the adopted estimates are chosen so as to converge eventually to the limit (if it exists). But since the long run is in fact never attained, even by immortal beings, it follows that the pragmatic defense yields no criteria for inductive decisions in short-run cases, to which inductive prediction is confined, and offers no differential reasons for preferring one inductive policy to another.

In spite of strenuous attempts (notably by Wesley Salmon) to improve Reichenbach's original conception by providing supplementary reasons for rejecting unwanted nonstandard policies, the prospects for vindicationism remain dubious. Even if some plausible way could be found of assigning, on vindicationist principles, a special status to the standard policy of induction, the approach would be vulnerable to the objection that it conceives inductive method in an eccentrically restricted fashion. The determination of limiting values of relative frequencies is at best a special problem of inductive method and by no means the most fundamental.

*Peirce's Views.* Peirce, whose views on induction have exerted a lasting influence on the subject since the posthumous appearance of his *Collected Papers,* had a more complex conception of scientific method than latter-day vindicationists.

Induction, conceived by him as a process of testing statistical hypotheses by examining random samples, has to be understood in its relations to two other procedures, statistical deduction and abduction.

Statistical deduction consists of inference from the frequency of occurrence of an attribute in a population to the probable and approximate occurrence of that attribute in a sample randomly drawn from it. Given Peirce's definition of probability as limiting frequency and his conception of randomness, it follows demonstratively that most of the samples drawn will have nearly the same composition as the parent population; statistical deduction is thus "valid" in the sense that it generates conclusions that are true most of the time.

Abduction, the creative formulation of statistical hypotheses and the only mode of scientific inference introducing new ideas, is a kind of inversion of statistical deduction. It has almost no probative force, its value being rather that it provides new generalizations needing independent verification and having "some chance of being true."

When the three procedures are used in combination, induction is seen to be a self-correcting method that if indefinitely followed must in the long run lead the scientific community, although not the individual reasoner, indefinitely close to the truth. In such asymptotic convergence to the truth lies the peculiar validity of induction.

Peirce cannot be held to have succeeded in his effort to defend the rationality of inductive policies in terms of long-range efficacy in generating conclusions approximately and for the most part true. Since the intended justification of induction depends essentially upon the randomness of the samples used, it must be objected that there is normally no way of guaranteeing in advance the presence of such randomness. (To this objection Peirce had only the lame and unsupported rejoinder that inductive inference retains some probative force even in the absence of the desired randomness.) The following are among the most obvious weaknesses of Peirce's views about induction.

The self-corrective tendency of induction, which Peirce, in his last writings on the subject, came to view as the heart and essence of inductive method, remains obscure, in spite of his eulogies. That inductive estimates will need, on Peirce's

principles, repeated adjustments as further evidence accumulates is clear enough, but that this process will show
any convergence toward a limiting value cannot be guaranteed *a priori*. If the samples to be examined were random in
Peirce's severe sense of that term, we could at least count
upon an over-all predominance of approximately correct
estimates, but even then we should have no reason, in the
absence of additional guarantees, to expect the better estimates to come near the end of the testing process. In any case,
supposing realistic conditions for the testing of hypotheses
(such as our necessary reliance on cases that we are in a position to examine), it seems clear that the conditions for the
kind of sampling demanded by Peirce cannot be fulfilled.

Peirce's references to the long run seem on the whole incoherent. Much of the time he seems to have been thinking
of what would prove to be the case in an actual but infinitely
extended series of trials. Toward the end of his life, however,
he appears to have recognized that his definitions of probability and of the validity of induction needed to be construed
more broadly, by reference to the "would be" of events, conceived as real general characters or habits. How such general
features of events can in fact be disclosed, even by very
lengthy series of trials, Peirce never made plain. Yet the need
for clarification is great for anybody attracted by his approach. The infinitely long run is a chimera, and to be told
that a certain method, if consistently pursued, would in such
a long run eventually lead as close as we pleased to the truth
is to be told nothing that can be useful for the actual process
of verification. All verification is necessarily performed in the
finite run, however extended in length, and what would
happen if *per impossibile* the "run" were infinite is not relevant to the relative appraisal of given hypotheses. We need a
method for adjudicating between rival hypotheses, if not now
then in the foreseeable future, and this Peirce's conception
cannot provide. Because of his reliance upon the infinitely
long run Peirce's pragmaticism, which initially seems so
hardheaded in its emphasis upon success and practical con-

[82]

sequences, ends by being as utopian as any of the metaphysical conceptions that he derided.

## JUSTIFICATION AS A PSEUDO PROBLEM

In view of the quandaries which beset all known attempts to answer Hume's challenge, it is reasonable to consider whether the problem itself may not have been misconceived. Indeed, it appears upon examination that the task of logical justification of induction, as classically conceived, is framed so as to be *a priori* impossible of solution. If induction is by definition nondeductive and if the demand for justification is, at bottom, that induction be shown to satisfy conditions of correctness appropriate only to deduction, then the task is certainly hopeless. But to conclude, for this reason, that induction is basically invalid or that a belief based upon inductive grounds can never be reasonable is to transfer, in a manner all too enticing, criteria of evaluation from one domain to another domain, in which they are inappropriate. Sound inductive conclusions do not follow (in the deductive sense of "follow") from even the best and strongest set of premises (in the inductive sense of "strongest"); there is no good reason why they should. Those who still seek a classical defense of induction may be challenged to show why deductive standards of justification should be appropriate.

Perhaps the retort will be that there is no clear sense in which assertion of a conclusion is justified except the sense in which it is known to follow strictly from premises known to be true, so the burden of argument rests upon anybody who claims the existence of some other sense.

*Linguistic Approach to the Problem.* The challenge to the claim that inductive arguments cannot be said to be justified might be met in the following way: Suppose a man has learned, partly from his own experience and partly from the testimony of others, that in a vast variety of circumstances, when stones are released they fall toward the ground. Let him consider the proposition $K$, that any stone chosen at random and released will do likewise. This is, in the writer's opinion, a paradigm case for saying that the man in question (any of us) has a good reason for asserting $K$ and is therefore justified in asserting $K$ rather than not-$K$. Similarly, this is a paradigm case for saying that the man in question is reasonable in asserting $K$ and would be unreasonable in asserting not-$K$, on the evidence at hand. Anybody who claimed otherwise would not be extraordinarily and admirably scrupulous but would be abusing language by violating some of the implicit criteria for the uses of "good reason," "justified," and "reasonable," to which he, like the interlocutor with whom he succeeds in communicating, is in fact committed.

Any man—say, one from Mars—who used these words according to criteria that would really make it improper for him to apply them in the kind of situation envisaged would not, in the end, be *understood* by us. Worse still, he would be trying, if he were consistent, to change our actual concepts of reason and reasonableness so that it would be logically impossible to have reasons for assertions concerning the unknown or to be reasonable in expecting one matter of fact rather than another on the basis of empirical evidence. (He would be behaving like a man who insisted that only stallions deserved to be called horses.) Nor would such distortion achieve anything significant, for the man who proposed to make "empirical reason" as impossible of application as "being in two places at once" would find himself forced to reintroduce essentially the same concept under some such label as "generally accepted as a reason" or "what commonly passes for a reason." The distinction between what ordinary men and what scientists call "good reasons" and "bad reasons" is made for a good purpose, has practical consequences, and is indispensable in practice. Thus, the dispute between the advocate of the linguistic approach and his opponent seems to reduce to a verbal one, ripe for oblivion.

Given the intertwined complexity of the concepts entering into alternative formulations of the problem of induction and the seductive plausibility of the distortions to which such concepts are subject, no brief reply such as the above can

[84]

be expected to clarify and to expose the conceptual confusions upon which traditional formulations of the problem rest. A full discussion would at least also have to consider the relevant senses of "knowledge" and "possibility" and related epistemological notions. The outline of the strategy is perhaps sufficiently plain; the line to be taken is that close and detailed examination of how the key words in the statement of the problem occur will show that criteria for the correct uses of such terms are violated in subtle and plausible ways. If this can be established, the celebrated problem of justifying induction will dissolve, and the confused supposition that induction needs philosophical justification or remains precarious in its absence will disappear.

The comparative problem and the analytical problem do not dissolve under this attack. Advocates of the linguistic approach can be fairly reproached for having been too often content to show to their own satisfaction that the general problem of justification is rooted in confusion, while neglecting the constructive tasks of rendering clearer the criteria for preferential appraisal of inductive arguments.

To those unsympathetic with the linguistic approach such an attack upon the traditional problem has sometimes seemed to be operating with dubious and insufficiently elaborated theories of meaning or use and to be altogether too glib in its attribution of semantical confusions. Moreover, a number of critics have thought that an appeal to ordinary language cannot be ultimately decisive from a philosophical standpoint. Even if it were established that it is a violation of ordinary language to describe the conclusion of some inductive arguments as supported by less than good reasons, the critics ask, what is there in the nature of things that requires us to continue talking in the ordinary way or to be bound by the encapsulated metaphysical prejudices of those originally responsible for establishing the rules of use to which appeal is now made? The linguistic philosopher necessarily uses such key words as "reasonable" in his polemic against the traditional approaches to the problem. But to use

[85]

the crucial terms in a discussion of the nature of the inductive problem, it might be urged, is to beg the very question at issue. A lunatic or an eccentric philosopher might well use the expression "good reason" in a way that would be blatantly improper, yet he might be able to prove, by appeal to his own criteria, that he had "good reasons" to use the phrase in the way he did. But are we ourselves in any better position? Are we not obligated to break through the linguistic barrier and at least to show why the alleged criteria for good reasons to which appeal is made should continue to receive our allegiance?

There is no short way of dealing with this type of objection. It may be helpful, however, to sketch the general view upon which the present writer, as defender of the linguistic approach, would rely.

*Defense of the Linguistic Approach.* All normal adult human beings follow the same broad and systematic patterns for drawing inferences concerning the unobserved and apply the same general principles for appraising such nondemonstrative inferences. For instance, all normal persons expect observed cases of association of attributes to be confirmed in further experience unless there are countervailing factors (the principle of simple enumeration), all count increase in the number of independent confirmatory instances of a law as strengthening (or at least not weakening) the probability of the law's truth, and all alike share the inductive beliefs that underpin causal notions. It is, therefore, not fanciful to conceive of all sane adult human beings as participating in a complex system of ways of learning from experience that might be called the inductive institution. Like other institutions (warfare, the law, and so on), it has a relatively fixed, though not immutable, structure, transmitted from one generation to the next and crystallized in the form of prohibitions and licenses, maxims of conduct, and informal precepts of performance. Like other institutions, the inductive institution requires that its participants have mastered a system of distinctive concepts (among them the concepts of good

[86]

reason, sound argument, and relative likelihood) having both descriptive and normative aspects. Such mastery is shown in capacity to use the corresponding language correctly—which, in turn, implies recognition of, though not invariable obedience to, associated rules for assertion, for evaluation, and for the appraisal of actions. Understanding what people mean by reasons for empirical conclusions requires acceptance of certain types of situations as paradigmatic of empirical evidence; to call given facts sound reasons for some conclusion is to imply the acceptability of certain criteria for judging one reason to be better than another; asserting that some belief about the hitherto unobserved is reasonable commits the speaker to holding that other things being equal, action based on such belief should be approved.

The philosophical problem of justifying induction can arise only for somebody who is a member of the inductive institution and is therefore already bound by its constitutive rules. A man can understand bridge without being a player, but all of us are necessarily players of the "inductive game" before we achieve the reflective self-consciousness characteristic of philosophical criticism.

The constitutive rules of the inductive institution (whose precise delineation remains a still unfinished task for philosophers of induction) are highly abstract, schematic, and limited in their practical usefulness. Indeed, the general principles of inductive inference are about as relevant to practice as the abstract principles of justice are to decisions on concrete legal issues. In particular situations concerning the soundness of empirical hypotheses the reasoner is compelled to fall back upon his specific knowledge of relevant facts and theories. In this way the conduct of concrete inductive inference resembles the exercise of a craft or skill more than it does the automatic application of a decision procedure. Yet the constitutive rules provide important general constraints that cannot be violated without generating nonsense.

To be in command of inductive language, whether as a

master of advanced techniques of statistical inference or as a layman constantly and more or less skillfully anticipating future experience, is necessarily to be subject to the implicit norms of belief and conduct imposed by the institution.

The inductive concepts that we acquire by example and formal education and modify through our own experiences are not exempt even from drastic revision. The norms may be usefully thought of as formal crystallizations into linguistic rules of general modes of response to the universe that our ancestors have, on the whole, found advantageous to survival, but the earlier experience of the race never has absolute authority. Piecemeal reform of the inductive institution can be observed in the history of modern science. What is clearly impossible, however, is the sort of wholesale revolution that would be involved in wiping the inductive slate clean and trying to revert to the condition of some hypothetical Adam setting out to learn from experience without previous indoctrination in relevant rules of inductive procedure. This would be tantamount to attempting to destroy the language we now use to talk about the world and about ourselves and thereby to destroy the concepts embodied in that language. The idea of ceasing to be an inductive reasoner is a monstrosity. The task is not impossibly difficult; rather, its very formulation fails to make sense. Yet it remains important to insist that the inductive institution, precisely because its *raison d'être* is learning from experience, is intrinsically self-critical. Induction, like the Sabbath, was made for man, not vice versa. Thus, constantly renewed experience of the successes and failures of the specific inductive procedures permitted within the general framework of the inductive institution provides a sound basis for gradual reform of the institution itself, without objectionable circularity.

Yet even if no feature of the institution is exempt, in principle, from criticism and reconstruction, the entire institution cannot be called into question all at once without destroying the very meaning of the words in which the

[88]

philosophical problems of induction are stated. Wholesale philosophical skepticism about matters of fact is senseless and must be shown to be so. If this is the "linguo-centric predicament," we must make the best of it.

The view here outlined must be carefully distinguished from what is commonly called conventionalism. The argument is not that the constitutive inductive rules hold by convention but rather that the sweeping question "Why should we accept *any* inductive rules?" can be shown to make no sense.

Our sketch may be usefully compared with Hume's view of induction as a habit or custom. Both views agree in regarding inductive practices as being, on the whole, social and contingent facts obtaining at given periods in human history. It is, after all, a contingent fact that there have existed animals sufficiently rational to be able to speak and hence to have inductive concepts. The present conception differs significantly from Hume's, however, in regarding the inductive institution as partly constituted by normative inductive rules to which the philosopher, like every reasoning man, finds himself already committed. Thus, the encompassing social fact of the existence of the inductive institution includes within itself the means for appraisal and criticism of inductive procedures; we cannot regard inductive inference as something merely "given," as a natural fact, like the Milky Way, that it would be absurd to criticize. To understand induction is necessarily to accept its authority. However (to repeat), questions about the general or ultimate justification of induction *as such,* questions of the form "Why should any induction be trusted?" must be recognized as senseless. If we persist in trying to raise them, we come, as Wittgenstein expressed it, to the "limits of language," and we can see that we have done so by perceiving that what we had hoped were important and fundamental questions are no better than nonsense masquerading as sense.

The foregoing will undoubtedly strike critics of the linguistic approach as too facile, for the tangle of philosophical problems that have been dubbed "the problem of induction" constitute, in their depth, their importance, their elusiveness, and their capacity to bewilder and confuse, a very paradigm of philosophical perplexity.

The foregoing survey indicates that no wholly satisfactory philosophy of induction is yet available. The work still to be done may be summarized as follows: for those who recognize the crucial role of probability in inductive inference, to develop a consistent, systematic, and relevant reconstruction of the concept of probability; for those who reject induction as an outmoded myth, to elaborate a detailed and comprehensive account of scientific practice that will be reasonably close to the best actual procedures used in reasoning about matters of fact; for those who pin their hopes on the construction of an inductive logic, to remove the constraints imposed by the study of artificially simplified languages and to show in detail how analytical statements of probability can be relevant to the practice of inductive prediction; for vindicationists, to solve the comparative problem of selecting competing hypotheses and to show how eventual convergence in the long run can bear upon short-run judgment; for those who regard induction as a pseudo problem, to articulate the theory of language presupposed and to demonstrate in convincing detail the origins and the character of the stubborn confusions that have infested the subject.

# VI

# *Probability*

OUR DISCUSSION of probability consists of three main parts. It seems advisable to trace in outline in the first part the "common sense of probability," the complex pattern of ordinary uses of "probably" and its semantic cognates that is the starting point for all attempts at philosophical analysis or reconstruction. Equally important is the well-established mathematical theory of probability, whose main outlines have been known for over two centuries and which is discussed in the second part. The concluding part outlines the main alternative types of philosophical interpretations of probability available at the time of writing. These three parts are relatively independent and can be read in any order.

It is unusual enough to be disconcerting when a philosopher, in his professional capacity, makes an assertion of the form "Probably P" or of the form "The probability of $P_2$, given D, is such and such." The natural context for a reference to probability is an assertion about matters of fact, about which philosophers are, by general consent, professionally indifferent. When a philosopher says that he hopes to have rendered it probable that arithmetic can be reduced to logic (Gottlob Frege) or urges that common sense has on the whole a higher probability of being right than any conflicting metaphysical theory (Bertrand Russell), he is perhaps merely reminding the reader of human fallibility. Indispensable references to probability are, however, a distinguishing feature of nondemonstrative arguments concerning matters of fact, which require more or less precise indications of the imputed reliability of both premises and conclusion. The rationale of nondemonstrative argument is a topic of great philosophical interest.

Corresponding interest in the concept of probability is heightened by its intimate connection with the still more elusive and important concept of rationality. Indeed, Pierre Simon de Laplace's dictum that the most important questions in life are usually those of probability is hardly overstated. Anybody who aspires to rationality must be guided by probabilities in the face of uncertainty: how this is to be done and with what justification are the main themes of the philosophy of probability.

Here, as elsewhere, the most pressing philosophical tasks are those of clarifying, analyzing, and, if need be, "reconstructing" the concept and its cognates. The "begin-all" of such work, as those who undertake it recognize, is the "ordinary" or "preanalytical" concept, whose relevant features are manifested in the accepted usages of the corresponding probability expressions.

## Common Sense of Probability

An adequate survey of laymen's talk about probability must take account of the uses of the words "probably," "probable," and "probability," together with their numerous synonyms, antonyms, and paronyms. However, it is plausible to assign logical primacy to the use of the adverb, in combination with singular sentences or "that"-clauses. It is at any rate convenient to start with the ordinary uses of such a sentence as "Probably a black ball will be drawn," where what may be called the *kernel sentence* ("A black ball will be drawn") refers to a particular event (the drawing of a ball from a bag) whose *outcome* (relevant feature—whether the ball is black or white) is unknown at the time of utterance.

The following comments are at least plausible:

(1) "Probably" is semantically akin to "possibly" and "certainly." More precisely, "probably" usually fits any sentence frame into which the other two adverbs fit, so that one may

[92]

be substituted for either of the others without violating syntax or logic.

(2) "Probably" implies "possibly" and excludes "certainly": what is probable is neither certain nor impossible. Anyone who says that a black ball will probably be drawn from an urn implies that it is possible for such a ball to be drawn and also that it is not certain that it will be—and similarly in other cases.

(3) In such contexts, the relevant sense of possibility is that of empirical, not "logical," possibility. A speaker who claims that a black ball may "possibly" be drawn is, to be sure, implying the absence of logical inconsistency between a statement of the known initial conditions (the nature and composition of the balls in the urn and the manner of drawing) and a prediction to the effect that a black ball will in fact be drawn. But he implies more. He means that in view of the urn's contents and the mode of selection the drawing of a black ball is not ruled out *by the facts* in the way that the drawing of a black bird would be. (Behind this is the idea that the nature of things excludes the occurrence of much that is logically possible.)

(4) As suggested by the last remark, there is implicit reference, in a statement of the form under consideration, to "initial conditions" (or, more colloquially, to the "way things are now"—that is to say, in advance of the trial). "Probably a black ball will be drawn" may be taken as elliptical for "Given that we have such and such an urn, containing such and such balls of known colors, etc., a black ball will probably be drawn." The initial conditions are identified by means of some abstract description: different descriptions of the state of the world may generate different estimates of probability. (Information about the electrical charge of the balls, for instance, may affect the probability of drawing a black one.)

(5) Often, a speaker will assert "Probably P" in partial or total ignorance of the initial conditions (with correspondingly weak reasons for his judgment); then the force of the state-

[93]

ment is, approximately, "In view of the unknown state of the universe prior to the trial, a black ball will probably be drawn."

(6) Grammatically speaking, the adverb "probably" modifies the entire "kernel sentence" (or, in other contexts, the entire "that"-clause) to which it is attached. This is suggested in English, as in other languages, by the "parenthetical" nature of this adverb—its capacity to appear, without grammatical impropriety, almost anywhere between the words of the kernel sentence.

(7) If a kernel sentence by itself ("A black ball will be drawn") is taken to express the occurrence of some yet-to-be-realized event, situation, or state of affairs, we shall have to say, in the material mode, that probability, like possibility and certainty, is ordinarily attributed to such a "situation"— to something expressed by the sentence. Thus, "probably" belongs, *prima facie,* to the object language, not to a metalanguage in which features of verbal expressions are mentioned rather than used. It is therefore misleading to say, as some writers do, that probability is an attribute of propositions. If this kind of idiom is to be employed, accuracy requires us to say that probability judgments concern the probability of a proposition's *being true* rather than the probability of the proposition *simpliciter.*

(8) In some uses, at least, "Probably a black ball will be drawn" implies that a black ball *will* be drawn. (This point, more controversial than its predecessors, would be denied by many theorists.) There is an absurdity in saying "Probably a black ball will be drawn, but all the same a black ball will not be drawn." Although the speaker's use of "probably" is intended to intimate that the initial conditions are insufficiently strong to render the designated outcome empirically certain, the whole assertion, however guarded by acknowledgment of fallibility, is intended to commit the speaker to the kernel's truth. A layman, uninfluenced by the supposed demands of a correct philosophical analysis, will say, after drawing a white ball, "I was wrong"—falsity of

[94]

the kernel counts as a setback, a failure. Of course the speaker may add, "But I was justified in saying what I did— namely, that a black ball would probably be drawn."

(9) We can accordingly distinguish between the appropriateness of a probability statement and its correctness. According to the view here recommended, a singular probability assertion has the double aim of seeking to make an appropriate attribution of probability while also seeking to predict the "outcome." Thus, the point of making a probability assertion is to make a prediction that is both sound (justified by the evidence) and successful (true); if it is the first, it may be called warranted, if the second, fulfilled. (It is interesting to note that "true" and "false" seem incongruous modifiers of entire probability sentences.) The assertive aspect of an adverbial probability assertion is often suppressed in adjectival uses of "probable" and is almost invariably absent from substantival uses of "probability."

(10) "Probably" admits of adverbs of comparison—probability is "gradable." The supplementary question, "How probable?" always in order after a "probably"-assertion has been made, may be answered by "Rather probable," "Highly probable," "Almost certain," and even, in special contexts to be discussed below, by an indication of numerical chances, or odds.

(11) Possibility is gradable in approximately the same way that probability is: the question "How possible?," odd as it might seem to some philosophers, occurs in ordinary talk and can be answered by "Very possible," "Almost certain," etc. "Certainly," on the other hand, functions as a boundary, which possibility and probability may approach without reaching. In ordinary uses, certainty is not a special case of probability. "Close to being certain" and "nearly certain" are natural locutions, whereas "highly certain" and "rather certain" sound decidedly absurd.

(12) Gradations in probability, indicated by such rough expressions as "more probable than not," "somewhat probable," "very probable," and "so probable as to be almost cer-

[95]

tain," seem to correspond precisely to the corresponding gradations in possibility. (The awkwardness in saying, in English, "more possible than not" and "so possible as to be almost certain" can be discounted as resulting from accidents of idiom.)

It is worth considering, indeed, whether the common notion of probability is not merely that of greater or less possibility relative to the "initial conditions," considered in the light of its "distance" from certainty. This is, of course, unacceptable as an analysis, but perhaps no formal definition should be demanded; a sufficiently detailed description of the ramifying uses of "probably" and its semantic cousins is perhaps all that can be expected.

(13) On this identification of probability with empirical possibility, a question of the form "What is the probability of P, given D?" (when appropriate) asks for an estimate of the extent of the possibility for the truth of "P" left open by the truth of "D." Similarly, "What is the length of B?" asks for a measure of the extension of B along a certain direction. However, length is not to be identified with the numerical result of the comparison of extension with a standard body; nor is probability to be identified, as is too often done, with its numerical measure.

(14) The "assertive aspect" of ordinary uses of "probably" (see 8, above) is bound up, in ways that are hard to make precise, with the practical function of probability estimates within a general practice of acting upon the conclusions of nondemonstrative arguments. It would count as an absurdity in common contexts to say, for instance, "P is so probable as to be as good as certain, but I don't think that P will be the case." It would be equally absurd to say, "P is as good as certain, but I propose to take no measures appropriate to P's being the case." Roughly speaking, it is required by the general practice of drawing "risky inferences" to prepare for what is almost certain and to neglect what is extremely improbable. (The estimation of how improbable a conclusion

has to be in order to be properly ignored must, in the end, be left to the judgment of the reasoner.)

A sufficiently detailed account of the uses of "probably" (which cannot be undertaken here) would require collateral exploration of the relevant uses of "expectation," "reasonable," and "justification."

(15) A paradigm case for the use of "probably" is the following: Imagine a marble contained in a box that is closed except for a hole large enough to permit the marble to pass. Imagine the box to be shaken vigorously for, say, thirty seconds. Common sense urges that the ball then "has a chance" of being shaken out, because it is possible for this to occur. That this empirical possibility is present can be shown by repeatedly shaking the box for the prescribed time: if the marble sometimes falls out, it was possible for it to do so; if this *never* happens, common sense will conclude that it is "impossible for the marble to escape" in the specified conditions. If a fairly long series of trials under the prescribed conditions results in the ball's being shaken out in a substantial majority of cases, common sense will conclude that the ball will "probably" be shaken out on the next trial.

(16) Suppose now that an extra hole of the same size is punched in the box. Then it looks "obvious" or "self-evident" that the marble has acquired "an extra chance" or extra possibility of escape and that, correspondingly, the probability of its emergence has been raised (or, more cautiously, not lowered). But since empirical possibility is in question, the assumption can be put to empirical trial. If under the new conditions the marble is found on the whole to emerge in a substantially larger proportion of cases than before, the assumption that "its chances" of being shaken out have increased will be sufficiently verified. (If the new hole left the frequency of success unchanged, the conclusion would be that one hole somehow "interfered" with the other.) Observation of repeated trials provides evidence for probability judgments. To identify probability with propor-

tionate frequency is, however, as implausible as to identify possibility with eventual occurrence.

(17) It will have been noted that we have been using "possibility" and its rough synonym "chance" as general nouns. In paradigmatic situations, common sense conceives of "chances," in the plural, as so many openings for bringing about a designated outcome (compare the common expression "Give me a chance," where "chance" has roughly the meaning of "opportunity"). If, given D, P is empirically impossible, then the initial situation that makes D true blocks all pathways to "success" (the marble is wholly enclosed in its box); if, however, the initial conditions are sufficiently relaxed, there is leeway for the outcome—the ball may or may not emerge, because there is now an exit, a tangible "chance" to get out. When one can justifiably say "Given D, probably P" the picture is one of "exits" predominating over "barriers."

(18) If a layman is pressed to explain in nonfigurative language what it means to say that exits "predominate" over barriers, a somewhat different picture may be offered. The "initial conditions" may now be conceived of as embodying forces or influences, some tending to bring about P but the others resisting. The underlying picture is of something like a tug of war between allies and adversaries.) From this perspective, to say "Probably P" is to claim that on balance the propitious influences will prevail over their opponents.

In a case of empirical certainty the initial conditions (the effective part of the state of the universe at a given time $t$) wholly constrain and determine the outcome. In a case of empirical possibility, however, the initial conditions determine the outcome only partially, so that at the time of utterance, $t$, some situations can be realized and others cannot. Finally, a case of probability is such that among the set of possible outcomes left open by the initial conditions, one (the situation expressed by the kernel of the "probably"-statement) is on the whole favored by the initial conditions and may therefore on balance be expected.

[98]

(19) The foregoing references to "pictures" are justified by the extent to which laymen's talk about probability is dominated by pictorial imagery and crude mythology, lurking just below the surface.

It is unclear how much influence such imagery exerts. The dramatic conceptions of "favorable" and "adverse" chances, of tangible pathways to realization, and the rest (all of which are necessarily attenuated in situations where they fit less plausibly than in the paradigmatic situation already considered), seem to leave the relevant verification conditions untouched: a man who dismisses them as fairy tales will adopt the same procedures for arriving at probabilities that anybody else will.

But reference to empirical possibility is not to be set aside so lightly. Too many philosophers display an unreasonable *horror possibilitatis*: a tough-minded positivist, for instance, is apt to regard all talk about empirical possibility as no better than picturesque nonsense and will seek to purge ordinary talk about probability of all implicit reference to the unobservable-in-principle. Yet talk about empirical possibility and empirical necessity seems no more objectionable in principle than talk about persons or tables; nor does there seem to be any harm in admitting a notion of partial empirical determination. The "pictures" that underlie ordinary probability talk, crude as they are, can perhaps be made as philosophically respectable as more fashionable general views concerning the universe.

(20) Conceptions of "partial determination," "favoring conditions," and the like, lend powerful support to certain general principles of probability that are needed in the mathematical theory of probability. Thus, it follows from what has already been said that any reinforcement of the "favoring chances" that leaves the original chances unimpaired cannot reduce the probability of P. (Hence, the second hole in the box could be expected not to diminish the chance of shaking the marble out.) This may be put more precisely, as follows: Suppose that P entails Q; then the probability of Q, given D,

is not less than the probability of P, given D. Similarly, increase in the relative superiority or "strength" of the favoring conditions for P cannot diminish the probability that P will be the case. (In a tug of war, adding another man to one team cannot lessen the team's prospect of success as long as the new man does not get in the way of those who were there already.) Most writers have agreed in treating these principles as axiomatic.

(21) Some philosophers will say that the cash value of ordinary probability talk, infected as it is with dubious metaphor, can reside only in the corresponding verification conditions.

There seem to be two main types of verification. The most basic has already been illustrated: it consists of appeal to relative frequency of occurrence in similar cases. If in initial conditions D, D', D'', . . . respectively, the outcomes P, P', P'', . . . are realized substantially more often than not (where the D's are all alike in relevant respects and the P's are all alike in relevant respects), then this is taken to establish that given D, P has a better chance of being realized than not-P. It will be noticed that this type of verification procedure uses inductive inference and hence presupposes the soundness of inductive methods.

(22) Less direct modes of verification, in common use, are based upon inspection of the given initial conditions rather than upon an inductive inference from the consequences of repeated trials. A man may (or may seem to) conclude from mere knowledge of the defining conditions that there is a better chance of drawing a black ball from an urn containing 99 per cent black ones than there is of drawing one from another urn containing 50 per cent black ones. Closer examination of the assumptions behind such reasoning will reveal the essential role played by previous experience—for example, about how shaking or shuffling will favor "random" distributions of outcomes.

(23) The last point suggests that certain commitments to uniformity play a large part in the common-sense view. Built

into the common talk about "forces," "reasons," and "determination," noted above, is the conception that like consequences must ensue upon like conditions. Thus, if a ball drawn in a certain way from a bag B that contains a given number of balls has a certain probability $p$ of being black, common sense requires that a ball drawn in the same way from another bag B′, similar in all relevant respects, notably in having the same number of balls, will have the same probability of being black. The associated proportionate frequencies of occurrence are also taken to be approximately equal. Probability talk is based upon a generalization of determinism: like conditions are expected to go with like distributions of probabilities and with like distributions of associated frequencies.

(24) The foregoing remarks have concerned what might be called an absolute sense of "probably," where the "initial conditions" to which explicit or implicit reference is made are identified with the relevant features of the "state of the world" at the moment of utterance. Attention should now be paid to an explicitly relative sense, exemplified in such uses as "On the evidence, he is probably guilty" or "Given that he is a wealthy American, there is a high probability that he is a Republican."

The "absolute" use of "probably" previously discussed can be assimilated to the explicitly relative use in the following way: in the formula "On evidence D, probably P (to such and such a degree)," take "D" to refer to what were previously called the initial conditions. In this way the "absolute" use can be regarded as a special case of the "relative" use, when the datum is the (known or assumed) condition of the universe at the instant of assertion. We can therefore acknowledge the large measure of truth in the commonly accepted dictum that probability is always relative to evidence. This is correct in its implication that any probability assertion, whether explicitly relational or not, harks back to assume enabling conditions—or, from another perspective, to conducive forces or propitious "chances"—that could be expressed in a more explicit version of the original assertion; it is, however, misleading if intended to imply that in the absence of such explicit indications of a basis, ordinary probability judgments are defective or in need of supplementation.

(25) The above view of ordinary uses of "probably" can be extended with little strain to cases in which the adverb is attached to a general statement. After inspecting a large and varied sample of crickets, a biologist may say, "Probably all crickets have ears on their legs." Common sense is inclined to think of the facts revealed in the examined sample as constraining and favoring a general possibility (that all crickets have ears on the leg) at the expense of competing possibilities. The available *information* about the universe now replaces the assumed initial conditions. In this use there need be no implication of objective uncertainty about the state of affairs to which probability is ascribed; a man who says, "On the evidence to hand, probably all A are B," may without inconsistency hold that there are conclusive reasons "in the world" for all A's being B. Thus, attributions of relative probability can be consistently made by a whole-hearted determinist, such as Laplace. That some general feature of "the facts" favors certain other large-scale features without wholly necessitating them is compatible with complete determination of the outcome in its full specificity. (This thought may have been behind Ludwig Wittgenstein's remark that probability assertions belong to a "myopic" view of the world.)

(26) The expression "it is probable that" sometimes functions as a synonym of "probably"; more characteristic, however, is its use to register the strength of the determining conditions as conducive, on balance, to the designated outcome. In many such cases the nonassertion of the kernel is patent.

With the use of the substantive, "probability," there is still greater epistemological distance from any act of assertion: to say something of the form "Given D, the probability that

P is such and such" is to formulate a theoretical judgment about the strength of the enabling conditions without facing the question whether P should be expected with sufficient confidence for its assertion to be warranted. Still, to probability thus theoretically conceived something of the more full-bodied adverbial use still clings, and there are logical transitions from the substantival assertions to the adverbial ones. For instance, no intervening link is required for the logical transition from "Given D, the probability that P is overwhelming" to "Given D, probably P" with assertive force.

(27) The extent to which precise measures can be assigned to degrees of probability (or—what comes to the same thing, according to the view here taken—to degrees of possibility) is moot. In some cases at least, comparative judgments of probability (see, for instance, 16, above), when coupled with the generalized principle of uniformity (21, above), readily persuade the layman to assign determinate measures of probability.

Suppose, for example, that ten similar cards, each white on one side and black on the other, are pasted on a vertical glass screen so that five white sides and five black are in view: let a man A on one side of the screen be asked to choose a card at random, and let another man B on the other side be given the same task. Then common sense is almost irresistibly inclined to say that the situations of A and B are alike in all relevant respects and consequently that the chance of A's choosing a white card is precisely the same as the chance of B's choosing a black one. With the conventional allocation of unity to certainty, it then follows that the chance of either A's or B's choosing a white card is precisely 1/2. (This is an example of the use of the "principle of indifference," discussed in the final part of this chapter.)

If one asks instead for the probability of, say, finding life on Mars, it would be hard to suppose any definite measure appropriate. But here again a layman would confidently set the probability at less than 99/100. Behind such a judgment

[103]

there may well be an imagined comparison with one's relative state of confidence in the occurrence of some designated outcome in a game of chance. If a man is convinced that he would rather bet on two consecutive sixes being shown by a fair die than on there being life on Mars, he can at least set an upper bound to his confidence in the truth of the latter proposition (see the discussion, in the last part of this chapter, of "subjective" interpretations of probability).

The correct view seems to be that ordinary uses of probability (influenced, no doubt, by exposure to discussion of odds in games of chance) employ rudimentary and limited measures of probability, but are willing to be led, by suitable devices, to extend such estimations to any desired degree of precision. Mathematical theories of probability superimpose a numerical grid upon the partially unstructured comparative probability judgments of naive common sense. The relations between such mathematical calculations and the common-sense matrix may be plausibly compared to those between thermometric readings of temperature and crude judgments of "warmth."

MULTIPLE SENSES OF PROBABILITY?

The propriety of what seems to be radically different ways of verifying ordinary probability judgments (say, counting the number of pips on a die—as opposed to consulting mortality tables) has led a number of writers to claim that "probability" is an equivocal term. The preferred number of senses is two, although some writers have argued for as many as five. The absence of any generally accepted criteria for identity of senses or identity of concepts makes such claims hard to assess. The most influential case for the recognition of radically distinct senses of probability has been made by Rudolf Carnap, who wishes to distinguish sharply between probability as "rational credibility" and probability as "limiting relative frequency of occurrence." But his argument proves, upon examination, to be based solely upon the different modes of verification of two probability assertions, one held to be *a priori,* the other empirical (although he later offers a "logical" interpretation even of the latter). Writers who wish to argue that the existence of *a priori* as well as empirical probability assertions justifies attribution of plurality of senses might be asked to consider whether "two" has different senses in "Jones has two hands" and "two and two makes four." There seem to be no compelling reasons for recognizing radically distinct senses of probability.

STRUCTURE OF THE COMMON-SENSE VIEW

In ordinary life, an assertion of the form "Probably P" where "P" expresses the realization of some possible event or situation has the function of committing the speaker to P's being true, on the basis of the existence of "enabling initial conditions" that favor P's realization without ensuring it. Thus, the use of the adverb signifies the supposed existence of such conditions and ensures that the assertion in which it occurs shall be circumspect, or "guarded." In the absence of other indications, the enabling conditions are understood to be the "state of the universe" (or the relevant part of it) at the moment of utterance. In explicitly relative probability assertions, however, the basis is expressed by a clause formulating information concerning some general feature of the universe, conceived of as favoring some other general feature (a relation of partial determination between attributes). In substantival uses ("Given D, the probability that P is such and such"), the assertive force of the adverbial use is bracketed or suppressed, the point of such uses being solely to estimate the strength with which the relevant enabling conditions (expressed by the reference to "D") favor the realization of the outcome P.

The view of probability here outlined differs from other current analyses in some or all of the following respects: (a) probability is not treated as an equivocal concept; (b) probability is regarded as legitimately attached to singular situations no less than to general features of the world; (c) probability is not identified with relative frequency or with

[105]

some definable logical relation between propositions or with some imputed state of mind of an ideally reasonable judge.

It will be noticed that the common-sense conception of probability has been taken to be thoroughly objective. It has been argued that the layman thinks of his probability assertions as referring to "something out there" rather than to logical relations between propositions, conceived of as conceptual or verbal entities. Still less plausible is it from the common-sense point of view to think of assertions of probability as intended to express merely the speaker's "confidence" in the designated outcome. There are, to be sure, pragmatic rules that require the speaker to be conventionally invested with a degree of confidence corresponding to the character of the probability assertion uttered, but the expression of such confidence is not the primary purpose of such utterances.

It may be generally acceptable as a conclusion from the foregoing survey that the patterns of ordinary use of "probably" and its cognates are dishearteningly complex. However, the various subtle differences between roughly synonymous modes of expression in terms of "probably," "the likelihood is," "the chances are," "it is to be expected that," and the like, are normally of no consequence in primary contexts of circumspect commitment to uncertain outcomes. Nor is it usually important to distinguish among, say, the content of the probability assertion itself, the grounds for its assertion (characteristically although not exclusively based upon relative frequencies of occurrences in similar cases), the degree of confidence conventionally attributed to the speaker, and his approvable epistemic attitudes and actions. Some theorists have therefore been able to exploit, quite plausibly, a single feature of this tangled web, whereas others have hoped to divide and conquer by imputing a variety of senses.

Monolithic theories tend to distort obstrusive features of ordinary probability talk in the service of some philosophical preconception, whereas fragmenting approaches are hard pressed to show any principle of connection between the divorced senses. It seems implausible, however, to saddle ordinary probability talk with an inexplicable propensity for punning. A fully satisfactory theory, which is yet to be found, would do justice to both the variability and the unity of ordinary probability talk.

## Mathematical Theory of Probability

### PROBABILITY AS A MEASURE OF SETS

Mathematicians have clarified the foundations of the mathematical theory of probability (or the "calculus of chances") to a point at which it can be rigorously presented as a branch of pure mathematics—more specifically, as part of the general theory of additive functions of sets.

The leading ideas in this approach can be illustrated as follows: Suppose we have a number of sets, composed of any objects whatsoever—for instance, the sets that can be formed by taking some or all of the inhabitants of a certain village. Let us call such a set $s_i$. The set of all the inhabitants of the village—S, say—is then a special case of an $s_i$, as is $\wedge$, the "null set" containing no inhabitants. We wish to find a way of assigning a number $m$ to each $s$, to indicate what may provisionally be conceived of as the "spread" or "extent" of that set. In order to do this we shall certainly want the measure of a set obtained by combining two sets with no common members to be the sum of the measures of the two original sets. Let us call this the additive condition. We shall now adopt the convention that the measure of S itself, $m(S)$, is 1.

With these understandings, the most natural way of defining $m$ would be to take its value each time to be simply the number of members of the set in question. It is easy to see, however, that as far as satisfying the proposed additive condition is concerned, the assignment of values to $m$ can be made in a large variety of ways. (There might be some practical point, for instance, in giving a set composed of adults a measure higher than that of a set composed of the same number of children.) Suppose we assign an arbitrary "weight" to each inhabitant (with the sum of all the weights being 1) and take the measure of a set to be the sum of the weights of all its members; it is easy to see that the additive condition is then satisfied.

More generally, consider some set S containing as members a finite set of individuals $a_1, a_2, \ldots, a_m$. (The interesting general case, where the members of S form an infinite set, not necessarily countable, will be ignored here for the sake of simplicity.) Consider next the set U of all the subsets of S, with members $s_1, s_2, \ldots, s_n$. (Since U is taken, by convention, to include both S itself and the null set, $\wedge$, it follows that $n = 2^m$.) Suppose, now, that each member $s_i$ of U is to be assigned a definite nonnegative number, represented as $m(s_i)$, to be regarded as the "measure" of the set in question. Let each individual $a_j$ be assigned a nonnegative "weight," $w(a_j)$. Finally, let $m(s_i)$ be defined as the sum of the weights of all the members of $s_i$. We add the convention that the measure of the set S (having all the $a_i$'s as its members) is unity.

The following are almost immediate consequences of these stipulations:

(a) The measure of the null set is zero: $m(\wedge) = 0$. (For $\wedge$ has no members at all.)

(b) The measure of a set and the measure of its complementary set, relative to U, add up to unity: $m(s) + m(\bar{s}) = 1$. (Here "$\bar{s}$" stands for the subset of S composed of all members of S that are not included in $s$.)

(c) The measure of a set composed by combining the membership of two sets is equal to the sum of their measures less the measure of their common part: $m(s_1 \cup s_2) = m(s_1) + m(s_2) - m(s_1 \cap s_2)$. (Here "$s_1 \cup s_2$" is used for the "union" of the two sets and "$s_1 \cap s_2$" for their "intersection," the set composed of their common members. The stated result follows at once from the adopted definition of measure.)

(d) In the special case in which the two sets have no common members, the measure of their union is the sum of the measures: If $s_1 \cap s_2 = \wedge$, then $m(s_1 \cup s_2) = m(s_1) + m(s_2)$.

Let us now introduce the notion of the relative measure of $s_1$ with respect to another set $s_2$, written $m(s_1 \mid s_2)$. The defini-

[108]

tion is, simply, $m(s_1 \mid s_2) = m(s_1 \cap s_2) / m(s_2)$—that is, the ratio of the measure of the intersection of the two sets to the measure of the reference class $s_2$.

(e) The measure of the intersection of two sets $s_1$ and $s_2$ is the product of the measure of the first and the relative measure of the second with respect to the first: $m(s_1 \cap s_2) = m(s_1 \mid s_2) \times m(s_2)$. (This follows immediately from the definition of relative measure already given.)

We can easily apply this simple mathematical apparatus to an illustrative case in which probability calculations are performed. Suppose we are interested in calculating various odds connected with outcomes, defined as the simultaneous throws of two coins. Then the most specific ways of describing the outcomes are "HH," "HT," "TH," and "TT." Let us refer to these "basic outcomes" as $a_1$, $a_2$, $a_3$, and $a_4$, respectively, and think of them as constituting a set S. Suppose them to have been given probabilities of occurrence (how these probabilities are known we do not here inquire) that are, respectively, $p_1$, $p_2$, $p_3$, and $p_4$.

A typical (but trivial) problem in mathematical probability is to determine the chance that at least one head will appear when both coins are tossed. The elementary reasoning runs as follows: "The event in question may arise from $a_1$ or $a_2$ or $a_3$; hence its probability is $\frac{3}{4}$." The analogy with the foregoing calculation of measures leaps to the eye. Think of any complex outcome as the set of all the basic outcomes compatible with it; identify the probabilities of the basic outcomes with weights; finally, identify probability and measure. Thus, we shall have

$$P(HH) = p_1 = w(a_1)$$
$$P(HT) = p_2 = w(a_2)$$
$$P(TH) = p_3 = w(a_3)$$
$$P(TT) = p_4 = w(a_4).$$

Since the complex outcome "at least one head" is compatible with $a_1$, $a_2$, and $a_3$, we shall have $P(HH \text{ or } HT \text{ or } TH) = m(\{a_1, a_2, a_3\}) = w(a_1) + w(a_2) + w(a_3) = p_1 + p_2 + p_3$.

In short, such a calculation as is illustrated here can be

conceived of as the determination of a measure, in the sense already explained, in accordance with the following dictionary:

| | |
|---|---|
| possible, fully analyzed, or "basic" outcome (such as "HH") | member of a given set S |
| a generalized nonbasic outcome (such as "at least one head"), conceived of as a disjunction of basic outcomes | nonunit subset of S |
| the initial probability ($p_1$, $p_2$, $p_3$, or $p_4$) of a given basic outcome | weight of the corresponding member of S |
| probability of occurrence of a generalized outcome | measure of the corresponding subset of S |
| the probability of no basic outcome resulting is zero | $m(\wedge) = 0$ |
| the probability of any outcome and the probability of the complementary outcome add up to unity | $m(s) + m(\bar{s}) = 1$ |

and so on. This scheme can be at once extended to include "conditional" probability, of the form $P(O_1 \mid O_2)$, read as "the probability of occurrence of $O_1$ if $O_2$ occurs":

| | |
|---|---|
| $P(O_1 \mid O_2)$, where $O_1$ and $O_2$ are the outcomes corresponding respectively to $s_1$ and $s_2$. | $m(s_1 \mid s_2)$ |

On this interpretation, propositions (c) and (e), above, correspond, respectively, to the "general addition theorem" and the "general multiplication theorem" that are the basic principles of the calculus of chances:

$$P(O_1 \text{ or } O_2) = P(O_1) + P(O_2) - P(O_1 \text{ and } O_2);$$
$$P(O_1 \text{ and } O_2) = P(O_1 \text{ given } O_2) \times P(O_2).$$

These fundamental propositions look almost self-evident on the suggested interpretation.

The suggested transition from preanalytical ideas about

probability to the abstract theory of measure has here been made via the notion of given basic outcomes, conceived of as abstract realizable features of a given configuration (the tossing of two coins, say). It is, however, possible to connect probability ideas with the abstract calculus in a variety of other ways. Suppose, for instance, that the desired weights are derived from observations of relative frequencies, so that to say $P(HH) = p_1$ is to claim that in a certain series of trials with the two pennies, HH turns up in the ratio $p_1 : 1 - p_1$ and similarly for $p_2$, $p_3$, and $p_4$. Then the transition to the calculus will be as feasible as before, for all that is needed for such a transition is that the individuals answering to the basic outcomes shall have numbers assigned to them in advance (and such that all these weights total unity). This very modest requirement can also be satisfied by somebody who purports to have *a priori* access to the requisite "weights"— or, again, by somebody who claims to be able to measure degrees of "rational confidence," or the like. Provided these competing philosophical interpretations issue, as they commonly do, in determinate measures of probability (however construed) satisfying the basic "additive condition" mentioned above, it will be possible to view the matter through the lenses of the set-measure conception. (The difficulty of directly connecting philosophical theories of probability with the mathematical theory will be precisely proportional to the extent that they imply that such measures cannot be provided. This is partly true, for instance, of J. M. Keynes's system of probability and to some extent true of Harold Jeffreys' system.)

The mathematical theory, accordingly, may be properly regarded as almost wholly neutral with respect to the conflicting philosophical analyses of the probability concept. It simply provides an abstract (but astonishingly fruitful) framework for calculating the values of complex probabilities in terms of the values of related ones. It gives us the former as calculable functions of the latter, ignoring any determinate values that either may have.

The last point can hardly be overemphasized, for its

[111]

neglect has often invited fallacy. The set-measure conception assumes that the weights are assigned (subject to stated restrictions) from "outside the theory": values of the probabilities of "basic" outcomes must be supplied *to* the theory and cannot be determined *inside* it. Nothing in the mathematical theory of probability is competent to settle the "proper" values of such probabilities. Now in all problems of application of the pure mathematics, determination of the values of these "basic" probabilities plays an essential part.

The mathematical theory of probability can be usefully compared to a (hypothetical) theory of length in which no determinate measures of lengths are available. Such a theory could show how the lengths of compound lines are related to the lengths of their components—l(AB) + l(BC) = l(AC), when A, B, and C are collinear, to take a simple example— but would be incompetent to determine the length of even a single segment. Were such a theory supplemented by conventions of congruence, permitting tests for equality of lengths, measurement would rapidly become possible. Precisely the same thing can be said for the theory of chances: in order to determine the requisite "weights" of basic outcomes it is sufficient—at any rate, in a large class of cases— to be able to determine when given outcomes are to be regarded as *equally* probable. (If certainty can be partitioned into a finite set of $n$ equiprobable alternatives, each of these will then have the determinate probability $1/n$ and the rest will follow without difficulty.) Equiprobability plays the same role in the pure theory of chances that congruence does in the mathematical theory of linear mensuration. In both cases the pure theory can receive specific application only by means of additional conventions not derivable from purely mathematical considerations. (This is a special case of the principle that pure mathematics cannot apply to the world without a nonmathematical link.)

### INVERSE PROBABILITY AND BAYES' FORMULA

A problem of calculation that constantly arises in practice is that of "inverting" a probability—that is, of computing the value of $P(L \mid K)$ when the value of $P(K \mid L)$ is known. Such a calculation—or something equivalent—is needed to perform the important task of inferring from observed frequencies to associated probabilities.

The calculation can be illustrated by the following simple example. Suppose that of a certain set of men 90 per cent own an automobile and that among those automobile owners 10 percent also own a bicycle, whereas among the non-automobile owners 20 per cent own a bicycle. We wish to know the probability that a man in the set considered, who owns a bicycle, also owns an automobile.

Writing "A" for "$x$ owns an automobile" and "B" for "$x$ owns a bicycle," we have:

$$p_1 = P(A) = .9 \qquad p_2 = P(\bar{A}) = .1 \text{ (given)}$$
$$q_1 = P(B|A = .1 \qquad q_2 = P(B|\bar{A}) = .2 \text{ (given)}.$$

Here $p_1$ and $p_2$ may be called the "prior" probabilities (a label to be preferred to the classical "*a priori* probabilities") and $q_1$ and $q_2$ the (conditional) "forward" or direct probabilities (sometimes called the likelihoods).

In this example, by the multiplication and addition rules we have:

$$P(AB) = p_1 q_1 = .9 \times .1 = .09$$
$$P(\bar{A}B) = p_2 q_2 = .1 \times .2 = .02$$
$$P(B) = P(AB) + P(\bar{A}B) = .09 + .02 = .11.$$

In order to find the "backward," or inverse, conditional probability, $P(A|B)$, we use the multiplication formula

$$P(A|B) \times P(B) = P(AB).$$

Writing "$r_1$" for "$P(A|B)$" and using the results already obtained, we rewrite the last equation as

(*) $$r_1 = (p_1 q_1)/(p_1 q_1 + p_2 q_2).$$

In the special case considered, we find that $r_1$, the inverse probability that a bicycle owner will also be an automobile owner, has the value $(.09)/(.11)$, or $9/11$. Similarly, the complementary probability that a bicycle owner will not also be an automobile owner is $2/11$.

The elementary formula (*) is a special case of the so-called Bayes' formula. Its essence is that the backward probability is proportional to the product of two numbers: the forward probability, $q_1$, and the corresponding prior probability, $p_1$. (This agrees with the "good sense" that Laplace wished to reduce to calculation. Common sense requires the chance that a bicycle owner shall also be an automobile owner to depend on two things—the prior probability that a man owns an automobile as well as the conditional probability that an automobile owner owns a bicycle. Formula (*) expresses this idea in a precise numerical form.)

The more general case, where we start with $n$ prior probabilities, $p_i$ and $n$ corresponding forward probabilities, $q_i$, follows by the same simple arithmetic. The corresponding value for the backward probability, $r_1$, is obviously

$$(**) \qquad r_1 = (p_1 q_1)/(p_1 q_1 + p_2 q_2 + \ldots + p_n q_n).$$

Given the values of the $p$'s and $q$'s, the value of each $r_i$ is readily obtained by simple arithmetic.

Bayes' formula, (**), is obviously legitimately applicable in the example illustrated. This is more than can immediately be said in instances where the values of the prior probabilities are unknown.

Consider the following example. A bag is known to contain 100 balls, all of which are either black or white. Of 10 balls drawn at random with replacement, 6 are found to be black and 4 white; it is required to calculate the (inverse) probability that the bag contains black and white balls in equal numbers.

Here there are 99 alternatives to be considered, corresponding to the 99 different possible compositions of the bag's contents. For each such alternative, the "forward" probability, $q_i$, can be computed. However, in order to apply Bayes' formula, we also need to know the prior probabilities of each of these alternatives. Thus, in computing the backward probability that on the evidence (6 black, 4 white balls in the sample), the original population was evenly divided

[114]

between black and white balls, we need to know the respective prior probabilities that the bag was composed of 99 white and 1 black, of 98 white and 2 black, and so on. Now, on the data given, no values can be assigned to these prior probabilities—not because we are ignorant but rather because the meaning of "prior probability" has not yet been established; hence, the problem is indeterminate and cannot be solved without further data.

In the earlier uses of Bayes' formula the assumption was made in such cases that in the absence of any specific knowledge of the prior probabilities, we are entitled to treat all of them as equal in value. It is easily seen that Bayes' formula then reduces to the special form

(†) $$r_i = (q_i)/(q_1 + q_2 + \cdots + q_n).$$

Since the $p_i$'s have now dropped out of the formula, the calculation is readily performed. It is however, hard to see what sense, let alone what justification, can be given to the assumption of the equality of the prior probabilities. Such a sense could be supplied in this particular illustration if a large number of similar drawings were made on other occasions from bags of different compositions. The requisite prior probabilities would then correspond to the proportionate frequencies of occurrence of differently composed bags in the series of trials considered. This resource will not, however, be available in the general case now to be considered.

The general situation in which considerations of inverse probability arise is one in which a number of hypotheses $H_i$ are compatible with given evidence E and in which the forward probabilities $P(E|H_i)$ are known or are computable. If one, or a certain subset, of the $H_i$ could be selected as relatively best-supported by E, it would then be possible to compute the forward probability that further data D would be found. In short, the situation is the basic one of inference from sample consequences to best-supported hypothesis and so, indirectly, to further consonant observations.

Here the analogy with the bags of balls, used above, breaks

down. Variously composed bags may indeed be used on different occasions, but universes are not available for inspection in repeatable series of trials. Since precisely one of the competing hypotheses $H_i$ is in fact true in this one and only universe, no good sense can be given, in general, to the ascription of an associated prior probability, and *a fortiori* no good sense can be given to the assumption of equality of such imputed probabilities.

This objection seems decisive against such uncritical use of Bayes' formula (or the interesting variants derivable from the assumption of infinitely many alternative hypotheses). Discussion of the subject has in the past sometimes paid undue attention to the supposedly absurd consequence known as Laplace's rule of succession—if $a$ successes have been observed in $a + b$ independent trials, the probability of success in a new trial is $(a + 1)/(a + b + 2)$. It would indeed be disquieting if we had to suppose that after rain on three successive days the chance of rain on the next day must be exactly $4/5$—but it may be doubted that the conditions for use of the rule of succession have here been satisfied. The objection previously formulated seems in any case more fundamental.

One nontrivial consequence of Bayes' formula is important to such theorists as the defenders of the "subjective" interpretation of probability to be discussed below, who still rely upon circumspect uses of inverse probability. We have seen that in such an example as the drawing of samples with replacement from a bag of unknown composition, the calculation from the composition of the sample to the backward probability depends on the unknown prior probabilities as well as on the conditional forward probabilities. It can be shown, however, that (speaking roughly) the influence of the values of the prior probabilities on the magnitude of the backward probability diminishes progressively as the size of the sample increases. Thus, a case can be made for arguing that an arbitrary but fixed distribution of the prior probabilities of the hypotheses considered will suffice for application of Bayes' formula if we are content to get results acceptable in the long run.

The issues are too technical and controversial for discussion here. Many, if not most, statisticians regard as dubious arguments from inverse probabilities in something like the traditional style. In many situations, at least, they can be bypassed in favor of "tests of significance," whose rationale is substantially different.

Suppose we are considering, in our example of the bag of colored balls, whether the evidence to hand (composition of a sample) will justify acceptance or rejection of a given hypothesis (say, that 90 per cent of the balls in the bag are black). Suppose the forward probability $P(E|H)$ is very low—say, less than .01. Then we may feel justified in rejecting H on the ground that it is unreasonable to believe in H if it commits us to the occurrence of so unlikely a consequence. If we were to accept H we would have to believe that some very improbable consequence (one whose probability of occurrence given H was less than .01) would have occurred—which may be enough to warrant our looking elsewhere for some other hypothesis compatible with the evidence.

The leading idea in this highly simplified train of thought is characteristic of much refined contemporary statistical method based upon the use of "confidence intervals" and "tests of significance." Its philosophical interest lies in its apparent avoidance of any dubious appeals to inverse probability. There does remain, however, the question of what justification, if any, can be given for the neglect of small probabilities—or, what comes to much the same thing—what justification can be given for the conventional choice by statisticians of a determinate confidence level.

## LAW OF LARGE NUMBERS

Let us suppose that a well-balanced, "fair," coin has been tossed a large number of times, $n$. Common sense would lead us to expect that the proportion of heads in the $n$ trials —call it "$p$"—should be approximately $\frac{1}{2}$ (that is, the same as the initial probability of a head). It is also reasonable to expect that the approximation gets "better" as $n$ gets larger. Our common ideas about probability seem to commit us to this loose kind of connection between the initial probability, $\frac{1}{2}$, and the approximate relative frequency of occurrence of heads in a long series of repeated trials. This important idea received exact mathematical expression in a striking result discovered by Jakob Bernoulli and often called Bernoulli's theorem.

The theorem applies to the present illustration in the following way: Suppose that after $n$ tosses the proportionate frequency is found to lie between $.5 + .1$ and $.5 - .1$; let us then say that $p$ has "*arrived* within .1 of the initial probability $\frac{1}{2}$," and let us call .1 the corresponding "distance." For a given $n$, say 1,000, the chances that $p$ will have arrived within the distance .1 of $\frac{1}{2}$ can be calculated; similarly, the corresponding chances can be calculated for other values of $n$ and other choices of the "distance." Let us call the chance in favor of $p$'s having arrived after $n$ throws within a given distance of the initial probability ($\frac{1}{2}$) the corresponding "prospect." It is obvious that the prospect is a function, in general, of the number of throws and also of the chosen distance.

Bernoulli's theorem implies the following information about this interdependence: For any given and fixed distance, the corresponding prospect after $n$ trials can be made indefinitely close to 1 as $n$ increases. In other words, if we want $p$ to be within a certain distance of $\frac{1}{2}$, settled in advance, our chance of being satisfied converges to 1 as $n$ increases.

An example may help to explain this. Let us take the distance to be 1 per cent. Then for $n = 40{,}000$, calculation shows that the odds in favor of the proportion of heads lying between $.5 + .01$ and $.5 - .01$ are better than 999 to 1 (that is, the prospect is then better than .999). Bernoulli's theorem assures us that had we held the 1 per cent distance fixed while considering a larger number of trials, the prospect would be

[118]

even closer to 1 than .999. Indeed, for that choice of distance, the prospect could be made as close to 1 as we pleased by taking $n$ to be sufficiently large. Had we chosen a smaller distance to start with, say .1 per cent, we would have needed a larger number than 40,000 trials to get equally favorable odds (999 to 1) in favor of the frequency's being within that distance of $\frac{1}{2}$, but otherwise all that has been said would still apply. All of this follows by nontrivial mathematical calculation from the stated assumptions.

In this sketch the initial probability of $\frac{1}{2}$ was chosen merely for the sake of simplicity in illustration. Had the initial probability been some other fraction, say $\frac{4}{5}$, corresponding remarks would apply.

Complicated as the foregoing may seem, it has seemed worthwhile to state the general character of the "law of great numbers" correctly, in order to forestall the misunderstandings of it and the consequent abuses that are surprisingly common in the literature. It is, for instance, quite wrong to say categorically that in the long run the observed relative frequency of occurrence of a character *will* be approximately the same as its initial probability of occurrence in a single trial. The correct formulation, as we have seen, concerns the *chance* that this will be the case. There is no direct "bridge" between probability and relative frequency: the law provides a connection between initial probability and a related *probability* (that can be made as close to unity as desired) of a certain specified kind of distribution of occurrences.

The validity of Bernoulli's theorem depends on two assumptions that restrict its usefulness in practice: (1) the initial probability of the single event ($\frac{1}{2}$ in our illustration) is assumed to be the same throughout; (2) the successive trials are assumed to be independent of one another. If a roulette wheel was to be continuously spun, without correction for wear and tear, the first condition would eventually be violated; if a dishonest croupier saw to it that no more than seven consecutive reds or blacks ever occurred, the second condition would be violated. (Modern refinements of Bernoulli's theorem, in which the two conditions can be somewhat relaxed, will not be considered here.)

It is possible to formulate a kind of inversion of the theorem, permitting a suitably circumspect inference from observed frequency to a prospect of the initial probability's being within a predetermined distance of the observed relative frequency $p$. This procedure has all the disadvantages of the "direct" use of Bernoulli's theorem.

The inference from "*a posteriori* probability" (that is, observation of relative frequency in a large number of trials) to approximate "*a priori* probability" (that is, "initial probability," in the terminology of the previous account) is, however, usually made in a somewhat different fashion. A certain hypothesis is considered concerning the approximate value of the unknown initial probability—call that hypothesis "H." Then the odds against the occurrence of the observed relative frequency are calculated on the assumption that not-H is the case—using Bernoulli's theorem or some consequence of it. If the odds against the observed distribution thus obtained are regarded as sufficiently high, not-H is rejected and H is accepted.

This may be regarded as the use of a "significance" test, for which the end of the section on inverse probability and Bayes' formula may be consulted. The basic methodological principle involved is—to speak roughly—that hypotheses that if true would make observed data sufficiently unlikely may be rejected. (To replace this crude formulation by precise procedures permitting reliable estimates of the risks involved is one of the main technical tasks of statistics.)

## The Meanings of "Probability"

Whether or not probability is as much the "guide of life" as Bishop Butler thought, probability estimates are highly useful for making determinate judgments concerning unobserved events and unverified hypotheses. No uninterpreted or "pure" mathematical theory of chances can be useful in this way until its undefined terms are given definite "interpretations" (semantical definitions) that will convert the axioms of the calculus into fully meaningful assertions. The student can choose, at this point, from an embarrassing variety of plausible interpretations of the basic probability expressions.

In weighing the merits of the rival claimants it is appropriate to consider how well they answer the following basic questions: (1) How well does the theory succeed in certifying the axioms of the mathematical theory of chances as correct? (As already explained, this hinges essentially upon the definition of equality of chances that is offered.) (2) What connection, if any, does the theory establish between probabilities and observed frequencies? (It is quite certain that frequencies, empirically determined, in practice often do establish reasonable judgments of probability). (3) Can the theory render intelligible and justify our trust in probabilities as a guide to the provisionally unknown? (This question is obviously connected with its predecessor.)

MATHEMATICAL DOGMATISM

Brief mention should be made of a view of a kind sometimes found in mathematical textbooks on probability and often recommended in the classroom. Roughly speaking, we are asked to conceive of probability as whatever can satisfy the axioms of the mathematical theory. The pure theory of chances is compared to a pure geometry, both viewed as "idealized model," having only a loose connection with reality, and the task of correlating the precise mathematical results with their imprecise counterparts in experience is held to be basically a practical one, needing no theoretical discussion.

As a solution to the problem of interpretation, this approach is merely an evasion. Formal obeisance to the "ideal-

[121]

ization" implicit in mathematical theory construction serves merely as an excuse for shirking the hard work of articulating the links between theory and practical applications.

CLASSICAL THEORY AND THE PRINCIPLE OF INDIFFERENCE

The label "classical theory" usually alludes to the influential views expressed in Laplace's famous "Essai philosophique sur les probabilités" (1814) and adopted by a hundred writers since. The fundamental notion of deriving equalities of probability from parity of favoring reasons is, however, at least a century older, having been stated by Jakob Bernoulli in his posthumously published *Ars Conjectandi* (1713).

In the absence of explicit information in the writings of Bernoulli and Laplace, it is uncertain how these pioneers would have chosen to define probability. On the whole, however, their practice suggests that the basic conception was, in effect, one of *justified degree of belief.* Probability concerns the "degree of certainty" (Bernoulli) of an ideal rather than an actual belief; its value measures the strength of a belief that would be held by a thinker (a perfectly reasonable man) who correctly adjusted his expectation to the evidence at his disposal.

To determine how strongly such a thinker would believe in a given alternative (or how anybody *ought* to think), we turn to the celebrated "principle of indifference" (so called following Keynes; formerly known as the "principle of nonsufficient reason," with a possible allusion to Leibniz' "principle of sufficient reason").

Suppose the question is whether a certain man is in New York or Chicago, given that he must be in one place or the other, and suppose every reason in favor of his being in New York (for example, that he said he would be there) is matched by a reason of the same form in favor of his being in Chicago (for example, that he also said he would be in Chicago); we are then, it is said, entitled to regard the probabilities of the two mutually exclusive alternatives as equal.

More generally: if there are $n$ mutually exclusive alternatives of the same form, backed by symmetrical reasons, then the $n$ probabilities are to be taken as equal. From this there follows at once the definition of measure of probability, to be found in innumerable mathematical textbooks, ancient and modern, as "the ratio of the number of favorable cases to the total number of cases." (To compute the probability of a 6 turning up in three throws of a die, for instance, we assume that the principle guarantees equal probabilities of the die's showing a given number on any throw; the rest is then a simple exercise in permutations and combination.)

The principle of indifference has been stated above in its most plausible form. When each reason we have for believing in A is matched by an exactly corresponding reason in favor of believing in B, common sense readily agrees that the probabilities properly assigned to the alternatives, on the evidence provided, should be equal. Less plausible is the application of the principle to cases where the required symmetry of supporting reasons derives from the total absence of reasons on either side. Arguments from what might be called "parity of ignorance" (which have seduced even so able a thinker as William Stanley Jevons) have tended to bring the principle into deserved disrepute. (It is hard, of course, to imagine a case in which the reasoner is *wholly* ignorant of evidence favoring either P or not-P and is therefore required to assign to each alternative the probability $\frac{1}{2}$. Is the present reader of these lines of the male sex? The writer fancies that women read philosophical articles less often than men do; if so, the relevant reasons are asymmetrical and the principle fails to apply.)

Even in more plausible contexts use of the principle can rapidly generate absurdities. For instance, the "alternatives" to which the principle is supposed to apply can normally be classified in a number of different ways, resulting in incompatible probability values. Suppose we wish to compute the probability that two cards drawn at random from a set composed of two red and two black cards will have the same color; shall we consider as equally probable alternatives the six possible "constitutions" of the hands (counting hands as different if different cards are drawn) or shall we pay attention only to the "complexions" of such hands (the number of red and black cards)? If the first, the probability will be $\frac{2}{6}$; if the second, $\frac{2}{3}$. Appeal to "parity of reasons" offers no guide to the right answer.

Even stronger objections can be raised when the variable whose value is to be determined runs over a continuous domain. To determine the probable mass $m$ of a body known to have a value between 0 and 1, shall we take it as equally likely that $m$ lies in the intervals $(0,\frac{1}{2})$ and $(\frac{1}{2},1)$? But then we also have "parity of reasons" for a similar distribution of the reciprocal, $1/m$—which would produce a different answer. (This type of objection has been forcefully upheld by Keynes.)

It has also been objected that the principle is never strictly applicable since evidence is never perfectly symmetrical with respect to a number of alternatives and that it is in any case useless in the numerous cases in which the alternatives to be examined cannot be analyzed into a set of ostensibly parallel alternatives.

The somewhat naive attempts by earlier exponents of the Bayesian approach to use the principle in the calculation of inverse probabilities (by assuming equiprobabilities of the hypotheses under test) have further contributed to the current ill repute of the principle.

It is clear that the principle is too weak to achieve unaided the desired results of assigning equiprobabilities. Some of the previously mentioned difficulties can perhaps be overcome by suitable supplementation of the principle. Variants of the principle of indifference will be found to figure prominently in the "logical" theories now to be discussed.

LOGICAL THEORIES

Any philosophical interpretation of probability deserves the title logical theory if its author claims that a basic probability statement, of the form "The probability of P on S is

p," is true *a priori*. This distinctive feature, shared, for instance, by the well-known theories of Keynes, W. E. Johnson,
Rudolf Carnap, and Harold Jeffreys, sets a "logical" interpretation apart from the "empiricist" and "subjective" views still
to be considered. (Roughly speaking, an "empiricist" sup-
poses a true basic probability statement to say something
about the inanimate world, whereas a "subjectivist" takes
it to say something about the belief or degree of confidence
of an ideal reasoner.)

Logical theories are in direct descent from the "classical"
standpoint of Bernoulli and Laplace, however superior they
may be in sophisticated elaboration of explicitly invoked
assumptions. Laplace and his followers, as we have seen,
characteristically conceived of the degree of probability as
being wholly determined by a calculable relation between
*given* information (or the lack of it) and a given hypothesis,
independently of appeal to associated frequencies or any
other matters of fact. Like the Laplacians, latter-day advocates of "logical" theories typically construe probability as
relative to evidence—indeed, the slogan "probability varies
with the evidence" is commonly taken by them to be as good
as self-evident.

Some confusion is often introduced by reference to "rational credibility," "warranted assertibility," or the like. This
has the appearance of an implicit appeal to some ideal judge
of strength of evidence, a perfectly reasonable man whose
verdicts determine the "correct," "rational," or "justifiable"
degree of probability. The fiction is, of course, transparent:
the ideally rational man does not answer when summoned,
and reference to him is merely a picturesque way of pointing
to an imputed logical relationship supposedly holding between a pair of given propositions solely in virtue of their
meanings. Indeed, the criteria of "rationality" include ob-
servance of proper rules for estimation of probabilities;
there is no independent test for rationality. The "ideally rational man" is as irrelevant to "logical" theories as the "ideal
calculator" would be to mathematics.

Keynes, whose eloquent defense of the logical approach

[125]

against its rivals is largely responsible for its present vogue, wished to treat the ultimate relation between "proposal" and "supposal" as indefinable. This has the serious disadvantage of making the truth of the ultimate basic propositions available only to intuition, which is even more unreliable in matters of probability than it is elsewhere.

Later writers, such as Carnap, committed to constructing a definition of the ultimate logical relation, have typically invoked the notion of relative "range" (Spielraum) or something equivalent.

This can be briefly explained as follows. Suppose the indefinable, or "primitive," propositional functions of a given language L have the form $P_i(x_1, x_2, \ldots, x_n)$. For each $P_i$, form all possible values of these functions by inserting all possible choices of names of the individuals in the domain to which L refers. Call these the "atomic" sentences of L. Now form a conjunction in which every atomic sentence or its negation appears. This is a so-called state description. Each such state description may be regarded as expressing a "possible universe" relative to the choice of the language L, because it is the most specific description in L of what such a universe might be like. By suitably weighting such state descriptions, each proposition P can then be assigned a measure $m(P)$ and the degree of probability of H on P can then be simply defined by the fraction $m(HP)/m(P)$. In this way it is theoretically possible to calculate the probability of H relative to P for every pair of propositions H and P expressible in L.

The arbitrariness in application of the "principle of indifference," previously noted, reappears here in the fact that the state descriptions can be weighed in infinitely many ways, each resulting in self-consistent attributions of probabilities to given pairs of propositions. (Carnap's detailed exploration of the consequences of such choices is a valuable contribution to this subject.)

Many critics regard the variability of the probability values relative to the choice of a language L as a further source of disquiet in Carnap's elaborate construction. (It should be

[126]

noted, also, that Carnap has so far succeeded in developing his theory only in connection with certain very highly simplified "languages." Whether his methods can be extended to some language rich enough to approximate the contemporary "language of science" is still an unsettled question.)

The most difficult question that any "logical" theory has to answer is how *a priori* truths can be expected to have any bearing upon the practical problem of anticipating the unknown on the basis of nondemonstrative reasons.

FREQUENCY THEORIES

All probability theorists agree with the common-sense approach in recognizing that knowledge of relative frequencies of occurrence sometimes properly influences probability judgments. Were this not so, actuaries would deserve no more credit than soothsayers and their interest in statistical information would be an idle folly. The warmest advocate of a neoclassical analysis of probability in terms of the relative strength of reasons is bound to recognize that such strength is sometimes affected by relevant information concerning frequency. A well-balanced coin may, in the absence of further information, invite application of the principle of indifference, but when repeated trials with it show heads markedly predominating over tails, the evidence ceases to be symmetrical.

The root idea of a "frequency" theory is to deny the existence of any logical gap between frequency and reasons: probability is, in all cases, to be identified with some suitably defined relative frequency. (Sophisticated modern versions of this approach identify probability, instead, with the "limiting value" of such frequency.)

This idea has great intrinsic appeal to empiricists who, hoping to interpret basic probability statements as contingent (and in this way guaranteeing their application to practice), have nowhere better to look than in the direction of observed frequencies.

An early and influential anticipation of "frequency" theories is Locke's characterization of probable argument as "proof . . . such as for the most part carries truth with it" (*Essay Concerning Human Understanding,* Bk. 4, Chap. 15, "Of Probability"). Locke, on the whole, with his definition of probability as "likeliness to be true . . . [of] a proposition, for which there be arguments or proofs, to make it pass or be received for true," is still close to the classical conception.

More than a century ago, Leslie Ellis proposed to make the theory of probabilities a "science relating to things as they really exist" by taking as axiomatic the principle that in a long series of trials "every possible event tends to recur in a definite ratio of frequency." John Venn used this suggestion in *The Logic of Chance* (1866), defined probability explicitly in terms of relative frequency of occurrence of events in "the long run" (Chap. 6, Sec. 35), and developed the consequences in much deail. C. S. Peirce, acknowledging indebtedness to both Locke and Venn, considered probability to belong to arguments rather than events. For him the relevant measure was the proportionate number of times that the argument leads from true premises to true conclusions and is to be established by empirical investigation of the "success of the argument in the long run.

The most ingenious and persuasive advocate of a frequency view in modern times has been Richard von Mises. Central to his conception is the original but controversial idea of a *Kollektiv,* a series of events in which the characters of interest occur randomly. Von Mises' own definition of the desired type of randomness can, it seems, survive the accusations of inconsistency first leveled against it. Hans Reichenbach's very detailed investigations of probability purport to be able to dispense with von Mises' problematic conditions of randomness.

Although the frequency approach attracts working statisticians and other scientists concerned with large populations of events (for example, in "statistical mechanics"), it has the disadvantage, from the broader standpoint of an adequately comprehensive philosophy of probability, of denying any meaning to the probability of a unique event. Probability, according to frequentists, must always be construed as a global character of some indefinitely large class or indefinitely extended series of events. That such series are never to be found in experience makes probability statements, on this interpretation, neither strictly verifiable nor strictly falsifiable. This limitation and the necessary exclusion of probability statements concerning single events combine to restrict the scope of probability, so interpreted, too drastically for comfort.

A further difficulty is the implausibility of assigning probability, conceived in the frequentist fashion, to general assertions of law. For laws can hardly be conceived of as "occurring" as members of relevant classes. In spite of Reichenbach's valiant attempts to overcome this defect, the frequency interpretation must be held to reflect at best only part of the truth about probability.

SUBJECTIVE THEORIES

Let someone—S, say—be asked to consider how confident he would be of the truth of the proposition "A black ball will be drawn next" (H, say) if he knew the truth of the proposition "Ten balls drawn with replacement from a bag have all been black" (E, say). It seems certain that S's attitude of expectation toward H, in such cases, would vary with the evidence, E; for instance, if H' is the proposition obtained from H, above, by replacing "ten" by "a hundred," it seems certain that every S can be counted upon to say that his confidence in E, given H', is greater than his confidence in E, given H. On the assumption of such comparability of expectations, we may introduce the symbol "$c_s(H|E)$" to stand for the degree of S's confidence in H, given E. (Some authors prefer to say "degree of belief.") It may also be assumed, pending further discussion, that numerical values can sometimes be attached to degrees of confidence. (For different choices of S, the values of $c_s(H|E)$ must in general be expected to be different.)

An extreme form of a "subjective" interpretation would

simply identify probability with $c_s$—that is, with a given person's intensity of confidence. No theorist has proposed this view, if only because it would make probabilities fluctuate too much to be worth considering.

The following modification has, however, been ably defended in recent times, notably by Leonard J. Savage and by Bruno de Finetti. Suppose our hypothetical subject, S, is called upon to make an indefinitely large number of judgments resulting in values of $c_s(H|E)$ for different choices of E and H. Some such assignments of values of $c_s$ would prove to be inconsistent or "incoherent," in senses soon to be explained. Let him then adjust all his assignments of values of $c_s$ in such a way as to remove such incoherence; his "confidence" in H, given E, may then be called "rectified" (most writers prefer some such term as "reasonable," which is here avoided because of its implications of some standard of objective rationality). The views to be discussed here identify probability with degree of rectified confidence. They are distinguished from all logical theories by the important assumption that rectified confidence (and hence probability) can vary from one person to another, without imputation of fault.

The requisite notion of "coherence" is broader than that of logical consistency, which is presupposed. (Thus, it is assumed that if $E_1$ is logically equivalent to $E_2$ and $H_1$ is logically equivalent to $H_2$, a given S will assign the same values to $c_s(H_1|E_1)$ and to $c_s(H_2|E_2)$.) Suppose a given S were willing to offer odds of two to one that H would be true, given E, and odds of three to one that not-H would be true, given E. Although this might be done without any formal contradiction resulting, a gambler, by accepting both bets at once, could be certain to defeat S. All he need do is to make E true and await the outcome: if H then proves to be true, he collects 3 — 1 points, while if H proves false he collects 2 — 1 points, ending as the winner in either case. In the jargon of the racetrack, this is called "making a Dutch book" against S.

Let us give the rectification of S's confidence values the

following meaning: S will so choose these values that it will be impossible for anybody to "make book" against him, by accepting odds that will guarantee a net profit. It is surprising but demonstrably true that if S's system of confidence values is coherent in this sense of rendering it impossible for anybody to make book against S, those values will obey the addition and multiplication rules of the mathematical theory of chances. This striking result gives the subjectivist access to the usual mathematical axioms and their consequences. By stipulating that the degrees of confidence in question shall be coherent in the sense now explained, the advocate of a subjective theory is able to find a firm foundation for the customary calculation of complex probabilities. All systems of rectified confidence-values will use the same calculations for deriving complex probabilities from simpler ones, however different their starting points.

Some reluctance may be felt in supposing that the "confidence-values" to which the theory refers can be accurately measured in all cases. The answer offered, based upon a suggestion of F. P. Ramsey, is, roughly speaking, to determine these values from a knowledge of the odds that the person in question would offer in betting for one outcome rather than another. Let S be asked to bet on the truth of H, given E: if he is willing to wager one dollar against fifty cents (or anything more, but nothing less), we may assume that his confidence in H, given E, is measured by the odds of 2 to 1 (or, in more conventional terminology, that he attributes to H, given E, the probability $2/3$) and similarly in other cases. (The complications resulting from the "diminishing utility" of money wagers, and the like, will be passed over here.) Even propositions at first sight incomparable because of diversity of content may in this way, at least in principle, have their corresponding degrees of confidence brought into a single system. This behavioristic conception of degrees of confidence, when due allowance is made for the inevitable idealization required by any comprehensive theory, seems to provide an intelligible link with observable fact.

[131]

In their approaches to the crucial problems of inverse probabilities, subjectivists like Savage and de Finetti are Bayesians. Since the prior probabilities entering into the calculations are supposed to reflect only the varying *opinions* of different reasoners, it might be thought that no generally acceptable estimates of the strength of given evidence could result. De Finetti, however, relies upon the asymptotically diminishing effect of such varying assignments of initial probabilities as empirical evidence accumulates. He is able to show, in effect, that in a large number of interesting cases the choices made of the initial probabilities have, in the long run, negligible influence on the conclusions of statistical inference. (This part of his work, with its introduction of the interesting notion of "exchangeable events," has mathematical significance independently of any final appraisal of his philosophical position.)

In spite of the admirable ingenuity of its defenders, and their great resourcefulness in answering criticism, it is hard to believe that this type of theory is satisfactory from a philosophical standpoint.

For instance, it is not clear why the desire to prevent others from "making a Dutch book" against oneself should be regarded as a necessary criterion of rationality, to be accepted without further ado. It might be objected that to be willing to accept simultaneous bets for and against a certain outcome at the same stakes (and thus to be as coherent as subjectivists require) would be to destroy the point of betting by ensuring that no money would change hands. It is only bookmakers, who are bound to accept a variety of bets on both sides of a given outcome, who need fear a "Dutch book." And even they, like traders in foreign exchange, are not to be counted as irrational in buying at a lower price than that at which they would sell. In any case, behavior that is prudent for bookmakers seems an inadequate basis for an analysis of rationality in general. A man would not be irrational if he insisted on betting on only one side of a question; nor would he necessarily be irrational if he offered odds of 1:3 on H and odds of 1:2 on H̄, with the stipulation that wagers on H must be at least three times as large as those on H̄.

In general, it seems doubtful that the subjective view provides an even approximately correct analysis of what probability statements normally mean. When a man says, for instance, "The chance of my dying within the next ten years is even," does he *mean* something like "On the evidence to hand, suitably rectified to prevent anybody from winning money from me without risk, I find I would accept the same odds against my death that I would against a fair penny's showing heads on a single toss"? This seems very doubtful, if only because the implication in ordinary language of there being a *correct* answer to the question raised is absent. The departure from the preanalytical, common-sense concept seems too drastic to be ultimately acceptable.

MERITS OF THE DIFFERENT THEORIES

None of the chief types of interpretation of probability now in favor can be accepted as wholly satisfactory. One reason may be that an acceptable philosophy of probability is called upon to perform a number of tasks that are hard to reconcile: to show why some probability judgments are *a priori* whereas others are contingent; to provide a firm basis for a calculus of probability while recognizing probability judgments that are incorrigibly inprecise; to account for and to defend the connection between "rationality" and specifiable degrees of confidence in conclusions following with probability from given premises; and, above all, to show how and why it is justifiable to act on probabilities.

To the extent that the theories briefly examined in this article do not respond to such problems by denying their existence (on the old principle of going to bed until the desire for exercise vanishes), they may be said to have emphasized, in their different ways, plausible approaches to some of these tasks at the expense of the others. The fashionable response of some mathematicians, who are too "pure" to take problems of interpretation seriously, is simply to turn a blind eye to the tasks of the philosophy of probability. Empiricist views would succeed in providing an intelligible basis for contingent probability judgments were they not driven to postulate, in the form of limiting frequencies, series of observations that cannot be performed. Logical views readily certify the credentials of a priori probability judgments but are hard pressed to identify the rationale of appeals to frequencies. Subjective views pay more attention than their rivals do to the relevance of the reasoner's attitude but operate with so schematic a conception of rationality as to render their position suspect. That all the theories can, with greater or less display of ingenuity, provide a basis for the calculus of chances testifies only to the remarkable economy and simplicity of the needed axioms.

A REMAINING PUZZLE

What still remains to be done can perhaps be sufficiently illustrated by some concluding remarks concerning the problem of application.

Suppose that a philosopher has the choice of publishing his first book with one of two publishers, A and B. Suppose also that he knows that of first philosophical manuscripts published by A and B the chances of a second edition's being required are $\frac{9}{10}$ in the case of publication by A but only $\frac{1}{10}$ in the case of publication by B. On the assumption that the philosopher wishes to have a second edition of his work and knows nothing else that is relevant, everybody would agree that he ought to prefer publication by A to publication by B. But why? It is generally admitted that the truth of the judgment that the book has a $\frac{9}{10}$ chance of having a second edition is logically compatible with its not in fact being reprinted. Thus, given that the author is interested in having his book continue in print and is not merely interested in the correctness of the probability estimate, why should he prefer A to B?

Peirce, Reichenbach, and many others, say that the answer is to be found by considering a class of similar cases and by

[134]

being content to achieve one's practical aims "in the long run." But even in the long run there can be only high *probability* of success on the whole, so that the question of why one should be guided by considerations of probability is only postponed. In any case, the very definition of our situation excludes repetition.

Some defenders of a logical interpretation argue, in effect, that it is an analytic truth that one must be guided by probabilities in order to be considered rational. But then why should one be rational, if rationality has nothing to do with "success" and the attainment of practical aims?

A currently fashionable appeal to "maximizing expected utility" invites a would-be reasonable man to choose that course of action that will provide him with the highest calculable "expected" value—but this is, after all, merely to invite him to choose a way that will *probably* lead to more gain.

The subjectivist, if he says anything, tells our imagined author to follow whatever course he is inclined to follow— provided he allows nobody to "make book" against him— which is not much help.

It may be that the root of this intractable puzzle—in which action based on considerations of probability is justified only by further considerations which never satisfy, just because they still refer to probabilities—is to be located in a persuasive metaphysical conception that is unable to find any place in the universe for anything but categorical facts—or, what comes to the same thing, for propositions that are unqualifiedly true or false. If a philosopher has the unshakable notion that everything in the universe is what it is and no other thing, that events either occur or else they do not, and that it is absurd to think of some "middle ground," the basic notions of probability are bound to seem mysterious. Foiled in the attempt to explain probability in terms of factual properties of aggregates or long-run sequences, he may revert, like many others, to thinking of probabilities as expressing degrees of ignorance or degrees of subjective belief or something of the sort. But then the problem of explaining why it should be rational to act on probability will seem even more intractable than ever.

Whatever may be the proper therapy for this philosophical "cramp," it still offers a formidable challenge to all students of philosophy of probability and induction.

# VII

# Some Half-Baked Thoughts
# about Induction

0. "Induction" stands here for any kind of nondemonstrative argument whose conclusion is not intended to follow from the premises by sheer logical necessity.

0.1. The negation of an inductive conclusion is compatible with the amalgamated premise (the conjunction of all the reasons offered in support of the conclusion). As Peirce said, induction, in this broad sense, is "ampliative"—"the facts summed up in the conclusion are not among those stated in the premises" (*Collected Papers*, 2.680).

0.2. It would be useful to have some short label for "nondemonstrative argument," to avoid confusion with generalization from particulars. My own candidate is "adduction," which contrasts neatly with "deduction."

0.3. Philosophers need to worry about adduction in general, and not especially with that primitive variety of it known as induction by simple enumeration.

1. There is such a thing as induction.

1.01. Induction, *pace* Popper, is not an illusion, a chimera, or a will-o'-the-wisp. Nor is it an invention of simpleminded philosophers of science.

1.02. Laymen, and scientists too, constantly offer as sufficient reasons for empirical conclusions the truth of propositions that do not entail those conclusions. In so doing, they think they are reasoning soundly. It is inconceivable that they should always, and necessarily, be mistaken.

1.03. Once in a while, we can prove an empirical conclusion by invoking empirical laws and observations. But in the absence of proof, we are not reduced to twiddling our thumbs. (The Chinese speak of riding an ox to find a horse. But the ox moves, too.)

1.1. Induction is an instrumental notion: Inductions must be good *for something*. If there is such a thing as induction, we must achieve something by sound inductive reasoning. But what? Why not: arriving, if all goes well, at new and true propositions, by means of a defensible procedure? (But *how* to defend the procedure? There's the rub.)

1.11. An inductive reasoner is like an archer: He wants to aim well but in order to *hit the target*. There is no point in aiming well, if it does not help you to hit the mark.

1.2. We ought to resist the persistent inclination of philosophers of induction to treat all inductions as deductive enthymemes—and not merely because this leads to wholesale skepticism.

1.21. The *Drang nach Beweis* can be made immensely plausible, for there is usually relevant background information that can be introduced to "strengthen" the argument. (You think there is a man in that car because you see it moving at high speed? But you would not think so unless you knew a great deal about cars and men. So why not write it down?)

1.211. Does the notion of a completely explicit argument always make sense?

1.3. When inductions are treated as partially inexplicit deductions, they must all be rejected as invalid, epistemically circular, or irrelevant.

1.31. An induction, the conjunction of whose premises is $P$ and conclusion $K$, can easily be rendered valid by supplying the additional premise, *If P then K*. But when $P$ expresses the reasoner's complete reasons for affirming $K$ (so that the original induction is fully explicit), no further reason is available, at the time at least, in support of the additional premise, *If P then K*. Reconstructed as a deductive argument, it has the defect of using a premise that its author has no good reason to think true.

[138]

1.311. In fact, the additional premise may very well be false.

1.312. If the additional premise is so weak that *If P then K* does *not* follow from it, in conjunction with *P*, the reconstructed argument, considered as a deduction, must be invalid.

1.313. If *If P then K* is offered as a reason for passing, inductively, from *P* to *K*, the circularity is patent.

1.314. But there is nothing to stop us from looking for additional information which might allow *If P then K,* or something stronger, to be established.

1.315. The foregoing strictures will apply, with even greater force, to any additional premise that is stronger than *If P then K.*

1.3151. The famous principles of Uniformity of Nature, Limitation of Variety, and the like are too strong to be established and too weak to imply the conditional link, *If P then K.*

1.31511. Furthermore, the chances are that one and all of them are false.

1.32. Those who cannot conceive induction to be legitimate sometimes try to weaken the conclusion by inserting a reference to probability.

1.321. On certain "logical" theories of probability (e.g., Carnap's) a weakened conclusion, *K* say, does follow strictly from *P*. But then such an argument fails to make the "inductive leap" and is therefore irrelevant to the purpose of induction.

1.3211. What is the use of telling me something that follows strictly from a proposition expressing my empirical evidence when I want to know something about what is *not* entailed by that proposition—something about the not-as-yet-verified? It would be more straightforward—more candid—to say that my purpose was misguided and impossible of achievement. (This way lies inductive skepticism.)

1.4. According to the hidden-assumption approach, inductive inference is *good for nothing* because it cannot serve the imputed purpose of being a partially explicit but sound deductive argument. According to the probability-seeking approach, inductive inference has not been shown *good for anything* because all the reputable work is accomplished in the calculation of the probability. One approach makes induction useless, the other makes it otiose.

2. Some inductive arguments are better than others and some are very good indeed.

2.1. Anybody who rejects all inductive arguments, indiscriminately, as "invalid" seems committed to holding that if I hear the sound "ku-ku" from a tree, it is no more reasonable to think there is a cuckoo in the tree than to think there is a lion there; and no more reasonable to expect to find a pebble on the sidewalk than to expect to find a thousand dollar bill.

2.11. If we hold $P$ to be true and are required to choose between $K$ and *not-K*, it is sometimes reasonable to say that there is nothing to choose between them; but sometimes this reply would be the height of absurdity. (Take $P$ to be: all but one of the 1,000 marbles in the bag are black and this ball was drawn at random from the bag; and $K$ to be: this ball is black.)

2.2. People whose common sense has not been weakened by philosophy will often agree in their judgments about the goodness or badness of given inductive arguments. This provides some hope for the codification of inductive procedures. But there is enough *dis*agreement to make us cautious.

2.3. If we ever met somebody who seemed to agree sincerely with that old bogey the "counterinductionist," we would have to treat him as a lunatic. And we should be right.

2.31. But how would such a lunatic behave? Can one commit the "gambler's fallacy" *all* the time?

3. There is no universal criterion for the soundness of an induction.

3.1. One might try as a criterion: The truth of the premises must be a good and sufficient reason for thinking the conclusion to be true. But this is circular in its use of "good"; and in any case, the application of such a criterion, if it deserves that name, would depend on recognizing *when* the reasons are "sufficient."

3.2. The question as to when inductive premises are sufficiently strong might be compared to the question as to when the foundations of a house are sufficiently strong. There are no infallible answers to either question—but it is not a matter of mere guesswork either.

3.3. It is worth remembering that there is no universal criterion for the validity of a deductive argument. Logicians comfort themselves by talk about the "truth-preserving" feature of a valid deductive argument; but upon reflection they are seen to be saying no more than that the conclusion *follows* from the premises.

4. There are *some* formal principles that are relevant in appraising inductions.

4.1. That all the observed $A$'s have been $B$ is *some* reason for thinking that *any* given $A$ is a $B$; that most $A$'s are $B$ is *some* reason for thinking that an $A$ drawn at random is a $B$; if $P$ inductively supports $K$, and $Q$ inductively supports $K$, and $P$ and $Q$ are compatible and independent, the argument from $P.Q$ to $K$ is at least as good as the argument from $P$ to $K$; and so on.

4.2. Principles such as these I hold to be "linguistically *a priori*," i.e., to be guaranteed by what we properly mean by "reason," "support," etc.

4.3. Such principles provide a meager harvest and serve rather to stigmatize as bad the inductive arguments that no sensible man would ever use than to provide guidelines for genuine inductive inferences.

5. Inductions yield *guarded* assertions.

5.01. By a "guarded assertion" I mean a proposition to which is attached some indication of the strength of support for that proposition in the light of the available evidence.

5.02. Assertions can be explicitly "guarded" by the use of expressions such as "almost certainly," "very likely," etc. which I call "confidence indicators." (When the risk is negligible, the indicator may be omitted.)

5.1. All inductions are precarious, in a way in which valid deductions are not, but not precarious in the way that a rickety footbridge might be. It is obviously useful to the hearer to know the speaker's estimate of the risk—or, what comes to the same thing, his estimate of the strength with which the premises support the conclusion.

5.2. If the confidence indicator is omitted, there is a danger of fallacious inference: Thus $P$ may "sufficiently" support $K_1$ and sufficiently support $K_2$ without sufficiently supporting the conjunction $K_1.K_2$.

5.21. There should be no particular difficulty in constructing, for what it is worth, a calculus of "guarded assertions."

5.3. A guarded assertion is still an *assertion*. I take the conclusion of an inductive inference to be "detached"—but with a cautionary signal attached. *Caveat auditor*: He has been warned.

6. Induction is an art, not a science or a system of mechanical routines.

6.1. The art of drawing risky inferences might be compared to the art of mountain climbing. The climber clings to his holds, estimates the security of the next footholds and handholds—and *leaps*. So also for induction.

6.2. There are useful inductive strategies and maxims but no infallible rules for getting right conclusions.

6.21. There are no infallible principles for climbing mountains *in general*. But when the task is narrowed to climbing a known mountain, it is possible to rely on determinate and helpful strategies. So also in induction: The better defined the inductive task, the more help we can get from previous experience of similar tasks and the obstacles to their fulfillment. Cf. the relatively definite rules for statistical inferences, discussed in treatises of statistical method.

6.3. Good inductive inferences call for *judgment*—in the sense in which one speaks of a good judge of wine or of livestock.

6.31. A miniature inductive problem: waking up, noticing that my watch has stopped and needing to decide whether it is time to get up yet. There are intelligent as well as stupid ways of attacking this task.

6.32. In a good inductive solution, there are present at least the following: recall and choice of *relevant* premises; estimation of the strength with which they support the conclusion under examination; conflation of several supporting strands to yield a judgment of the resultant strength of the conclusion; a decision whether a suitable "detachment point" has been reached, or whether suspension of belief is in order.

6.321. At point after point in this process, the reasoner's flair, skill, *good judgment*, are crucial.

6.4. All sound inductive judgment is made against a background of detailed knowledge that activates the skill and expertise built up by repeated exercises of inductive judgment.

6.41. Asking somebody to form an inductive judgment about a skeleton argument, presented in all the nakedness of abstract symbols, is like asking a connoisseur to evaluate an imaginary painting.

6.5. One way to find out whether a man is a good inductive judge is to notice how often he goes wrong without extenuating circumstances. A good inductive judge must not fail too often.

6.51. But how often is "too often"? It takes a good inductive judge to judge an inductive judge—if only because the arguments in question have to be independently appraised.

6.52. We learn to become better inductive judges by scrutinizing our failures and retroactively criticizing the trains of thought that produced them.

7. Induction needs no general philosophical justification—and can receive none.

7.1. Again, it is worth insisting that the same is true of

deduction. Addicts of deduction should not harbor flattering illusions.

7.2. An inductive inference purports to justify the assertions of its conclusion. So a demand for justification of induction *as such* is as odd as a demand for an explanation of explanation as such or a proof of proof as such.

7.3. *Specific* challenges (demands for justification) of specific inductions are often in order: The critic may question the imputed strength of the reasons offered, their cumulative force, the appropriateness of the chosen "detachment point," and so on. Sometimes, such challenges are properly met by further inductive arguments.

7.31. But a point is eventually reached where the best that can be said is "That's how it looks to me." There is no substitute in the end for the reasoner's judgment.

7.32. If anything is clear in this whole subject, it is that *no* defense—deductive, inductive, or "pragmatic"—will satisfy the resolute inductive skeptic.

7.321. Offering the skeptic an inductive "justification" of induction is as futile as telling a dipsomaniac that the snakes he sees are not poisonous. (The psychotic *knows* that two and two make four, but can't stop worrying about it.)

7.4. The only way to cope with a *general* challenge to induction is to show that no philosophical task has been defined by the challenger. ("If only the fool would persist in his folly he would become wise"—Blake.) How *could* one "justify" mountain climbing *in general?* There is nothing to justify— and the same applies to induction.

7.41. Isn't the trick in philosophy, sometimes, in knowing when to *stop* worrying?

# VIII

# *The* Raison d'Etre
# *of Inductive Argument*

### 1 Some Definitions and Assumptions

BY AN inductive argument I mean a set of declarative propositions (the premises), together with another declarative
proposition (the conclusion), that purports to be supported
by those premises *without following from them.* By definition, therefore, no inductive argument is a deductive argument. All of the inductive arguments I shall consider are
intended to be fully explicit: the intended degree of support
for the conclusion is supposed to be provided wholly by the
stated premises, without assitance from unstated assumptions.[1]

A correct deductive argument is usually called "valid"; to
avoid confusion, a correct inductive argument may be called
"sound." Since an inductive argument does not aspire—or
should not aspire—to satisfy the standards of deductive correctness, it would be misleading to call it invalid. I shall be

[1] In practice, it is not always easy to distinguish an inductive argument, as here defined, from a deductive enthymeme. Consider the following example. *Pippa is a bird so Pippa has wings:* is this to count as
a deductive argument or as an incomplete inductive one? If the suppressed premise is *All birds have wings,* the argument will have to
count as a deductive enthymeme; if it should be *Most birds have wings,*
it will be an inductive argument (of the sort called a "proportional
syllogism") or an invalid deductive one, depending upon whether the
conclusion is or is not intended to follow demonstratively from the
premises. If the argument is actually presented by a speaker available
for interrogation, he can sometimes be asked how he intends the argument to be taken. I shall not consider any further difficulties involved
in identifying inductive arguments.

assuming, without argument, that some inductive arguments are sound and some are not.[2]

The foregoing definition deviates from the main traditions of the philosophy of induction in two ways. Classical writers take induction to be "generalisation from experience" (Mill) or "the logical processes employed in the inductive sciences, so far as these infer from particular facts the principles that explain them" (W. E. Johnson, *Logic*, III, 395), or something similar. However, I find it useful to consider all forms of "nondemonstrative" argument together. Besides generalization from particulars, inductive arguments, thus comprehensively viewed, include "eduction" (Johnson), or "argument from particulars to particulars," and "direct inductive arguments" from imperfect generalizations to their instances.

In the second place, there is a powerful tradition in the philosophy of induction that is committed to viewing allegedly inductive arguments as special kinds of inexplicit deductions.[3] Mill, and many other writers influenced by him, have insisted that every argument that would commonly be called "inductive" needs supplementation by some grand major premise concerning the uniformity of nature. Other writers claim that an inductive argument can be justified only if its conclusion is sufficiently weakened, by including explicit reference to probability, for the conclusion to be entailed by the given premises. If either demand is accepted, what is commonly called an inductive argument becomes a special case of a deductive one. By contrast, I wish to explore the conse-

---

[2] Anybody who denies this must presumably hold that it is no better to argue from *Pippa is a bird and Most birds have wings* to *Pippa has wings* than it would be to argue from the same premises to the contrary conclusion. This seems plainly absurd. The premises, by themselves, provide some reason for thinking that Pippa has wings and hence, some reason for not thinking that Pippa does not have wings. Even if the argument about Pippa be regarded as very weak, it should be recognized as sound, so far as it goes.

[3] "What is called induction appears to me to be either disguised deduction, or a mere method of making plausible guesses" (Bertrand Russell, *Principles of Mathematics*, p. 11n.).

quences of treating induction, in the broad sense, as a distinctive mode of argument having its own special *rationale,* and subject to standards of correctness that are not those of deduction.

Accordingly, I set out the general form of a complete inductive argument as follows:

$$P_1$$
$$P_2$$
$$\cdot$$
$$\cdot$$
$$\cdot$$
$$P_n$$

*Therefore (probably),*

$$K$$

Here, the qualifier "probably" may be conceived to be attached, as shown, to the "Therefore" (the sign of illation); when the conclusion appears detached from its premises, it is useful to attach the "probably" qualifier to it ("Probably, *K*") as a reminder.[4]

The word "probably," which might be called a *reliability indicator,* has something of the force of "more likely than not."[5] Its occurrence shows that the argument is intended to be inductive, not deductive. Other reliability indicators in common use are "very probably," "almost certainly," "the chances are," and "beyond all reasonable doubt." In sophisticated contexts, such as those of statistical argument, the reliability in question may be indicated by some number or range of numbers.

It will be noticed that I am taking the conclusion of an inductive argument to be *detached* (although I am aware of the

[4] In an ampler context, this might be a convenient place at which to develop a notion of *guarded assertion.*

[5] If the truth of the premises tips the balance in favor of the conclusion as against its negation only very slightly, one might hesitate to *assert* the favored proposition. So, a more plausible expansion of "Therefore (probably)": might be "Therefore (more likely than not by a sufficient margin)."

difficulties that may arise from this decision).[6] I wish to take the conclusion as K, *simpliciter,* without the intrusion of any indication of probability in the conclusion itself.[7] I shall not be able to discuss in this paper arguments whose conclusions are propositions that include reference *to* probabilities.

I propose now to consider the drawing of inductive *inferences,* i.e., the affirmation of inductive conclusions because they are, or are taken to be, sufficiently supported by true premises of sound inductive arguments. I wish to view such inferences as falling within the scope of a *purposive, rule-governed, practice.*

To be more explicit: Let us call an episode, in which some inductive conclusion is actually drawn by somebody, an *inductive performance.* I conceive of each such performance as determining a class of arguments, all of whose members are appraised as sound or unsound in virtue of rules that determine what is to count as inductive correctness for the class of

[6] For discussion of these, see especially C. G. Hempel, "Inductive Inconsistencies," *Synthese,* 12 (1960), 439–469. One of Hempel's objections to "detaching" the conclusion is that contrary conclusions may need to be inferred from alternative sets of true premises (p. 442). This seems to me a peculiarity of inductive inference that simply has to be accepted. More troublesome, I think, is the fact that K may be soundly inferred from P, and L from K, without L being a sound inference from P, i.e., the difficulty that the relation of inductive implication is apparently not transitive. Again P may sufficiently support $K_1$, and also sufficiently support $K_2$ without sufficiently supporting the conjunction $K_1 . K_2$. The notion of "guarded assertion," mentioned in footnote 4, above, offers some prospect of handling such difficulties.

[7] I would argue for the necessity for this by urging that only in this way can inductive inference have any bearing upon subsequent verification. If the conclusion is of the form *The probability of K (relative to P) is such and such,* its truth-value is independent of whatever proves to be the case (whether on the "logical" or on the "frequency" interpretations of probability). Attempts, such as those of Carnap, to provide a link between probability and verification—or, at least, between probability estimates and rational action—by relying on some principle for the maximizing of utility are, in my opinion, unsuccessful. For the most that can be assured by any such principle is "expected" gain, i.e., the *probability* of some desired, theoretical or practical, outcome.

[148]

cases in question.[8] Various rules of this sort, in their totality and interaction, constitute a formalized *practice*—or, if the reader prefers, an institution, a tradition—that defines inductive correctness and prescribes associated modes of conduct. Such conduct I take to be, notably, a readiness to "stand by" an asserted inductive conclusion, to defend it against attack, to use it as a premise for further arguments, to accept it as a premise when it is offered by another person, and so on. A short formula for this complex maze of related activities might be the *public expression and elaboration of the consequences of belief.* The practice or institution of inductive inference is a social device for regulating and appraising the publication of beliefs purporting to be derived from other beliefs but not entailed by them.

## 2 The Problem Stated

Given this conception of inductive inference, I now feel obliged to seek some account of the *rationale* of the inductive

---

[8] Some will wish to object that inference has to do with belief—which is not a matter of choice or decision and, therefore, not subject to the control of rules. Judith Jarvis Thomson says, of a proposed rule of inference: "To put it in the form of an imperative . . . would unfortunately be mad. Must I really be inferring statements from each other all the time? So also for attempts to set it out as a conditional imperative. Infer this from that, whenever—whenever I want to infer this from something?" ("Reasons and Reasoning," in Max Black, ed., *Philosophy in America* [1965], p. 287). She complains that it is not clear what "actions" could be enjoined by rules of inference, since they must tell the reasoner "to think something, and not merely to say or write something" (p. 289). The implied separation between thought and action seems hard to maintain. In any case, Mrs. Thomson takes too narrow a view of the character of the rules in question. They could, reasonably, be taken as rules of evaluation, specifying when inductive arguments are to *count as* being correct. Whether or not given reasoners find themselves able to obey the rules is therefore irrelevant. So long as they can understand that certain patterns of thought have to be criticized as incorrect, that will suffice for the practical utility of such rules.

practice and of the specific activities falling within its ambit. Induction, like the Sabbath, was made for man—and not vice versa. Accordingly, it should be possible to exhibit the overall purposes served, or intended to be served, by the encompassing practice, and the ways in which the rules and procedures enjoined by that practice contribute to the fulfillment of these purposes.

The peculiar urgency of this program for exhibiting the *rationale* of induction can be shown by contrasting the case of deductive inference. There, the *rationale* seems straightforward enough, at first sight. When the premises of a deductive inference are true and the argument is valid (is correctly conducted according to the prescriptions of the deductive practice), the conclusion is also true: valid deduction is truth-preserving, truth-transmitting. Thus, from knowledge of the truth of premises, we can sometimes acquire explicit knowledge of the truth of other propositions implicated by those premises. The benefits are obvious. If we desire to increase available knowledge, without recourse to experience or some other external source, deduction will sometimes satisfy the desire. Deduction is like a dredge that brings hidden cognitive treasure to light—or like the cashing of a draft on a fund of potential knowledge. Given an antecedent interest in increasing our store of available knowledge, the point of deduction is clear enough and no further rationalization is needed. (This sketch is, of course, incomplete, if only because we often wish to argue from the falsity of a conclusion to the falsity of one of its premises, or to draw the deductive consequences of premises only hypothetically entertained.)

Now contrast the case of inductive inference. Any inductive performance must be connected in some way with an antecedent interest in discovering the truth. But it is a striking feature of inductive inference, in which it differs importantly from deductive inference, that a sound inductive argument with true premises may have a false conclusion. Anybody who reasons deductively from true premises to a false conclusion must have made a mistake; but if he derives a false inductive conclusion from true premises, he may have been only unlucky. This makes the aim of inductive performances puzzling. A sceptic might reasonably ask: If the object of induction is to arrive at the truth, and if even the best inductive inference may fail to achieve this object, what *is* the point of such a performance or of the practice to which it belongs?

## 3 Some Distinctions Applicable to Purposive Activities

A few distinctions, applicable to all purposive activities, may help us to find our bearings. I shall distinguish between a *performance*, the *activity* of which it is an instantiation, and the general *practice* encompassing the activity and determining its proper mode of execution. (Thus, the particular episode consisting of somebody's opening a game of chess by moving his King's pawn on a particular occasion will be his *performance*; the corresponding "activity" will be identified as *moving P-K₄ on the first move*: and the enveloping "practice" is, of course, that of playing chess. An activity, in the sense here understood, is more abstract than a performance: the latter must occur at a specified place and time, while the former is, roughly speaking, the same as *what* is performed, or as I shall often say, "instantiated.")

I wish to distinguish, also, between the *immediate purpose* of the performance, the *general purpose* of the relevant activity, and the *global purpose* of the encompassing practice. (The immediate purpose of a dressmaker may be to put a stitch of a certain form in a particular place on the material; the general purpose of stitching may be that of holding pieces of material together in the desired shape; and the global purpose of dressmaking is, say, that of making garments that are comfortable and pleasing.) The threefold distinction I have introduced is somewhat rough-and-ready, but it will serve our purpose.

In the cases to be discussed, we may assume that the immediate purpose of a performance is *conducive* to the general purpose, and that the general purpose of an activity is *conformable* to the global purpose of the practice.

We may, with advantage, also introduce a cross-classification of purposes as *substantive* and *procedural*. Typically, the immediate purpose of a performance is to achieve a certain end state or result (the substantive purpose) but also to do so in a certain fashion, mode, or style (the procedural purpose). (Sometimes, the "procedural purpose" alone is relevant—as when a pianist plays a sonata. Here there is no "end state" to be produced—no artifact to be generated.)

The procedural purpose is usually intended to be conducive to the substantive purpose. Thus, a golfer addresses himself to the ball in a certain way, with the hope that making the stroke in "proper form" will serve his immediate purpose of getting the ball as close to the hole as possible. When achievement of the subordinate procedural purpose is certain to lead to achievement of the immediate purpose, I shall say that the former is *strongly* or categorically conducive to the latter. (Thus the tactic of keeping contact with one bounding wall of a maze is strongly conducive to the immediate purpose of getting out of that maze, since it constitutes an achievement procedure for that task.) When achievement of the procedural purpose contributes to, but does not guarantee, achievement of the immediate purpose, I shall say that it is *weakly* conducive to it. (Thus, aiming a gun at the target is weakly, but only weakly, conducive to the purpose of hitting that target.)

To sum up: I am thinking of the particular inductive performance of drawing a conclusion from given premises as having an immediate purpose that is both substantive and procedural; I think of the corresponding inductive activity that is thereby instantiated as having some general cognitive purpose; and I assume that the immediate purpose is at least weakly conducive to the general purpose, while the latter is such as to contribute in some way, still to be determined, to the overall global purpose, whatever that may be, of the inductive practice.

[152]

## 4 The Problem Restated in Application to an Example

Consider, now, somebody who argues as follows:

Most businessmen are Conservatives.

Grumbacker is a businessman.

*Therefore (probably)*, Grumbacker is a Conservative.

I take the *activity* of which this performance is an instantiation to be that of arguing from *Most B are C and A is a B* to a conclusion of the form *A is a C*. I want to ask, first, whether the *performance* has an immediate substantive purpose and, if so, what that purpose is.

It seems to me quite implausible to say, as some philosophers of induction do, that there is no immediate purpose, apart from the procedural one of performing correctly, i.e., of reasoning soundly. Those who take this position sometimes proceed to say that the only rational purpose of a particular inductive performance is that of providing a conclusion conducive to the general long-term purpose of the activity—or, perhaps, still more indirectly, to the global purpose of the encompassing practice. They are implying, I think, that so far as a particular inductive inference is concerned, all that the reasoner is immediately trying to achieve is a sound argument, with possible implications for wider purposes (behaving rationally on the whole—or sustaining a rational practice). This is no more plausible, I think, than contending that a man who gives a promise has no immediate interest in the outcome of his performance, but is solely interested in being judged to be a morally trustworthy person—or, is perhaps solely interested in maintaining the institution of promising. It seems to me clear enough that anybody, not a lunatic, who does perform an inductive inference is trying to achieve something immediately—and something more than reasoning soundly.

If there is an immediate substantive purpose, it could hardly be anything else but one of the following: either, to reach a conclusion that is true—or, alternatively, to reach one that is at least more likely than not to be true. Should the less ambitious of these alternatives be adopted as correct, the global purpose of the entire practice could not be anything more grandiose than that of arriving at a body of empirical belief that is on the whole well confirmed—is more likely than not to be true. For if nothing better than probable truth is to be expected of the individual conclusions, only probability or likelihood can be expected of their totality. Many able philosophers of science have acquiesced, or have positively gloried in, this deflationary conception of empirical inquiry, and they might conceivably be right. I shall, however, adopt the more interesting hypothesis that the immediate substantive purpose of an inductive performance is to arrive at a true conclusion. I believe, indeed, that anybody inductively reasoning from true premises has two immediate ends in view: to reason correctly and also to get a true conclusion. To be sure, all that even the best reasoner can guarantee is that he has made no mistake in reasoning, for whether his conclusion turns out to be true, as he hopes, is something that depends on more than his skill. (There is an element of risk in all inductive reasoning.) Nevertheless, to arrive by sound reasoning at a false conclusion must be judged to be a setback: the reasoner has failed in his immediate purpose, though through no fault of his own.

That the substantive purpose of getting a true conclusion may not be achieved is no objection to this view. When I play the patience game called Spider, I know that the chances of success are small, yet my object in playing each hand is correctly described as that of "getting the cards out" *this* time. So long as I know that success is not impossible, there is no absurdity in setting myself to perform a task that I may fail to accomplish. So also in the case of the inductive inference. So long as the reasoner knows, as he does, that it is not impossible for him to reach a true conclusion of the sort he desires, it is quite sensible for him to aim at getting such a conclusion each time he tries. (The higher the likelihood of truth, the more confidently he may set himself in pursuit of it.)

The inductive reasoner tries to obtain a true conclusion, not by accident but by means of a sound argument. His procedural purpose is, therefore, simply that of reasoning soundly in accordance with the relevant rules governing such reasoning. From what has already been said, we can see that this procedural purpose could at best be *weakly* conducive to the substantive aim of getting a true conclusion, for the conclusion's truth is never guaranteed. But it is not obvious how it can be even weakly conducive. How does conformity to rules of sound inductive reasoning contribute to the immediate purpose of arriving at a true conclusion? In order to see this, we shall need to reflect upon the relation between the premises and the conclusion of a sound inductive argument.

## 5 Relations between Premises and Conclusion of a Sound Induction

If we unite the two premises of our specimen inductive argument, we get the amalgamated premise: *Most businessmen are Conservatives and Grumbacker is a businessman.* Call it *P*. What is the connection between this proposition and the conclusion, *Grumbacker is a Conservative* (call it *K*) that entitles us to say that the passage from the former to the latter is sound? I can think of the following two answers, and no others: (*a*) Belief in the truth of *P* is a good reason for belief in the truth of *K*; and (*b*) if *P* is true, then *K* is more likely than not to be true.

There is a sense in which both answers amount to very nearly the same. First, it seems to me that acceptance of *b* necessarily requires acceptance of *a*: If you think that *K* is more likely than not to be true, given that *P* is true, you are obliged to hold that belief in the truth of *P* is, so far, a good reason for belief in the truth of *K*. In the second place, the

[155]

converse also seems true: If you hold that belief in the truth of $P$, by itself, is a good reason for holding $K$ to be true, you are obliged to hold that if $P$ is true, $K$ is more likely to be true than not. Moreover, the two conditionals seem to be necessary truths, depending, roughly speaking, upon what we mean by "belief," "good reason," and "likelihood." It is not a contingent matter of fact that "good reason" and "likelihood" are connected in the manner I have indicated; it is part of what we mean by the two expressions that they should be thus connected. (We could not make sense of somebody who urged that because $A$ was likely than not to be true, given $B$, *therefore* belief in the truth of $B$, by itself, would be a good reason for belief in the truth of $A$.) One difference between the two formulations is that talk about "good reasons" belongs to a context of evaluation, with fairly direct consequences for practice, while talk about "likelihood" is more theoretical, and does not trail practical consequences so obviously. To say something is a "good reason" is to prod your hearer, while to speak merely of likelihood is to adopt a cooler, more dispassionate posture. (Cf. the difference between asking somebody to close a window and merely remarking that it would be nice to have the window closed.)

It follows, if I am not mistaken, that a question about the weak conduciveness of the procedural purpose of *this* kind of inductive performance can be answered with remarkably little trouble.

If $K$ is the conclusion of a sound inductive argument from $P$, it is a necessary truth that $K$ is more likely than not to be true, given $P$—and a necessary truth that belief in the truth of $P$ is, by itself and so far, a good reason for belief in the truth of $K$. Hence, it follows at once that performing the inductive inference in correct form is weakly conducive to the desired substantive goal of getting a true conclusion. For that accomplishing $A$ is *likely* to lead to the accomplishment of $B$ is precisely what we mean by saying that $A$ is weakly conducive to $B$. If reasoning correctly is *likely* to lead to a true conclusion, we have all that can reasonably be desired in

[156]

seeking a link between the mode of performance and its desired end product.

This line of thought, although perfectly correct, will probably seem too glib to be satisfactory: it may well have the unsatisfying appearance of producing an invisible rabbit from a nonexistent hat.

Consider the following interchange between a critic of this standpoint and its defender:

A. Given that I am primarily interested in getting a *K* that is true, why should I bother about arguing from *P* "soundly"?

B. Because *P* is a good reason for *K*, so the truth of *P* makes it more likely than not that *K* is true. Thus *P* is conducive to the truth of *K*, which is what you want.

A. But how do we know that *P* is a good reason for *K*?

B. That is a necessary truth. To use "good reason" correctly is, *inter alia*, to consent to call *this* kind of argument one that supplies a good reason for the conclusion. To do anything else would be to violate a linguistic practice to which you are as firmly committed as I am.

What B says is perfectly right, but it will be singularly unsatisfying to anybody who has a genuine philosophical perplexity about the status and rationale of inductive procedures. One might say that B's account is too sensible to be persuasive. With respect to a limited practical aim, say that of curing a patient suffering from a disease, it is a perfectly satisfactory answer to an inquiry about the relevance of a given means that it is more *likely* than not to effect the desired end. Now B's answer has quite the air of responding to such a limited practical inquiry. (One recalls Moore pointing to a hand to dispel a philosophical doubt about the existence of material objects.) But once the rationale of the entire inductive practice has been brought into question and made to seem problematic, in a fashion that is sufficiently familiar after centuries of debate about the "justification of induction," any *use* of the key terms "good reason" and "likelihood" will be apt to seem question-begging or circular.

We can imagine our questioner elaborating his perplexity as follows:

A. Let me grant, at least for the sake of argument, that the way in which we talk about reasons and likelihood does require me, on pain of violating ordinary language, to call $P$ a good reason for $K$. But why should we—why should I—talk in that way? If you *use* the crucial terms in your defence, you are begging the very question at issue. A lunatic who used the term "good reason" in what would seem to us a crazily improper way, might be able to *prove* to us that, in accordance with *his* use of "good reason," he had good reason to use the phrase in the way he does. But that would not show him to be right. Why, then, should your answer be any better?

I believe that a challenge of this sort cannot be brushed aside as absurd on the face of it. To retort: "We talk the way that we talk and have the concepts that we have—and that's the end of it" must seem insufferably dogmatic to anybody of a genuinely philosophical turn of mind. Why *should* we talk as we do? Why can't we change the way we talk, if that should seem desirable? What is there to show that, after all, reliance upon inductive arguments is better than mere superstition?

Instead of meeting the challenge head on, I propose first to see whether any connection can be established between the procedural purpose of our inference and the *general* purpose of the activity that it instantiates. For we must bear in mind the possibility that what underlies the ordinary language link between "good reason" and "likelihood" is a more intelligible connection between sound reasoning "on the whole" and the general aims of inductive reasoning. I shall need, first, to recall some familiar points.

## 6 The Generality of Inductive Reasons

Philosophers have often commented on the "implicit generality" of reasons. To offer a reason, whether for a belief, an action, a moral verdict, or something else, is necessarily to rely upon some real or fancied character of the situation in question. To imply that this character is relevant to whatever is being defended is necessarily to hold that some general connection obtains between the invoked character and something else. If I say that the risk of fire is a reason for not smoking in bed, I imply that the relevant character, smoking in bed, is generally connected with a risk of fire. The relevant generalization need not be the unqualified one, *Whenever anybody smokes in bed, there is risk of fire* (although that is roughly true and relevant) but may be the more guarded one, *Whenever anybody smokes in bed in such and such circumstances, there is risk of fire*. But unless one has some such generalization in reverse, talk about a "reason" is improper. It follows that what is claimed to be a reason in one case is necessarily put forward as something that *would be* a reason in a class of similar cases, where the definition of that class depends upon what is taken to be relevant in the case in hand. The reference to what *would be* the case is essential —in other words, the supporting generalization must be "lawlike" and not merely "accidental." [9] If I say, to vary the ex-

---

[9] A valuable feature of Peirce's last discussions of probability is his frequent insistence upon the importance of bearing in mind what *would be* the case and not merely what *will be* so. For example: "I am, then, to define the meanings of the statement that the *probability,* that if a die be thrown from a dice box it will turn up a number divisible by three, is one-third. The statement means that the die has a certain "would-be"; and to say that a die has a "would-be" is to say that it has a property, quite analogous to any *habit* that a man might have" (*Collected Papers,* 2.664, p. 409). Also: "A probable deductive argument is valid, if the conclusion of precisely such arguments (from true premises) *would* be true, in the long run, in a proportion of time equal to the probability which this argument assigns to its conclusion; for that is all that is pretended" (*ibid.* 2.781, p. 501, italics added). On the other hand, Peirce often slipped into talking, mistakenly in my judgment, about what *will* be the case: "The validity of a presumptive adoption of a hypothesis for examination consists in this, that the hypothesis . . . is selected according to a method which *must* ultimately lead to the discovery of the truth, so far as the truth is capable of being discovered, with an indefinite approximation to accuracy" (*ibid.*). Peirce's reasons for thinking that the truth *must* ultimately be approximated to by inductive methods seem to me incorrect.

ample, "His inflicting unnecessary cruelty in vivisecting the cat is a reason for morally censuring him," I must imply that infliction of unnecessary cruelty to animals by anybody *would*, so far, be a reason for moral censure. There would be a patent absurdity in saying, for instance, "This act in which somebody inflicted unnecessary pain is morally censurable, but some cases, differing in no relevant respect, *would not be*."

Let us apply these elementary considerations to our specimen inductive argument. I said that belief in the truth of the amalgamated premise, *Most businessmen are Conservatives and Grumbacker is a businessman* is a good reason for belief in the truth of *Grumbacker is a Conservative*. Here, the class of cases similar in all relevant respects is easy to discern: In calling the argument sound, I am committed to holding that belief in the truth of any premise of the form *Most B are C and A is a B* would always be a good reason, so far, for belief in the truth of a conclusion of the form *A is a C*. And, conversely, if the general statement about a good reason is true, its application to the case in hand necessarily follows.

This offers some hope of connecting the general purpose of what I have called the inductive activity with the immediate purposes of the particular inductive performances instantiating that activity. We may hope to pass from what *would be* a good reason in each of a class of cases of inductive inference to what *is* a good reason in any given case. Let us see how this might be attempted.

## 7  A Deductive Link between General Inductive Purpose and Immediate Inductive Purpose

Consider the following example. I draw a ticket from a lottery of a thousand tickets, knowing that just one of those tickets will earn a prize. I argue as follows: "Nearly all the tickets will fail to win a prize; therefore (almost certainly), my ticket will fail to win a prize." If the soundness of this argument is challenged, I can defend it as follows: "Each and every one of the other 999 persons who draw a ticket will be in the same cognitive situation as I am. What counts as a good reason for me must equally count as a good reason for each of them. Now if all the thousand ticket holders were to argue as I did, it necessarily follows that 999 would affirm a true conclusion and only one would (though with good reason) affirm a false one. Thus the activity is certain to lead to true conclusions *on the whole*, which is more than can be said, with certainty, of any other procedure for reaching the desired conclusion. Conversely, if the general purpose of the activity is taken to be that of getting true conclusions on the whole, it follows that *each* of the ticket holders has a good reason for arguing as I originally did, and for not arguing to the contrary conclusion. What is a good reason for all is necessarily a good reason for each."

This defense seems to be sufficient if the general purpose is acceptable. Of course, if a prospective buyer of a lottery ticket were to say that he had no interest whatever in what would happen to the other ticket holders, but wished only to know the fate of his own ticket, the defense I have suggested would seem pointless to him. But then he would be unable to consider *reasons* for having one belief about the outcome rather than another. To weigh inductive reasons is necessarily to be in a posture of considering what *would* happen in a class of relevantly similar cases—not, as Peirce wrongly suggested, because the individual identifies his interest with that of the unbounded community,[10] but rather because it is of the essence of reasons to be "implicitly general."

[10] "It seems to me that we are driven to this, that logicality inexorably requires that our interests shall *not* be limited. They must not stop at our own fate, but must embrace the whole community. This community, again, must not be limited, but must extend to all races of beings with whom we can come into immediate or mediate intellectual relation. It must reach, however vaguely, beyond this geological epoch, beyond all bounds. He who would not sacrifice his own soul to save the whole world, is, as it seems to me, illogical in all his inferences, collectively. Logic is rooted in the social principle" (*Collected Papers*, 2.654).

I wish now to urge that the defense I have offered for my conclusion about the lottery ticket holds good whether or not the remaining tickets are in fact all drawn. Even if some of the tickets remain unsold and undrawn, we can still argue as I did before; it will still be true that 999 reasoners drawing the parallel conclusion *would be* right. For, to be right "on the whole" can only mean, for the reasons I have already sketched, to be such as to yield a majority of true answers in a set of *would-be*'s. Take the extreme case in which I draw a ticket, on the terms already stated, knowing in advance that all the other 999 tickets will immediately be destroyed. Even then, appeal to what would happen "on the whole" is as relevant and as conclusive as before.

In some such way as the foregoing, connection can be demonstrated between the immediate procedural purpose of using a statistical syllogism and the general purpose of the activity instantiated by such a performance.

I do not think I need to discuss the rationality of the general purpose of being right—of getting a true conclusion—"on the whole." If we desire truth about the unknown, but cannot hope to get it each time, we must be satisfied with a method that would serve most of the time. But the line of defense adopted will hardly suffice, without important modification, to justify other modes of inductive argument that have an equal title to be regarded as basic.[11] For instance, it is hard to see how the defense can be adapted to fit a case where the reference class is indefinite or potentially infinite in membership (as when a ball is drawn from an urn with

[11] One of the most important of these is the argument from the composition of a sample to the approximate composition of the population from which the sample is drawn. Suppose $m/n$ members of the population have a certain character $C$. Then, most samples containing $n$ members will have a frequency of occurrence of $C$ falling within the range $m/n + \delta$, for suitable choice of $\delta$. This would allow us to argue that *most* samples will approximately match the population and so to construct a defence somewhat like that already offered. Cf. D. C. Williams, *The Ground of Induction* (Cambridge, Mass., 1947), for a similar argument.

replacement); and it is even harder to see what sense could be made of the notion of "being right on the whole" in arguments whose conclusions are general.[12]

In order to illustrate further some of the problems that can arise, I shall now consider the type of inductive inference sometimes called *eduction* (inference from particulars to particulars) and will try to discover how far one could get in establishing in this type of case a deductive connection between immediate and general purpose.

## 8 A Quasi-Pragmatic Vindication of Proportional Eduction

By a *proportional eduction* I mean an inductive argument of the following form: *Most of the observed A's have been B; therefore (probably), The next A to be observed will be B.* My aim, as it was in the case of the statistical syllogism, is to see how far one can hope to go in establishing some necessary connection between the "immediate purpose" and the "general purpose." Since I see no prospect of finding a line of argument closely analogous to the one I have already used, I propose instead to follow a somewhat different tack.

A slight change of perspective will be helpful. For we can, without substantially changing our task, now conceive of the principle of the proportional eduction as governed by a certain *policy*, rather than by the corresponding principle. We can think of any particular eduction as exemplifying and conforming to the policy, "When most observed *A's* have been *B*, expect the next *A* to be *B*, unless there are sufficiently strong countervailing reasons to think otherwise." I want to

---

12 It is worth recalling that Peirce did not rest the "validity" of inductions upon success "on the whole." On the contrary, he said, "The validity of induction is entirely different; for it is by no means certain that the conclusion actually drawn in a given case would turn out true in the majority of cases where precisely such a method was followed" (*Collected Papers,* 2.781, p. 501). And in the same vein: "It is nonsense to talk of the probability of a law, as if we could pick universes out of a grab-bag and find in what proportion of them the law held good" (*ibid.,* 2.780, p. 500).

see what can be said for this policy in terms of success "on the whole." In order to do so, I shall now describe the following, highly artificial situation in which the policy might be applied.

THE FINITE PREDICTION TASK

Imagine that you are to be shown, one by one, a hundred objects, each having one or other of two qualities (call them 1 and 0, respectively). Before each object is shown, you are to predict its character (i.e., whether it will be 1 or 0), whereupon you will at once be told the right answer. You are allowed to keep a cumulative record of your predictions and of the right answers. The object of the exercise is to get the highest number of correct answers by the end of the test run. I shall also stipulate that no further information is available: you are completely in the dark about the nature of the two characters here called 1 and 0, and you have absolutely no information about whether the series of 1's and 0's will be a random one, whether the experimenter who supplies the objects will make his choice depend upon your own performance—in short you are and will remain until the end of the test run completely uninformed about the design of the series and the plan, if any, behind its generation. Given all this, is it possible to have a rational policy for performing the set task? [13]

[13] The test situation described is essentially that used in many simple experiments on choice under uncertainty. See, for instance, William K. Estes, "Individual Behavior in Uncertain Situations: An Interpretation in Terms of Statistical Association Theory," in R. M. Thrall, ed., *Decision Processes* (New York, 1954), pp. 127–137.

"In these experiments the outcome of the situation has no utility for the individual (except that of being right or wrong in his guess) and the information available to the individual is restricted to what he can obtain from observing a series of replications of the situation. . . . The subject is given no information about the conditions of the experiment except that one of the $E_j$ [the events to be predicted] will follow the signal S on each trial; he is instructed to do his best to make a good score (in terms of correct predictions), and to make a prediction on each trial regardless of how uncertain he may feel about the outcome" (p. 128).

Some men of good judgment will say that in the situation envisaged we are so close to the condition of "complete nescience" envisaged by certain writers on induction as the setting for ultimate justification of inductive procedures [14] that no rational policy is defensible and blind guessing would be as reasonable as anything else. I shall however try to defend the following policy (call it *P*): (i) Whenever the observed segment of the run shows a predominance of one character over the other (more 1's than 0's, or vice versa), to predict the immediate occurrence of that character; (ii) whenever the 1's and 0's have occurred equally often in the observed segment, to predict 1 and 0 alternately (i.e., predict 1 the first time this happens, 0 the next time, and so on); [15] (iii) to scrutinize the observed segment constantly for evidence of order, and to modify the application of the first two clauses accordingly (I shall explain the meaning of this very soon).

The first clause in this statement of the policy in effect prescribes the use of proportional eduction whenever it is applicable; the second is merely an arbitrary way of ensuring a determinate prediction when the proportional eduction fails; and the last is a somewhat vague injunction to override the eductions specified, whenever sufficient evidence of regularity appears in the series. Vague as it is, the last clause seems essential. To conform solely to the first two clauses when faced by a series that continued to deliver a 1 and an 0 alternately would, plainly, be highly unreasonable.

Let us put aside, for the moment, complications arising from the presence of the last clause in the statement of the recommended policy, by supposing that we are dealing, for

[14] "Simple induction . . . is the first step in the emergence from total nescience" (Roy F. Harrod, *Foundations of Inductive Logic* [New York, 1956], p. 67). He seeks a defense of inverse probability "as a method of rescuing us from initial nescience" (p. 87), construed as a state where, notably, we cannot employ a Bayesian resort to *a priori* probabilities of the hypotheses under test.

[15] Or use *any* device that will ensure a definite decision. The purpose of this clause is merely to avoid any indeterminacy in applying the policy.

the time being, only with series in which the initial segments manifest no evidence of any special order (series which are random in the distribution of 1's and 0's, although with a possible predominance of the one character over the other). We can then argue in defense of $P$ in the following way: Suppose one character, say the 1, predominates in the entire test run of 100 items; then in that run there will be a certain number, $n$, by which the total number of 1's exceeds the total number of 0's. Let us call $n - 1$ the *security*. Then it is a fact, though one that is not quite obvious, that by following $P$, we can be certain, in advance, of ending with a final score of successes *equal to or greater than the "security."* Furthermore, any deviation from the recommended policy runs the risk of reducing the final score below that guaranteed lower bound. $P$ is what game-theorists call a "maximin" policy, since the worst that can happen by following it is no worse than the worst that could happen upon adopting some other policy.

It is not hard to see why the final score obtained by following the recommended policy, $P$, must be equal to or greater than what I have called the "security." Let us call the character (1 or 0) that has occurred more frequently at a given point in the test run, the *leader*, and let us call predicting the immediate recurrence of that character, *backing the leader*. Suppose 1 ends up as the ultimate leader—the *winner*, let us say—by a margin of $n$ more total occurrences than 0 has. Then, obviously, 1 must have been the leader at least $n$ times: it needs to have been ahead at least $n$ times in order to build up its final lead (more often than $n$ times if 0 is ever ahead). At the outset we do not know which character will end as the winner, but by always backing whichever character happens to be in the lead at a given point we can be *sure* of ending on the right side.

A helpful way of looking at the matter is this. Since we want to be right in our predictions as often as possible, we should like to know whether most of the items to be shown to us are 1's or whether most of them are 0's. Had we been told at the outset that most of the items were 1's, say, the rational policy would clearly have been to back a 1 all the way, for this would have guaranteed a final score equal to the total number of occurrences of the more frequent character. By the policy of constantly backing the leader, we do end by backing the winner—the character that occurs the more frequently—and meanwhile we have been backing it at all times when it was ahead, without knowing that we *were* backing the winner. So the recommended policy for the task can also be thought of as a way of approximating to the truth about the total run—or at least to the truth about which character finally predominates.

The suggested defense of policy $P$ can now be set out as follows: For each given test run, $R$, there is an associated but unknown number, $s$, greater or equal to zero, i.e., the number that we have called the "security." If $s$ is equal to zero, we have nothing to lose by following $P$, for, on the special assumption made, that no regularity can be detected in the successively revealed initial segments of $R$, $R$ will be random and no policy is any better than any other. On the other hand, if $s$ should be greater than zero, which it may be, we would have the advantage, by following $P$, of having a built-in guarantee against ending with less than $s$ as our final score. Since no other policy has this advantage, $P$ is preferable to any competitor.[16]

It must be admitted that this is, at best, a very weak defense. It does, to be sure, establish *some* necessary connection between the proximate procedural purpose of drawing the predictive conclusion in a certain stipulated way and the more remote general purpose of doing well—or as well as can reasonably be hoped for—"on the whole." It guarantees the

[16] It might be noticed that $P$ is a very conservative policy that cannot at best produce a very high score. Let $t$ be the total number of occurrences of 1 (the character assumed to predominate). If the arrangement of the terms of the series is sufficiently favorable we might get an assured score of $t - 1$, but no more (apart from lucky guesses at points where neither character is in the lead). Let $e$ be the number of points at which the 1's and 0's have occurred equally often; then, all that we could count upon is $t - e - 1$, which cannot be less than $s$, but need not be more.

modest prospect of insurance against a very low score *in a particular case*—but is that enough to satisfy us?

Here I am, with a particular test run before me and the task of getting a true eductive conclusion as many times as I can in my 100 tries; why should I follow $P$? Well, if the series manifests sufficient regularity for me to detect it, $P$ may well lead me astray (as we shall see very soon); and if the series is irregular, with equal occurrences of the two characters, $P$ is no worse than any other policy—i.e., to be candid, no good at all; but if $P$ is thoroughly irregular, with a predominance of one character over the other, then following $P$ will make it certain that my score will not fall below a certain, unknown, number $s$. This defense of $P$ is so hedged about with provisos as to be less than persuasive.

Would it be a good policy to follow $P$ if I had to take the experiment a large number of times? There is no argument to show that it would. The recommended efficacy of the policy depends upon the same procedure being applied, without interruption, from the very start of the run. Now, if I am required to repeat the experiment on another occasion, I cannot consider the next test run as an extension of the old one, because I presumably have no record of that earlier one. The most one can say is that if the policy was rational in one case, it is rational in every similiar case.

A serious weakness of this policy is that it considers only possible losses, without balancing them against possible gains. What is at stake can be brought out by contrasting $P$ with a modified policy, which I will call P′. The modified policy is simply that of following $P$ for the first fifty terms and then starting afresh for the last fifty predictions, as if they constituted a new test run. Let the "securities" of the two halves of the test run, considered separately, be $s_1$ and $s_2$ respectively (and let $s$ as before be the security for the whole run). Then it is easy to see that if the same character predominates in the two halves, we must have

$$s_1 + s_2 = s - 1.$$

That is to say, by performing our task in two independent installments, we risk losing one point in the overall guarantee. (The first member of the second half of the total run, where we can only guess, might have been a place where we ought to have been backing a 1.) But now suppose that the two halves show *different* predominating characters, say with 1's predominating in the first half, o's in the second, and 1's predominating over all. Then the equation between the securities will be

$$s_1 - s_2 = s - 1.$$

Our total guarantee in the interrupted procedure, $P'$, viz. $s_1 + s_2$, will then be greater than the security, $s$, obtainable on $P$. In short, we stand to gain something that may be substantial, at the risk of a small loss (one point off the total security) if the two halves are not homogeneous with respect to the predominance of one and the same character. By using $P$ rather than $P'$ we are, as it were, counting on the homogeneity of the series; by preferring $P'$ to $P$ we would be counting on the heterogeneity of the series. (Similar considerations would apply to a proposal to use another policy, say $P''$, involving separate consideration of three successive partial segments of the test run.)

In the absence of any consideration of probabilities (and perhaps associated utilities of success and failure) there seems to be no rational way of deciding between $P$ and $P'$—or indeed between $P$ and many other policies. One might say the choice depends upon the subject's relative interest in winning or losing. If he is more concerned to avoid loss than to acquire gain, he should prefer $P$, but then he runs a risk of failing to pocket a considerable gain. If, however, he would rather take a slightly increased risk of loss for the sake of having a chance of great gain, he might well prefer $P'$.[17]

---

[17] In experiments of the kind cited in footnote 13, groups of subjects, considered as a whole, tend to approximate asymptotically to a strategy which "matches" the frequency in which the characters to be predicted occur in the (random) series of their presentations. (Thus, in

Let us now return to what we have so far excluded, the use of the third clause of the policy, which was, it will be remembered, to check each observed segment for possible evidence of regularity. Suppose we have had the following initial segment: 1010101. Adherence to the policy $P$ would require the subject to predict a 1, but if he thinks that there is now good evidence for a regularity in the series he might well prefer to predict an 0. Here, there is a sharp conflict, which I can see no way to resolve without recourse to questions of probability (and perhaps utility). To abandon $P$ at this point is certainly to diminish the "security"; but perhaps that is worthwhile, in view of the gain to be expected if the hypothesis of regularity is verified.

Is the chance of gain on the hypothesis of regularity worth the reduction of security involved in abandoning the conservative maximum policy? I see no way of answering this question in the absence of further information. In practice, I imagine, anybody actually faced with the task I have described would decide, sooner or later, that a long initial segment of alternating 1's and 0's justified him in betting on its continuation. Called upon to rationalize this, one would probably argue that the conservative policy $P$ is tailored to the case of random distribution (for it is only then that its safeguards are least in doubt), while a *long* run of alternating 1's and 0's makes the hypothesis of randomness progressively less likely. This argument is, clearly, an exercise in inverse probability, or in the rational choice of hypotheses—at any rate, is based upon considerations a great deal more complicated than anything that I am here seeking to defend.

---

my own statement of the conditions, if 1's appear twice as often as 0's, without any noticeable regularities in occurrence, the average behavior of a large group of subjects approximates to predicting 1 twice as often as 0.) This is clearly *not* the policy I have been recommending, which is approximately the same as the "pure strategy" which would be recommended by game-theoretical considerations.

## 9 The Moral of the Preceding Exercise

The outcome of our attempted quasi-pragmatic vindication of proportional eduction is disappointing, for the connection between the rule governing the performance of eduction and the presumptive aims of the activity instantiated is tenuous to the point of nonexistence. The chief lesson to be drawn from the exercise is perhaps the implausibility of hoping to establish a necessary connection, even of so tenuous a sort, between the purpose of the performance and the purpose of the associated activity, so nakedly conceived. It would hardly be a parody on the defense we have attempted to compare it to an effort to justify the wearing of a hat by arguing that if we were to wear a hat in a state of otherwise complete nudity, we might have a better chance of keeping at least our head warm than if we went bareheaded. A state of almost total ignorance concerning the relevant empirical situation is about as rare, and needs as much special contrivance, as a state of complete nudity. Were we to be actually faced with the kind of predictive task I have envisaged, we would, I believe, try to assimilate it to a condition of substantial antecedent knowledge. Thus, it would certainly be rational to speculate concerning the motives of the experimenter, what plan he might be using in generating the terms of the series, and so on—in short, to formulate hypotheses, however ill-supported by evidence, as we should normally do in any authentic empirical investigation. In the absence of any access to relevant information about the background of the set task, our inductive procedures will be, at best, pallid and ineffectual efforts to behave as if we had a solid basis for full-blooded inductive inference.

If challenged to defend "eduction" as an isolated procedure we might, of course, fall back upon the linguistic argument I used before. It is, I think, correct to say that all the observed *A*'s having been seen to be *B* is *so far* a good reason for thinking that the next *A* will (probably) be a *B*, and to

[171]

appeal to the way we use the key terms in justification. But that gets us a very little way, at best, and leaves us exposed to the old accusation of circularity.

## 10 Links with the Entire Practice?

The reason for our setback may, of course, be simply lack of competence. It is notoriously hard to establish a negative, and correspondingly hard to show that there is *no* necessary connection between success in performing a "proportional eduction" correctly and some intelligible general purpose of the activity instantiated. Instead of what I called the "security," it may be possible to find some other feature of a long series of applications of the type of inductive argument in question that would supply the missing link between the short-term and the long-term purpose. I am strongly inclined to doubt this, however, if only because so many talented philosophers have tried it without success.[18] I would therefore like to raise now the possibility that there is something wrong with the approach adopted. Perhaps it was a mistake to seek to isolate the activity of "proportional eduction" from the wider practice to which it belongs (as it would be to seek to establish the utility of addition, without reference to the function of the whole of arithmetic). Perhaps the place to find a connection between induction and intelligible human interests in arriving at the truth is in the entire *practice* and not in some artificially dissected component of it.

Well, what is the overall purpose of the inductive practice? Can it be anything but arriving at an approximation to the truth? And is not the past experience of the race some evidence of its success in achieving that purpose? Certainly there is a strong inclination, on the part of the sophisticated no less than the naïve, to point to the past successes of the whole inductive practice as some kind of justification. Surely, one is inclined to say, the fact that the inductive practice, broadly

[18] See, in this connection, especially D. C. Williams, *op. cit.* and Roy F. Harrod, *op. cit.*

[172]

conceived, has worked so well in the past *must be* a good reason for continuing to trust it.[19] Well, much depends upon how the inductive practice and its global purpose are conceived—whether as revelation of the most general and systematic truth about the universe, or as a series of interconnected assertions having high confirmation, or as a progressively "self-correcting" procedure for approximating in the infinitely long run to the truth (Peirce) or, as a rigorous and sophisticated strategy for eliminating plausible and interesting errors (Popper). Whatever answer is given, there will be many who will be quick to level the charge of circularity against *any* such attempt. Suppose the global purpose of inductive inference be isolated as $Q$ ($Q$ being such as to make the more immediate purposes of particular inductive activities intelligible in their relation to it) and suppose also that there is no dispute as to the practice having sufficiently achieved $Q$ in the past. Consider, now, an argument having the form: *P has achieved Q in the past; therefore (probably), P will continue to achieve Q in the future.* Is there any reprehensible circularity in an argument of this form?

I believe the following assertions concerning this kind of argument are correct:

[19] Cf. the following answer to the question whether the Laws of Nature will continue to hold: "I reply that, unless the constitution of the Universe shall be changed to an extent which I cannot now even conceive, they will so continue, and that no reasonable man has any practical doubt as to their continuance. And why? *Because they are confirmed by the whole of our own experiences*, which . . . is of enormous extent and variety, *by the experiences of our ancestors, and by all that we can ascertain of the past history of nature* [he is speaking of the law of gravitation and the proposition than animal and vegetable life cannot exist without moisture], while their reversal would involve the reversal of almost all the other laws with which we are acquainted" (Thomas Fowler, *The Elements of Inductive Logic*, 6th ed. (Oxford, 1904), p. xi, italics added). In the tradition of Mill, Fowler makes this belief in the "continuance" of laws of nature depend upon the "hypothesis" that "the same causes will continue to produce the same effects." He concludes: "What would happen if this expectation were ever frustrated, it is absolutely impossible for us to say, so completely is it assumed in all our plans and reasonings" (*ibid.*).

1. The argument is *sound*. That is to say, anybody who believes in the truth of the premise would be justified on inductive grounds in believing in the truth of the conclusion and, consequently, in asserting that conclusion.

2. We have, for the reason set out in the premise of the argument, strong grounds for holding that the inductive practice will continue as it has done in the past to serve its distinctive purposes.

3. There is no *formal circularity* in the argument, i.e., nobody using the argument needs to assume *as a premise* that the inductive practice will continue to work successfully in the future—or anything from which this would follow.

4. Nor is there any more subtle circularity such as would be involved in anybody's necessarily having to believe (or even to know) the conclusion to be true before he could be justified in presenting the argument as sound.[20]

What, then, does the accusation of circularity, commonly brought against any argument of this form, amount to? The accusation reduces to something like the following, I believe: "In offering the inductive argument in support of the continuing efficacy of the inductive practice, you must be at least believing (if not actually assuming) that your argument is sound. But then you must be believing (or actually assuming) that a certain mode of inductive activity (simple eduction) *will* continue to work in the future. Now this is part of what is in question here. For unless simple eduction works, the entire practice cannot continue to be efficacious. You are, in part at least, assuming the very thing to be proved."

The following rejoinders can be made. It must be conceded to the critic that anybody offering the inductive defense of the inductive practice in good faith must hold (as he undoubtedly will) that the form of inductive argument he

---

[20] I have argued in the past, more narrowly, for the noncircularity of inductive support of an inductive rule. See my controversy about this with Peter Achinstein in *Analysis,* 22 (1961–62), 138–141; 23 (1962–63), 43–44 and 123–127; also Henry Kyburg's comment on the dispute in *American Philosophical Quarterly,* 1 (1964), 260–261.

is using is sound. But, on the type of view here being outlined, that is not the same thing as holding that the argument "works" in the sense of being right "on the whole"—
indeed we have had serious reasons to doubt whether *that*
view can be defended. The most that can be said is that the
type of inductive activity called "eduction" is conducive to
the aims of the overall activity—and that is guaranteed, not
by any contingent empirical considerations, but by an a
priori connection between that particular activity and the
entire practice. What we *mean* by the "inductive practice"
includes eduction; and what we mean by "more likely than
not" guarantees that the conclusion of an eduction will be
more likely to be true than the contrary conclusion. The
critic who raises the objection of circularity is really objecting to the use of inductive language and the concepts expressed by such language. He is objecting to the use of typically inductive concepts in advance of a demonstration that
will justify such use. He is, it might be added, in a radically
incoherent position. In using, as all of us do, language that
purports to refer to persisting physical objects, he is himself
committed to inductive beliefs at least as sweeping as those
he wishes us to forego. But an argument *ad hominem* will accomplish little at this juncture.

We may grant that, without the use of inductive concepts,
no inductive defense of the inductive institution can get off
the ground. It is worth pointing out that in this respect the
defense of induction is in no worse case than the defense of
deduction. For after all what is to be said by way of justifying deduction? Is it not, essentially, that if the premises of a
valid deductive argument are true, and if the argument is
valid then, necessarily, the conclusion is true (with an implicit appeal to our interest in deriving new truths from old).
But how is *this* established? How else except by appeal to the
ways in which we do actually use the key terms—or, if preferred, by the use of deductive concepts of validity and the
like, which presuppose the correctness of certain deductive
inferences? If the alleged circularity obtains in the case of

induction, it must be held to obtain equally in the defense of deduction that we commonly advance without any qualms. If our trust in induction is held to be dogmatic, the same must be said for our confidence in deduction.

If objection to the use of inductive language and inductive concepts is indeed the burden of the skeptic's complaint, skepticism concerning induction is introduced by the very terms of the demand. Given that induction differs from deduction by its very definition, a deductive proof of its efficacy is impossible in principle. If the demand is also made that no *inductive* concepts be used in justification, then an inductive defense will also be ruled out *ab initio*. But then the allegedly skeptical conclusions will spring from the arbitrary blinkers imposed by the philosophical critic. Once it has been understood that the demand for "justification of induction" has been so constructed that it can be seen *a priori* to be impossible of fulfillment, the skeptical conclusions drawn from the impossibility of fulfilling an impossible task will seem somewhat less than compelling. If a Zen master imposes upon me the task of jumping without moving a limb, the impossibility of satisfying *him* will reveal only something about the taskmaster and could be regarded as a symptom of human incapacity only by a very muddled thinker. Now the same can be said, *mutatis mutandis,* about the alleged impossibility of solving the philosophical "problem of induction." If we seem unable to make the "inductive leap," that is because philosophers, excessively influenced by the deductive conception of inference, insist upon defining the task in a way that renders it logically impossible to jump. But if we ignore the arbitrary distortions implicit in this persuasive maneuver, we shall find that we can jump perfectly well. *Solvitur saltando.*

In order to forestall possible misapprehension, I would like to add that I am not proposing the inductive argument from the past successes of the inductive practice as a solution to the philosophical problem of the justification of induction. (This would be as misconceived, in my opinion, as trying to deal with somebody who thought he could see snakes everywhere by arguing that at least they don't bite.) The roots of the philosophical problem are to be found in the imposition of arbitrary and inappropriate standards of rationality. There is no way to cope with the "problem" that, in my opinion, offers any prospect of satisfying those to whom its solution seems necessary except by patiently exposing the underlying confusions until the alleged problem withers away. I have been trying to draw attention to a much less exciting point. I have thought it proper to ask, as we might of any human practice or institution, whether there is reason to think that it has fulfilled and will continue to fulfill the human purposes it is presumably intended to serve. My answer is the commonplace one that there is indeed good inductive evidence for thinking that our universe is of such a character that continued trust in the inductive practice is reasonable. That no stultifying circularity is involved in such a claim, and on such grounds, is a point of considerable importance —if only because so many wise men, steeped in the subject, still think otherwise. A fuller and more adequate defense against the charge of circularity would need more space than I here have at my disposal.

## 11 Retrospect

I have here been adopting a somewhat heterodox conception of inductive argument that takes it to be subject to distinctive rules of sound procedure not reducible to the canons of deductive argument. I have further assumed that at least *some* conclusions of good inductive arguments can be "detached" so that one can, in favorable instances, proceed from the assertion of true premises to the justified assertion of other propositions, sufficiently supported, though not entailed by, those premises. Throughout, I have chosen to think of induction as a public practice embodying distinctive rule-governed activities, each of which is instantiated in indefinitely many inductive performances, actual or possible. Conceiving, as seems reasonable, that the practice as a whole is

[177]

concerned with the rational acquisition of truth, it has seemed plausible to expect links between the "immediate purpose" or goal of the individual inductive performance and the more general purpose of the activity instantiated—and between the latter and the overall purpose of the supporting practice. Such links are, in a way, easily found. It is an *a priori* truth that inductive arguments of given forms are *more likely than not to* lead from true premises to true conclusions based upon those premises. Thus, the performances are weakly conducive to the general purpose of arriving at the truth. It is tempting to hope for a stronger connection than this—to establish that certain cognitive benefits *must* ensue from the use of inductive methods. Glimpses of such connections are indeed to be captured: We can see, for instance, that the "proportional syllogism" is *bound* to yield true answers from true premises in most of the cases of its application. And even in the more problematic instance of "simple eduction," I showed that some case can be made for an associated guarantee or "security" against an excessive number of predictive failures. But it had to be admitted that the outcome of such argument was extremely meager, which suggested, in turn, that a basic fallacy of method might be involved in seeking to detach particular inductive methods from the global practice to which they belong. I argued that the practice, considered as whole, could be shown, by a sound and noncircular inductive argument, to be as deserving of our rational confidence as in our unreflective moments we hold it to be. I also urged that such commonsensical reflections upon the utility and relevance of the inductive practice held little promise of being able to cope with the philosophical problems associated with induction. Having deeper roots, those stubborn perplexities demand a more fundamental therapy than the appeal to common sense.

[178]

# IX

# *Notes on the "Paradoxes*
# *of Confirmation"*

### 1 Formulation of the Paradoxes

THE LABEL "paradoxes of confirmation" was assigned by Professor C. G. Hempel, in his well-known paper ("Studies in the Logic of Confirmation," *Mind*, 54 [1945], 1–26, 91–21), to the following sheaf of arguments.

Consider the proposition, *All ravens are black* (which I shall call "the raven hypothesis"). Common sense is inclined to say the following three things about it:

(i) The hypothesis is, or would be, shown to be false by the existence of a single nonblack raven.

(ii) The existence of a black raven supports, or would support, the hypothesis—is, or would be, empirical evidence favoring its truth.

(iii) Not all objects bear upon the hypothesis, negatively or positively, in these ways: for instance, the existence of Halley's comet neither falsifies nor supports the raven hypothesis.

In short, the common sense position is that the existence of *some*, but not all, things is relevant to the raven hypothesis. This might be called the principle of limited relevance.

Hempel now offers the following arguments against this principle:

The raven hypothesis can be symbolically represented as

$$(x)(Rx \supset Bx), \tag{1}$$

and a positive instance of it will accordingly have the form

$$Ra \cdot Ba. \tag{2}$$

Now 1 is logically equivalent to its "contrapositive":

$$(x)(\sim Bx \supset \sim Rx), \tag{3}$$

a positive instance of which has the form

$$\sim Bb \cdot \sim Rb, \tag{4}$$

and is also logically equivalent to what I shall call its "comprehensive,"

$$(x)[(Rx \mathbf{v} \sim Rx) \supset (\sim Rx \mathbf{v} Bx)], \tag{5}$$

a positive instance of which has the form

$$(Rc \mathbf{v} \sim Rc) \cdot (\sim Rc \mathbf{v} Bc). \tag{6}$$

On the assumption that logically equivalent hypotheses are "confirmed" (Hempel's term, which I shall discuss later) by the same instances, we are led to the following conclusions:

(iv) Any nonblack nonraven confirms the raven hypothesis (cf. formula 4 above).

(v) Any nonraven also confirms the same hypothesis (because any object, $c$, for which $\sim Rc$ is the case, will satisfy formula 6 above).

(vi) Any black thing will also confirm the hypothesis (for $Bc$ will logically imply 6 above).

Thus it would seem that the raven hypothesis is, or would be, "confirmed," for instance, by the existence of a white handkerchief (cf. iv), by the existence of a stone (cf. v), and by the existence of a black pearl (cf. vi). These conclusions are certainly startling.

The foregoing arguments purport to show that any object, $o$, without exception, is relevant to the raven hypothesis, in the sense of either confirming it or falsifying it. For if $\sim Ro$ holds, the hypothesis will be confirmed (see v above); and if $Ro$ holds we must also have $Bo$ (which provides a confirming instance) or else $\sim Bo$ (which provides a falsifying instance). This result flatly contradicts the principle of limited relevance" (cf. iii above). Hence a suitably descriptive label for

Hempel's argument might be "the paradox of universal relevance."

## 2 The Intended Context

It is important to remember that Hempel was trying to construct a formal and "purely syntactical" concept of confirmation.[1] If such a project could be successfully executed, the "confirmation" conferred upon formula 1 above by formulas 2 or 4 or 6 could be considered in abstraction from any meanings that might be attached to "*R*" or to "*B*" and hence without reference to any "background knowledge" which we might normally regard as relevant. Now it is argued that common sense's reluctance to accept *some* of the paradoxical instances produced in the last section can be explained by our possession of relevant "background knowledge": if we think the existence of a stone does nothing to strengthen the empirical evidence supporting the raven hypothesis, that is because we *already* know that no stones are ravens and are therefore receiving no additional information that is relevant.[2]

---

[1] See, for instance, Hempel's explicit statement: ". . . it seems reasonable to require that the criteria of empirical confirmation, besides being objective in character, should contain no reference to the specific subject-matter of the hypothesis or of the evidence in question; it ought to be possible, one feels, to set up purely formal criteria of confirmation in a manner similar to that in which deductive logic provides purely formal criteria for the validity of deductive inferences" *ibid.,* p. 9). This is a program for a unified and comprehensive *inductive logic.* The "paradoxes" are philosophically interesting to the extent to which they highlight some of the implications of such a program.

[2] Cf. Hempel's discussion of an attempt to "support" the assertion *All sodium salts burn yellow* by burning a piece of ice: ". . . we happen to 'know anyhow' that ice contains no sodium salt; this has the consequence that the outcome of the flame-colour test becomes entirely irrelevant for the confirmation of the hypothesis and thus can yield no new evidence for us" (*ibid.,* p. 19). So far as I can see, this kind of defense could be used only in connection with "contrapositive instances"

It is extremely difficult, however, to suppress, ignore or "bracket" the knowledge we in fact have about ravens, colored things—and, more generally, about birds, other physical objects, and other relevant broad-scale features of the universe.[3] One might, however, deliberately construct an artificial context in which covert appeal to "background knowledge" would be impossible.

Suppose somebody invites me to consider a proposition, $H$, say, of the form, *All A are B*, where "*A*" and "*B*" stand for definite characters, known to my interlocutor, but deliberately concealed from me. Let it be further supposed that my interrogator now tells me that, to his knowledge, a certain object, not further described or identified, is in fact both $A$ and $B$: I am asked to say whether, in my opinion, the likelihood of $H$ being true has been increased by this information.

The correct answer seems to me that I am in no position to have any rational opinion about the matter. For one thing, my enforced ignorance concerning the identity of the hypothesis in question prevents me from any reasonable opinion concerning the *initial* likelihood of $H$. (To have any opinion about this would be as absurd as to have an opinion

_____

(cf. 4 above) and would leave the still more puzzling cases of "comprehensive instances" (stones, lumps of coal) to be explained. However, all three types of instances are made to seem relevant by Hempel's original argument, and in the end the relevance of all three types of cases must be explained or explained away.

[3] I am strongly inclined to think that nobody who lacked such knowledge could qualify as *understanding* the raven hypothesis or as knowing the language in which it is expressed. Could somebody who had never seen or heard of animals understand our intention in saying "All ravens are black"? And would not an effort to teach him the intended meaning naturally begin with a recital of certain *facts*, familiar to us, but surprising to him—"There are creatures, like us in certain respects, but unlike in others, who do such and such, etc. etc."? If we did not need to understand the raven hypothesis in order to assess its confirmation by given empirical facts (as an advocate of a formal concept of confirmation expects), what I have just said would be irrelevant. But I shall be arguing that reference to meaning is necessary if apparently "paradoxical" consequences are to be generated.

about the height of some object, known to the questioner, but completely unknown to me.) Given this condition of almost total nescience on my part, it would seem absurd for me to say that I now have *more* empirical support for $H$ than I had a moment ago. Of course, the report of a confirming instance does tend, in general, to favor a hypothesis, but it may be a long step from "tends to favor" to "positively supports." [4] I am inclined to say that if the presupposition of total ignorance of relevant background were taken seriously, a question concerning the empirical support for a given hypothesis could not yet arise. "Empirical support" may well be a *threshold concept* whose application requires appeal to some background knowledge and hence one that fails to apply if such background knowledge is lacking.

### 3 Some Pecularities of the Stock Example

I have been following the practice of previous writers in using Hempel's illustration—for it is intended to be no more than that—of the "raven hypothesis." Attention to some specific illustration is indeed essential, if what some philosophers like to call our "preanalytical intuitions" are to be consulted and, if necessary, rectified. For common sense speaks with an uncertain voice at best about abstract relations of "confirmation" between propositions about unidentified $A$'s and $B$'s (as I have just been arguing) However, the stock example may be held to have been an unfortunate choice, considering certain of its features which I shall now enumerate. (These oddities might plausibly be held respon-

---

[4] The following analogy may help: Suppose I am told about some chess game, not otherwise identified, that White has just captured a pawn: should I conclude that White has a better chance of winning than he had before making that move? Well, other things being equal, capturing a pawn tends to help a chessplayer to win. But then so much depends upon the state of the game! Finding empirical support for a hypothesis may well resemble playing well at chess, rather than conducting a valid argument. (We can sometimes *prove* that a move is bad, but whether a move is *good* is usually debatable.)

sible for at least some of the air of "paradox" that clings to Hempel's conclusions.)

There is a noticeable artificiality about the contrapositive, *All nonblack things are nonravens,* and a still greater artificiality about what I have called the "comprehensive," *Everything that is either a raven or a nonraven is either not a raven or black or both.* If it is hard to imagine anybody seriously undertaking to put the contrapositive to empirical test, one reason may be that *nonblack* is a nonindividuating predicate, that omits any specification of the logical type of the things to which it is intended to apply. (Is a rainbow to count as a nonblack thing? And what about an electron—or even a prime number?) Here may be one source of our resistance to the claim that any nonblack thing, without exception, "confirms" the raven hypothesis.[5]

If we replace the original example by one in which predicate and subject are both individuating terms, we may get such a proposition as *All vertebrate animals are warm-blooded animals,* which might be symbolized as

$$(x)(Ax \cdot Vx \supset Ax \cdot Wx). \tag{7}$$

The corresponding "restricted contrapositive," as it might be called, would be *All cold-blooded animals are invertebrate animals,* symbolized as

$$(x)(Ax \cdot \sim Wx \supset Ax \cdot \sim Vx). \tag{8}$$

---

[5] Consider instead the statement, *Anything whatever is either a nonraven or black or both (k,* say). If my own "intuitions" can be trusted, no corresponding resistance is evoked: it seems reasonable enough to say that *k* is "confirmed" by a rainbow, by an electron, by the number 5—or, more generally, by anything that is not black. The soundness of Hempel's conclusions accordingly turns on whether the raven hypothesis can properly be regarded as identical with, or at least logically equivalent to, the statement *k*. If the answer is Yes, Hempel is quite right.

Here it is by no means implausible, or shocking to common sense, that the existence of a cold-blooded invertebrate should support the hypothesis. We might therefore conjecture that one source of the "paradoxes" is the choice, as a paradigm, of a proposition of the form 1 rather than one of the form 8. Let us call objects that are $A$'s (i.e., animals, in our example) members of the *range* of the hypothesis: we would still have to explain why members inside the range seem eligible, while objects outside the range do not, to be treated as relevant instances of the hypothesis. For it is easy to transform 7 or 8 into a "comprehensive" form like 5.[6] And when this has been done, the old perplexities about apparently paradoxical instances (about unlimited relevance) will reappear.

UNCERTAINTY ABOUT THE MEANING
OF THE RAVEN HYPOTHESIS

It is natural to understand the assertion that all ravens are black as intending to attribute to all ravens some typical *species-identifying* character (like some identifying shape of beak). But if so, the hypothesis would express a "lawlike" association of attributes, applicable to possible as well as to actual specimens of the class of animals in question. And then any serious investigation of the truth of the hypothesis, thus construed, would be far more complicated than the symbolic formulas so far used would suggest. (If falsification of the hypothesis required only the existence of some nonblack nonraven, why not "falsify" the hypothesis by painting some raven pink all over?)

It seems clear, however, that neither Hempel nor other writers on this topic have understood the raven hypothesis in this natural way. It is not unfair to them, I think, to say that they conceive of the blackness of any given object as determinable by immediate inspection. What is more important, however, is their conception of the hypothesis in question as an indefinite *accidental* association of attributes—as the use

---

[6] Thus 7 is logically equivalent to $(x)[(Ax \lor \sim Av) \supset ((\sim Ax \lor \sim Vx) \lor (Ax \cdot Wx))]$.

of the sign for *material* implication in such formulas as 1 above shows.[7] Now, if the allegedly universal blackness of ravens is conceived as a tremendous cosmic accident, with each raven merely happening to be black (if it is black), as a die might happen to throw a six, independently of what happens to any other raven, we are dealing with a proposition so unlikely, on general principles, to be true that it is hard to take the notion of "confirming" it seriously. This brings me to a final source of dissatisfaction with the stock example.

### UNCERTAINTY ABOUT THE TRUTH-VALUE OF THE HYPOTHESIS

One is inclined to think that the truth of the raven hypothesis is a commonplace—to assume that "everybody knows" that ravens are black, just as everybody is supposed to know that robins are red. (*This* "background knowledge," if we genuinely possess it, will interfere massively with our efforts to scrutinize the allegedly abstract logical relationship of "confirmation.") But the hypothesis is a commonplace—if indeed it really is true—only when construed in the "lawlike" way. Taken however, as intended, as an enormously, perhaps infinitely, extended conjunction of independent singular accidental assertions, it seems almost certainly false. (If there is any nonzero probability against the "accidental" coincidence of two attributes in a given instance, the chance of these attributes coinciding indefinitely often becomes in the long run vanishingly small—the blackness of *all* ravens would eventually become as unlikely as an uninterrupted run of sixes from a fair die.)

It is worth noticing that, on the view of "confirmation" advocated by Hempel (and also, with some variations, by Carnap) the increment in the degree of "confirmation" contributed to the raven hypothesis by even a straightforward positive instance of a black raven is zero. For in this type

[7] Formal logic, for all its sophistication, is still notoriously embarrassed by the task of distinguishing a "lawlike" from an "accidental" generalization.

of confirmation theory, every generalization has an *a priori* probability of zero, that cannot be raised by any finite number of positive instances.[8] Now, if this were correct, it would be hard to evoke the "intuitions" to which we are supposed to appeal. If the raven hypothesis remains infinitely unlikely to be true after any amount of empirical evidence has been found, it is perhaps not so paradoxical after all that a white shoe might make the same negligible contribution as anything else.[9]

## CONCLUSION

I have been objecting—pedantically, as some will think [10]—to my predecessors' preoccupation with the stock illustration of the ravens because it does not lend itself to contraposition and other relevant logical transformations, because its intended meaning is unclear (with a dangerous oscillation between a "lawlike" and an "accidental" interpretation), and because its presumed truth-value is uncertain (so that we don't know whether to treat it as a tiresome commonplace or a wildly implausible prediction).

Can we find another simple example, free of these blemishes? Perhaps the following might serve: *All American taxpayers turned on the radio at least once in the course of 1965.*[11] Considering, in connection with *this* hypothesis the

[8] This is plausible enough if a generalization is viewed as an extended logical product of indefinitely many singular statements about the independently existing individuals in the universe. Roughly speaking, the "width" of the singular confirming proposition is always negligibly small when compared with the "logical width" of the generalization under test.

[9] Yet one is *still* inclined to think the white shoe irrelevant in a way in which the black raven is not! This is what still needs to be explained —or explained away.

[10] But if empirical support is not a wholly formal notion—contrary to the hopes of the architects of inductive logic—such pedantry is quite in order. If the appropriate methods for an empirical test of a given hypothesis depend on the meaning of that hypothesis, clarification of such meaning is essential if paralogism is to be avoided.

[11] In order to stay as close to Hempel's program as possible, I have

three types of *prima facie* "paradoxical" instances produced
by Hempel, we can perhaps say the following: *restricted* "contrapositive instances" (Americans who did not use a radio
in 1965 and paid no taxes) still seem somewhat odd [12]—
though perhaps less so than in the case of the raven hypothesis; on the other hand, the remaining types (e.g., non-
Americans, also those who use their radios, whether Americans or not) still seem—with whatever justice—to be plainly
irrelevant. I therefore conclude that the puzzle will not be
resolved by introducing better illustrations: its roots must be
deeper.

### 4 The Technical Sense of "Confirmation" and the Common Notion of "Empirical Evidence"

"Confirmation" is, of course, a term of art,[13] however
firmly established in the writings of English-speaking philosophers of science. It is plainly intended to be a technical
surrogate for the common notion that I have been referring
to as *"constituting empirical support"*—or, at least, some
component of that notion.[14] Now, that common notion is

---

deliberately chosen a hypothesis in which there can be no serious suggestion of a "lawlike" connection—one could hardly suppose that
being an American taxpayer is a *reason* for listening to the radio. It
seems to me an open question whether the taxpayer hypothesis is true:
a statistical test, by sampling American taxpayers, would therefore have
some point—if anybody were interested in the answer.

[12] Some reasons for this lingering oddity will be suggested later.

[13] It is good English to speak of "confirming a rumor" or "confirming
a statement"—approximately in the sense of citing an independent
statement by a trustworthy source—but in nontechnical contexts "confirming an hypothesis" would sound so odd as to be barely intelligible.

[14] In the 1945 article, Hempel uses a number of ordinary, nontechnical expressions, intended to indicate, at least roughly, the "preanalytical" concept he hopes to "reconstruct." He speaks of the raven
hypothesis as "being tested by confrontation with experimental findings" (p. 1), of its receiving "favourable evidence" (p. 2), of data being
"in accord with" the hypothesis (*ibid.*), and so on. He also speaks of
"relevant evidence" (p. 3) and asks how a fact could "affect . . . [the]

closely connected with the notion of what might be called a *deliberate investigation* of a given hypothesis. Anybody who becomes seriously interested in determining the truth-value of some hypothesis, $H$, will normally initiate a search for relevant empirical data that may reasonably be expected to establish $H$, to refute it—or, failing either of these results, to alter the initial plausibility of $H$. (I shall ignore, for the purpose in hand, any questions about the coherence of $H$ with provisionally accepted generalizations and theories.) A full-blooded, authentic, empirical inquiry of this sort (as, for instance, in contemporary investigations of the suspected causal links between cigarette-smoking and cancer) has the following characteristic features:

(i) It is conducted against a background of at least provisionally accepted relevant information, notably including a large number of generalizations: the empirical investigator never begins with a clean slate.[15]

(ii) The investigation is typically selective or comparative: the merits of $H$ are weighed, in the light of acquired empirical findings, against those of a finite number of rival hypotheses, $H'$, $H''$, . . . .[16]

(iii) The inquiry may be viewed as a finite series of *investigation-episodes,* each of which is conducted according to a predetermined plan of operations and prearranged understandings (rules of valuation) as to how and to what degree the possible outcomes of the episode are to count in $H$'s favor. An empirical investigation, as here conceived, is not a fishing expedition conducted at random, but an orderly ser-

---

probability of a given hypothesis" (p. 9). It is doubtful whether these various expressions that Hempel treats as synonyms really do have the same meanings and the same presuppositions: for instance, some writers would refuse to assign probability to hypotheses or other general statements, while readily admitting that hypotheses can be empirically *tested.*

15 Try to imagine Sherlock Holmes operating with no experience of human nature, no preconceptions about criminal behavior, and so on!

16 In current statistical procedure, a choice is usually made between *two* hypotheses, antecedently designated. (The choice of the hypotheses partially determines the character of the subsequent inquiry.)

ies of consecutive operations, performed according to a well-defined *modus operandi* that may not be changed, without good reason, during the course of the investigation in question.

When a hypothesis, *H*, has successfully withstood a rigorous examination of this kind it may be said to have been *empirically supported*, in a strong sense of that expression. Alternatively it may be said to have acquired (a certain amout of) *empirical evidence*. The notion of empirical support, as I have depicted it, is of course thoroughly "pragmatic": whether a given hypothesis has been supported (and in what degree) depends upon historical facts concerning the identity and competence of the investigators in question and the soundness of the procedures employed by them, as well as upon the character of the facts uncovered. It is particularly important to stress that the amount of support that acquired data yield normally depends strongly upon the method employed in finding those data: [17] If I merely hear by accident of a hundred black ravens in Jerusalem, that cannot appreciably strengthen my belief in the raven hypothesis; the case would be different if the batch had been selected from scattered regions in accordance with a rigorous sampling technique.

My sketch of the main features of the empirical investigation of hypotheses is somewhat idealized: important scientific discoveries have been made by accident and we often do, in practice, admit, as empirical evidence, data stumbled upon in the absence of prior commitment to a rigorous searching procedure. (We can sometimes accommodate such uncovenanted findings retroactively, by treating them *as if* we had set out to find them—we might then, perhaps, speak of *"virtual* empirical support.") There are, therefore, weaker senses of "empirically supports" and "constitutes empirical evidence for"

[17] This point was repeatedly and emphatically made by Peirce. In this respect, he saw further than his commentators who have, for instance, tended to pooh-pooh Peirce's insistence upon the importance of "predesignation."

which do not imply the deliberate contrivance, adherence to explicit rules of procedure, and so on, that are characteristic of what I have above called the "stronger" senses of these expressions.

Yet something of the stronger senses still clings to the weaker senses: if we count the fact $F$, however it came to our knowledge, as *supporting H*, that is normally so—in view of the nature of empirical support here advocated—because we can, after the event, concoct a defensible and appropriate procedure by which $F$ *might* have been discovered in such a way as to have rendered $H$ more credible than its designated rivals. When this is *not* the case, there will be something distinctly misleading about using such expressions as "empirical support" or "empirical evidence."

Let us see how these ideas apply to Hempel's discussion. He says that the existence of a black raven "confirms" the raven hypothesis. If one agrees, that is—I suggest—because we substitute "empirically support" for "confirms" and naturally think (retroactively!) of the admissible procedure of selecting a raven *at random* in order to determine whether or not it is black. But even this example suffices to highlight the gap between Hempel's designedly formal concept of "confirmation" and the *pragmatic* concept of empirical support outlined above. For it is one procedure to select a raven at random in order to determine whether it is black, and a different procedure to select a black thing at random (assuming that makes sense, which seems very questionable) in order to see whether it is a raven. In general, a hypothesis, *All A are B*, will receive different amounts of empirical support from *A random A has been found to be B* and from *A random B has been found to be A*, respectively, while the hypothesis of course receives the same "confirmation" from $Aa \cdot Bb$ as from $Bb \cdot Aa$.[18]

18 Cf. G. H. von Wright's discussion of the paradoxes in *The Logical Problem of Induction* (New York: Macmillan, 1957), pp. 125–127, in which he relies upon the difference made by the order in which an investigator comes to observe an $A$ or a $B$.

[191]

The gap between the two concepts becomes still more glaring when we consider the paradoxical but allegedly confirming instance of a nonraven. What would be the corresponding *modus operandi* of an "investigation episode" to inquire into the raven hypothesis? Could it be: to look at *anything one pleases,* with the prior understanding that if it turns out to be not a raven that will count as *supporting* the hypothesis? Apart from the intrinsic absurdity of such a rule of operation, there is a conclusive objection to it, viz., that the outcome would not discriminate between the raven hypothesis and its contradictory, *No ravens are black.*[19] Hence, finding a nonraven would not count as a *test* of the hypothesis,[20] would not count as empirical *support* for it.

To sum up, there seems to be an appreciable and important gap between the formal and artificially constructed concept of confirmation and certain familiar if somewhat ill-defined concepts in common use ("empirical support," "empirical evidence") of which it is intended to be a technical "reconstruction." Whatever empirically supports a hypothesis must at least be in logical agreement with it—but the converse is untrue. Now one explanation for the "paradoxes" may well be that we naturally think of them in terms of the pragmatic concept, rather than in terms of the technical concept of "confirmation." Of course, Hempel might retort that he can hardly be held responsible for any such confusion between the two concepts: let us remember what *he* means by "confirmation" and all risk of confusion will be obviated.[21]

---

[19] On the customary symbolization, $(x)$ $(Rx \supset Bx)$ is compatible with $(x)$ $(Rx \supset \sim Bx)$. But cf. the discussion below of "ordinary" uses of conditionals.

[20] This point has been well made by Nelson Goodman and, following him, by I. Scheffler, *The Anatomy of Inquiry* (New York: Alfred A. Knopf, 1963).

[21] One may recall the disputes between Spearman and those psychologists who rejected his definition of "intelligence" as inadequate. Spearman and his defenders used to say that by *"g"* they meant *"g"* (as technically defined, e.g., in connection with factor analysis). If anybody wanted to identify *"g"* with "intelligence" that was his affair!

But the issue is neither so simple, nor so clear-cut. The whole interest of Hempel's studies in confirmation (and of similar essays by those who hope to develop a formal inductive logic) depends upon the "adequacy" of his technical surrogate for the common notions of support and empirical evidence. Any striking disparity between the two notions is a *prima facie* ground for distrusting the "logical reconstruction" offered. (This, as I have already said, is what makes the "paradoxes of confirmation" philosophically significant—something more than substitutes for the daily crossword puzzle.)

## 5 Possible Ways Out

It may be useful at this point to survey the various strategies that have been used—or that might plausibly be used—for dealing with the paradoxes.

We might (a) reject Hempel's original argument as unsound in some identified respect; or, we might (b) accept the soundness of his argument. If the latter course seems right, we shall need to explain why the argument's conclusions should seem "paradoxical." In so doing, we might rely $(b_1)$ upon the temptation to invoke "background knowledge"; or $(b_2)$ upon disparities between the technical notion of "material implication," as used in the paradox-generating arguments, with "ordinary" uses of "if-then"; or $(b_3)$ upon confusion between low (or negligible) confirmation and irrelevance; or, finally, $(b_4)$ upon some other significant differences between "confirmation" and other notions with which it might easily be confused. (The last four are obviously compatible strategies.) I shall now make brief comments upon these possible solutions, reserving $(b_2)$ and $(b_3)$ for more extended treatment later.

### REJECTING THE PARADOX-ENGENDERING ARGUMENT

Given the relative simplicity and perspicuity of Hempel's original exposition, there seem to be only three ways in which this might plausibly be done.

($a_1$) We might try to reject the assumption that logically equivalent propositions receive exactly the same confirmation from given data. This is a decidedly uninviting stratagem. If "logically equivalent propositions" are understood to be such as are, of logical necessity, rendered true or false by precisely the same states-of-affairs, the conclusion seems inescapable that they cannot be confirmed in different degrees by the same evidence. (This verdict remains correct if we substitute "empirical support" for "confirmation.")

($a_2$) We might try to reject the remaining assumption that an instance of a simple generalization always confirms it.[22] This is somewhat more plausible (given what we know, at the back of our minds, about the lurking notion of "empirical support"). However, I find it hard to see any reasonable way in which this assumption could be denied, once a *formal* definition of confirmation had been adopted.

($a_3$) We might try to question the alleged logical equivalence between the original raven hypothesis and its "contrapositive" (formula 3 above) or between it and its "comprehensive" (formula 5 above). There can be no question, however, that the three propositions, *as expressed,* are indeed logically equivalent. (Any lingering doubts about the equivalence of these expressions—or, rather, the ordinary-language expressions corresponding to them—might better be dismissed under one of the subheadings that immediately follow.)

On the whole, then, it seems to me that Hempel's argument, *taken as intended,* must be regarded as perfectly sound. There is no prospect of finding an internal flaw in it: if we are startled by its conclusions, the fault must lie in some stubborn confusion or prejudice.

### ACCEPTING THE PARADOX-ENGENDERING ARGUMENT

Hempel has made a strong case for the view that the common sense principle of limited relevance, which I mentioned earlier, arises only from a "misleading intuition": he claims

[22] That is to say, that a truth of the form $Aa \cdot Ba$ always confirms the corresponding hypothesis $(x) (Ax \supset Bx)$.

that "the impression of a paradoxical situation is not objectively sound; it is a psychological illusion" (Hempel, *op. cit.*, p. 18). We tend, he suggests, to confuse "practical" with "logical" considerations: for the very form of the raven hypothesis reveals a practical interest in the application of the hypothesis to ravens—and a relative lack of interest in its bearing upon nonravens, nonblack things, etc.[23] Yet, in this case, as in others like it, ". . . the hypothesis nevertheless asserts something about, and indeed imposes restrictions upon, *all* objects (within the logical type of the variable occurring in the hypothesis . . .)" (Hempel, *op. cit.*). The raven hypothesis, we need to see, is indeed an assertion about [24] every physical object in the world, claiming of each such thing that it is either a nonraven or a black thing; and, for similar reasons, any generalization whatever is about each and every thing of the appropriate logical type in the universe. Once we grasp this point, it should no longer appear startling or paradoxical that every physical object, without exception, bears one way or the other upon the truth of the raven hypothesis.

On the whole, Hempel's analysis impresses me as attractively straightforward and persuasive, by contrast with some of the more elaborate explanations of the "psychological illusion" that some subsequent writers have proposed.

If further explanation seems needed in order to account for our proneness to overlook the simple logical point that Hempel mainly relies upon (the logical equivalence of formulas 1, 3, and 5, above), we have a choice between a number of plausible options (see $b_1$–$b_4$ above). Since enough has already been said about the possible influence of "background

---

[23] Is it always true—or even generally true—that the subject of an assertion "interests" us more than the predicate, and that what is explicitly mentioned interests us more than what is implicit? How would "interest," in the relevant sense, be defined or detected?

[24] There is surely a covert extension here of the common notion of *about?* Even philosophers don't talk "about" everything whenever they utter generalizations.

[195]

knowledge" (i.e., $b_1$), I shall proceed at once to discuss the possible influence of the logical gap between material implication and ordinary uses of "if-then" (option $b_2$).

## 6 Some Relevant Peculiarities of Material Implications

### ORDINARY USES OF SINGULAR CONDITIONALS

I wish to recall some familiar features of ordinary uses of sentences of the form *If A then C*, or of similar sentences obtainable from such sentences by changes of mood. The "logic" of such ordinary singular conditionals is closely related to the "logic" of general statements of the form *All A are B* and may be expected to throw some useful light on the latter.

We shall find it convenient to distinguish between *indicative* singular conditionals, such as "If the temperature falls, we shall have snow," *subjunctive* singular conditionals, such as "If you were to touch that plate you would get burned," and *counterfactual* singular conditionals, such as "If I had betted on Excelsior, I would have won." I can think of no other types that are relevant to the present discussion.

It has often been observed that when a speaker asserts an indicative singular conditional, he normally implies some *connection* between the antecedent and the consequent. Suppose I say, "if you interrupt Robinson now he will be angry." If you do proceed to interrupt Robinson and he does become angry, that will not necessarily show that my original assertion was true: for if Robinson became angry because somebody entered the room at the moment you interrupted him, we should have to say that the truth of my original assertion remained unsettled. Thus the force of my original remark was approximately the same as that of "If you interrupt Robinson he will become angry *because you interrupt him.*" In this more explicit form, the word "because" expresses the intended presence of some reason (often, though not always of a causal sort) why the antecedent and consequent should have the same truth-value.

The character of the imputed connection between antecedent and consequent varies from case to case: antecedent and consequent may be intended to be both true in virtue of some common cause, or the implied link may be supplied by somebody's promise, decision, and so on. The general formula seems to be that the truth of the antecedent $A$ is such as to provide a *reason,* of some sort, for the truth of $B$. (Hence, somebody who in ordinary life says "If $A$ then $B$" can always properly be asked, in the kind of case I here have in mind, *why* the truth of $A$ should make $B$ also true.) When a singular sentence is used in this familiar way, I shall speak of the statement as a *connected* singular conditional.

For the reasons I have explained, a connected singular conditional statement is a stronger statement than the corresponding material conditional, symbolized as "$A \supset B$."

Although if-then sentences are normally used in the way I have described, there are I believe, special and exceptional occasions when a speaker wishes to be understood as making only the weaker statement. When I say "If that penny comes down heads when tossed now, so will that other penny," I cannot mean that the truth of the antecedent will constitute a *reason* for the truth of the consequent: my intended meaning is simply that if $A$ is made true, $B$ will as a matter of fact, and not for any specifiable reason, also be true—just that and nothing more. In such a case one might speak of an unconnected or, perhaps an *accidental* singular *conditional*. Of course, a connected singular conditional logically implies the corresponding accidental singular conditional—but not *vice versa*.

I do not wish to argue here that "if-then" has different meanings or senses in the types of cases I have called "unconnected" and "accidental." If I had to choose, I would say that the same meaning was involved each time.

TRUTH-CONDITIONS AND DIRECT VERIFICATION
OF ACCIDENTAL CONDITIONALS

It is obvious that an accidental singular conditional is directly verified by $A \cdot B$ and is directly falsified by $A \cdot \sim B$. If you toss both pennies and both show heads, my original assertion was true (since I made no further claim about there being any connection between the two states of affairs); if you toss them and the first shows heads, but the second tails, my original assertion was false. But suppose you throw the first penny into the fire as soon as I have made the prediction, so that the antecedent $A$ remains unfulfilled. Then it seems that the truth-value of the conditional remains *open*; and the original assertion has received and can henceforward receive no *direct* test. (If this is correct, there is a sharp contrast with the truth conditions for a material implication of the form $A \supset B$.) We need not abrogate the law of excluded middle in such a case: even if you refuse to make the test, I can still sensibly maintain, "What I said was true—if you had tossed both pennies, the second would have come down heads if the first did." But in the absence of direct test, any further argument about the conditional's truth-value will have to rest upon indirect evidence. (If I had some hidden device that would allow me to produce heads at will, I might have a good reason for reaffirming the truth of the original accidental conditional, in the absence of direct verification.)

Let us now compare these results with the corresponding results for the contrapositive, *If not-B then not-A*. It is seen at once that while this proposition is directly verified by $\sim B \cdot \sim A$ and directly falsified by $\sim B \cdot A$, it has no direct verification or falsification if $B$ is true. Thus we see that whereas the original proposition and its contrapositive are both falsified by the same complex state of affairs, $A \cdot \sim B$, $A \cdot B$, which directly verifies the original proposition, leaves its contrapositive's truth-value open, while $\sim B \cdot \sim A$, which directly verifies the contrapositive, leaves the truth-value of

[198]

the original proposition open. In the case of $\sim A \cdot B$, neither of the two propositions receives direct verification. If we write $P$ for the original proposition and $Q$ for its contrapositive, we shall obtain the following summary:

$P$ is verified by $A \cdot B$, falsified by $A \cdot \sim B$, left open by $\sim A \cdot B$ and by $\sim A \cdot \sim B$.

$Q$ is verified by $\sim A \cdot \sim B$, falsified by $A \cdot \sim B$, left open by $\sim A \cdot B$ and by $A \cdot B$.

Thus $P$ and $Q$ have different *ranges of direct verification*: if two men betted on $P$ and $Q$ respectively, then if one lost so would the other, but one might win while the other neither lost nor won. It seems, therefore, that in ordinary uses an accidental singular conditional and its contrapositive are not logically equivalent. This point can be clinched by showing that situations can arise in which one of the two propositions is directly verified while the other is actually false.

Suppose $P$ is "If you now press the switch, the light will go on" and $Q$ is the corresponding contrapositive, "If the light does not now go on, you will not in fact have pressed the switch," where both are intended to be taken "accidentally." Then if you do not press the switch and the light does not go on (i.e., if $\sim A \cdot \sim B$ is the case) $Q$ will be directly verified. But this result is compatible with the falsity of $P$: we might know, for instance, that the lamp was broken and therefore be in a position to assert, in retrospect, "If you had pressed the switch, the light would not have gone on," and hence to derive the falsity of $P$. Such results as these are so unlike the corresponding results for material conditionals, that conclusions based, as in Hempel's arguments, upon theorems of the standard propositional calculus must be interpreted with great caution.

Before leaving this topic, we may notice the following simple way of representing "accidental singular conditionals" in terms of the familiar symbolism of the propositional calculus. Using the technique of Carnap's "reduction sentences" we may write the following formulas:

$$A \supset (P \equiv B)$$
$$\sim B \supset (Q \equiv \sim A)$$

which highlight the indeterminacy of direct verification previously noticed. These expressions can, in turn, be "solved" for $P$ and $Q$, respectively yielding:

$$P \equiv A \cdot B \mathbf{v} \sim A \cdot X$$
$$Q \equiv \sim A \cdot \sim B \mathbf{v} B \cdot Y$$

where $X$ and $Y$ are to be taken as indeterminate parameters —propositions of unspecified truth-values.[25] As I have already suggested, values of $X$ or $Y$, respectively, can sometimes be supplied by indirect reasoning from similar cases or, what comes almost to the same thing, by indirect reasoning from relevant generalizations.

THE VERIFICATION OF RESTRICTED
ACCIDENTAL GENERALIZATIONS

Let us now apply the results already obtained to the verification of the general statement *All the white balls in this urn are solid* ($P'$, say). I have chosen a statement that, to common sense at least, seems to be about a finite, although unknown, number of objects, viz., the white balls contained in the urn in question. The corresponding "restricted" contrapositive may be taken to be *All the nonsolid balls in this urn are nonwhite* ($Q'$, say).

Our generalization, $P'$, may reasonably be construed as a finite conjunction of an indefinite number of accidental singular conditionals: it says of each ball in the urn that if it is white, then, as a matter of fact (and not for any special "connection" or reason) that ball is also solid. The asymmetry between the conditions for direct test of an accidental singular

---

[25] It is easy to see that these parameters must be functions of $A$ and $B$. Suppose we have $P_1 \equiv A \cdot B \mathbf{v} \sim A \cdot X_1$ and $P_2 \equiv A \cdot \sim B_1 \mathbf{v} \sim A \cdot X_2$. We want $P_1$ and $P_2$ to be contradictories, which will require $\sim A \supset \sim (X_1 \cdot X_2)$ to be the case. Thus the "parameters" cannot be chosen altogether freely, if the ordinary conventions for "if-then" are to be respected. I shall not pursue this topic here.

conditional and its contrapositive will obviously reappear in the present case. When $P'$ is directly tested by examining each ball in the urn separately, a given ball may be found to agree with $P'$ by being both white and solid $(W \cdot S)$ or it may disagree with it by being white and not solid $(W \cdot \sim S)$, whereupon the testing process will terminate; but if it should be nonwhite, the instance will be dismissed as irrelevant. If, however, the restricted contrapositive, $Q'$, is being directly tested, different judgments will be in point (except in the case of falsification).

Let $a$ be the class of white-and-solid balls in the urn; $b$ the class of white-and-nonsolid balls in the urn; $c$ the class of nonwhite-and-solid balls in the urn; and, finally $d$ the class of nonwhite-and-nonsolid balls in the urn. Then $P'$ is partially verified by each member of $a$, is falsified by each member of $b$, and is unaffected by each member of $c$ and by each member of $d$; while the restricted contrapositive, $Q'$, is unaffected by each member of $a$, is falsified by each member of $b$, is unaffected by each member of $c$ and is partially verified by each member of $d$. We have, once again, the pattern previously observed of different though overlapping verification conditions but identical falsification conditions.

There is, however, the following new point. In order to establish $P'$ directly, we must eventually examine each ball in the urn, in order to record it as partially verifying the hypothesis, or as irrelevant to it. If $P'$ is in fact true (and not void on account of the absence of any white balls) completion of the entire process of direct testing will also, thereby, supply all the data we need for direct verification of the contrapositive, $Q'$.

It is easily seen that if we have found by direct test that $P'$ is true, then $Q'$, if not vacuous (through the absence of non-solid balls in the urn) must likewise be true. We may therefore say, without doing any violence to our "intuitions," that any direct test of $P'$ will be an indirect test of $Q'$, and vice versa. This will sometimes make it plausible to examine cases of nonsolid balls, even if we are setting out to test the direct generalization, $P'$. For example, if we knew that we could locate three balls that were known to be the only non-solid ones in the urn, examination of each of them for their color would provide us with a rapid way of indirectly testing $P'$, without the lengthy and tedious routine of successively examining each ball in the urn. This might be regarded as a scrutiny of all the possible negative instances—those that might be of the form $\sim S \cdot W$. On the other hand, it would never be appropriate to consider cases that are $\sim W \cdot S$—whether we were testing $P'$ or $Q'$. If we knew that we could extract a certain subset of the balls, each known to be both nonwhite and solid $(\sim W \cdot S)$, we should at once discard them as being irrelevant to the testing of either $P'$ or $Q'$.

If we now apply these results to a modified form of Hempel's example, such as the hypothesis, *All ravens in the New York Zoo are black* $(R,$ say$)$, we shall want to say that each black raven in the Zoo directly confirms $R$, each nonblack raven in the Zoo falsifies it, each white or other nonblack object is irrelevant (so far as direct test goes), and each black thing in the Zoo either confirms it or is irrelevant, depending on whether or not it is a raven. Furthermore, each thing outside the New York Zoo must count as irrelevant.

But suppose Hempel, or someone who agrees with his approach, asks us to consider instead the original raven hypothesis, *All ravens are black?* If this is intended to be understood as an unrestricted accidental generalization, to the effect that each raven (past, present, and future) is in fact black, it is doubtful whether the notion of "direct verification" with its implication of successive scrutiny of every physical object, without exception, continues to make sense.[26] At any rate, the chance of such a tremendous cosmic "accident" occurring is so small, on general grounds, that there would

[26] In the case of the balls in the urn, discussed above, the examination of a single ball is one step forward in a procedure which I know, in advance, will terminate *at a known instant*. But to undertake to scrutinise "everything in the universe" would be to start something which could never be *known* to have been accomplished.

be something odd about saying that observation of a single black raven should count as "partial" verification.

Here, perhaps, "verification" assumes the negative sense of "absence of falsification" and with this understanding the sting is removed from the paradoxes. There is certainly nothing paradoxical about saying that both a white shoe and a black cat fail to falsify the raven hypothesis—although even here we might wish to make a distinction between an object, like the first, that might have falsified the hypothesis, and one like the second that could not have done so. Paradoxical suggestions would be conveyed by this manner of description only if we were led to suppose that an appropriate method of testing an unrestricted accidental generalization might reasonably consist of an unsystematic and exhaustive scrutiny of every object of the appropriate logical type in the entire universe.

### TRANSITION TO THE CASE OF CONNECTED CONDITIONALS

I have been arguing that an "accidental" singular conditional of the form *If A then B*, does not have the same direct truth-conditions as its contrapositive, *If not-B then not-A*, and may therefore be treated as a distinct proposition. I now wish to consider whether a similar point can be made with respect to "connected" singular conditionals.

Take, as an example, *If I press the switch the light will go on* (If *A* then *B*—or *P*) with the intended implication that fulfillment of the antecedent will be a *reason* for the fulfillment of the consequent. The possibilities for *direct* testing of this strong conditional are even more restricted than in the case of the corresponding weak, accidental, conditional. For even if I do press the switch and the light does go on ($A \cdot B$), that might still have been just a coincidence, and more evidence of an indirect sort (e.g., concerning the mechanism of the switch) will be needed before the assertion can be regarded as established. Similar remarks apply to the contrapositive, *If the light will not go on, then I will not have pressed the switch* (*Q*). So, with respect to both *P* and *Q* we

[203]

now have the situation that each of them is falsified by $A \cdot \sim B$ and neither is directly verified by any of the three remaining possibilities, $A \cdot B$, $\sim A \cdot B$, and $\sim A \cdot \sim B$. It looks as if the asymmetry of the truth-conditions upon which I previously relied has vanished.

Common sense, however, will still wish to make a distinction between the bearing upon $P$ of the case $A \cdot B$ and the bearing upon it of the cases $\sim A \cdot B$ or $\sim A \cdot \sim B$. Consider the first: If I press the switch, then for all I know the light may not go on, in which case $P$ would be false; if, therefore, the light does go on, I have, to be sure, obtained no conclusive evidence of $P$'s truth, but I have obtained *some* relevant information. A natural way to describe this would be to say that I have obtained some *partial* verification of $P$. (This would be all the more natural if we were to think of $P$ as a conjunction of an accidental conditional and an assertion about the imputed "reason" or "connection"; the observation of $A \cdot B$ then directly verifies the first conjunct, while leaving the second open.) On the other hand, if I do not press the switch, then there is no chance of my falsifying $P$, so nothing that subsequently happens, whether the light goes on or not, can give me any direct information. These cases, one is inclined to say, are *irrelevant*.

If we apply similar considerations to $Q$, we get the following patterns of truth conditions for the original assertion and its contrapositive:

$P$ is falsified by $A \cdot \sim B$, is partially verified by $A \cdot B$, and is unaffected by $\sim A \cdot B$ and by $\sim A \cdot \sim B$.

$Q$ is falsified by $A \cdot \sim B$, is partially verified by $\sim A \cdot \sim B$, and is unaffected by $\sim A \cdot B$ and by $A \cdot B$.

Thus we get a modified asymmetry, somewhat resembling what we found in the case of accidental conditionals, and can proceed as before.

We must notice, however, that the logical relations between "strong" conditionals such as $P$ and $Q$ differ from those of the corresponding "weak" conditionals. It is easy to see, indeed, that if P is true, Q must also be true; and if P is false, $Q$ cannot be true. Thus we must admit a relation of logical equivalence between the two propositions. It follows that any case that partially verifies $P$ by direct test $(A \cdot C)$ will also indirectly and partially verify its contrapositive $Q$. Our analysis must acordingly be modified as follows:

### TABLE OF TRUTH CONDITIONS

$A \cdot \sim B$ directly falsifies $P$, directly falsifies $Q$.

$\quad A \cdot B$ partially and directly verifies $P$; and hence partially and indirectly verifies $Q$.

$\sim A \cdot \sim B$ partially and directly verifies $Q$; and hence partially and indirectly verifies $P$.

$\quad \sim A \cdot B$ leaves $P$ unaffected; leaves $Q$ unaffected.

### CONCLUSIONS

I believe that a *prima facie* case has now been made for thinking that the discomfort produced by the paradoxical cases of confirmation is partly due to the logical gap between material implication and "ordinary" implication. However, it is hard to be sure of this in the absence of any thorough and comprehensive examination of the discrepancies between the two concepts.[27]

## 7 Bayesian Approaches

I have left for the last a type of "solution," involving considerations of "inverse probability," that has been astonishingly popular,[28] considering the notorious difficulties that

---

[27] A valuable contribution to this neglected task is a recent paper by E. W. Adams, "The Logic of Conditionals," *Inquiry*, 8 (1965), 166–197.

[28] See, for instance, J. Hosiasson–Lindenbaum, "On Confirmation," *Journal of Symbolic Logic*, 5 (1940), 138–148. This contains one of the best attempts to deal with the paradoxes in the way now to be explained. For critical comments, see Hempel *op. cit.*, p. 21, n. 2. A recent attempt of this sort is J. L. Mackie, "The Paradox of Confirmation," *British Journal for Philosophy of Science*, 13 (1963), 265–277, which contains references to other essays in the same vein.

have generally discredited the classical "Bayesian" approach to the confirmation of empirical generalizations.[29]

The argument fastens upon the circumstances that the number of ravens in the universe is very much smaller than the number of non-black things. This being admitted, an attempt is made to show that the "prior" or antecedent likelihood of finding a raven to be black is smaller than the likelihood of finding a nonblack thing to be a nonraven. Indeed, if the class of ravens is *much* smaller than the class of nonblack things, the first likelihood is *much* smaller than the second. (Call this last contention *Step one*.) It is now urged that, on the basis of *Step one*, the increase in degree of confirmation produced by finding a raven to be black is much greater than the increase produced by finding a nonblack thing to be a nonraven (call this last claim *Step two*). We now explain our initial reluctance to see that a white shoe, or any other nonblack nonraven, is an authentically confirming instance of the raven hypothesis, as arising from a confusion between *low confirmation* and *irrelevance*: intuitively grasping, as we are supposed to do, the negligible contribution to the confirmation of the hypothesis made by a "paradoxical" instance, we mistakenly suppose that it makes no contribution at all. Once this error has been detected, there is no further reason to reject such an instance as irrelevant, even though it makes a trifling contribution in practice to the support of the hypothesis that interests us.

I believe I can here dispense with a detailed examination of the ingenious arguments by which this approach has been supported, since the following considerations seem sufficient to show its inadequacy.

(i) The defense of what I have called *Step two* (the crucial

---

[29] There is a useful summary of such difficulties in Von Wright *op. cit.*, pp. 112–117. Von Wright says that ". . . such uses of inverse probability as those of determining the probability that the sun will rise to-morrow or that the next raven will be black are illegitimate" (p. 115). Anybody who agrees will reject the "Bayesian approach" to the paradoxes at the very outset.

link in the argument offered) is admittedly intricate and problematic.[30]

(ii) Hence, even if *Step two* is correct (which I doubt), common sense—if it does rely upon the supposedly different contributions made by the two sets of instances—must be using a fallacious argument.

(iii) No reason has been given to believe that "common sense" does in fact believe in *Step two*—indeed the empirical evidence (and this is an empirical question!) suggests that common sense simply holds the paradoxical cases to be irrelevant.

(iv) Consider the contrapositive, $H'$, of the raven hypothesis, i.e., *All nonblack things are nonravens* (or *Nothing that is not black is a raven*). On the solution proposed, "common sense" ought to treat direct instances of $H'$ (nonblack things that are nonravens) as irrelevant.[31] (For the subject

---

[30] One might be inclined to think it obvious that an instance antecedently less likely to arise supports the hypothesis ($H$, say) more strongly than does an instance that is antecedently more likely to arise. (Roughly speaking, the less surprising an observed consequence of a law under empirical test, the less support such an observation gives to the law.) But any careful attempt to calculate the relevant degrees of "confirmation" quickly reveals the implicit fallacy. Call the positive instance (a black raven) $a$ and the contrapositive instance (e.g., a white shoe) $b$. Let the probability of $a$ being observed if $H$ is true, $P(a|H)$, be $p_1$ and similarly, let $P(b|H) = q_1$; let $P(a|\sim H) = p_2$; and, finally $P(b|\sim H) = q_2$. Then, the observation of $a$ raises the antecedent odds in favor of $H$ in the ratio $p_1/p_2$; and the observation of $b$ raises those same odds in the ratio of $q_1/q_2$. Whether the positive instance, $a$, supports $H$ more strongly than the contrapositive instance, $b$, therefore depends on whether $p_1/p_2$ is greater than $q_1/q_2$. Clearly, more is involved than the sizes of the classes of ravens and nonblack things respectively. What is at stake may, with some simplification, be said to be whether a predominance of contrapositive instances over positive instances is more likely on the supposition that $H$ is true than upon the supposition that $H$ is false. It is hard to see how this question could possibly be answered. As Peirce said, universes are not as plentiful as blackberries; and hence speculation about the number of white shoes to be expected if not all ravens are black is bound to be idle.

[31] This point has been well made by Professor I. Scheffler, *op. cit.*

class of $H'$, the nonblack things, is supposed to have enormously more members than the complement of its predicate class.) This is as paradoxical as what is supposed to be explained.

On the whole, the Bayesian approach seems to me wrong in principle and ineffective in practice.

## 8 Postscript

Considering the amount of sophisticated discussion that the paradoxes have received, the lack of some generally acceptable solution is disappointing. The preceding remarks have no claim to serve as a satisfactory basis for such a solution. If they have any merit, it may be that of drawing attention to some subtleties that have been overlooked in the past. I have been concerned throughout to stress the gap between the syntactical notion of confirmation and the common notion of "empirical evidence" (see especially section 4). But the latter notion is still shrouded in unnecessary obscurity.

# X

## *Austin on Performatives*

THE LATE John Austin's William James Lectures [1] might well have born the subtitle "In Pursuit of a Vanishing Distinction." Although the chase is remorseless, glimpses of the quarry become increasingly equivocal, and the hunter is left empty-handed at last. It is hard to know what has gone awry. Has the wrong game been pursued—and in the wrong direction?

There seems deceptively little mystery about the starting point. It is by now a commonplace that in uttering a sentence a speaker need not always be saying something true or false, but may be doing something other than or more than that.[2] The point has been well remembered since Austin's provocative paper on "Other Minds."[3] Austin's original example of "I promise [such and such]," spoken in a situation in which uttering the words counts as the making of a promise, is a good illustration. It would require a perverse attachment to what Austin used to call the "descriptive fallacy"[4]

---

[1] J. L. Austin, *How to Do Things with Words*, J. O. Urmson, ed. (Oxford University Press, 1962), pp. vii, 166.

[2] It is worth recalling Wittgenstein's remark about "the multiplicity of the tools in language": "But how many kinds of sentence are there? Say assertion, question and command?—There are *countless* kinds: countless kinds of use of what we call 'symbols,' 'words,' 'sentences'" (*Philosophical Investigations*, Sec. 23). The long list of examples of linguistic activities given in the same section should be consulted.

[3] Originally part of a symposium in *Aristotelian Society Proceedings*, supp. vol. 20 (1946), reprinted in J. L. Austin, *Philosophical Papers* (Oxford, 1961).

[4] "To suppose that 'I know' is a descriptive phrase, is only one example of the *descriptive fallacy*, so common in philosophy. Even if

to insist that the promise-maker is primarily making a truth-claim: one might as well argue that a chessplayer who moves a bishop is primarily *saying that* he is moving the piece. (Still less plausible would it be to contend that the player is saying anything else.) The analogy with promising is still closer when the move is "announced" at blindfold chess: in both cases, words are used in order to do something other than making an assertion. There is a manifest contrast between the first-person promise and the corresponding third-person remark *about* the episode ("Austin promised [such and such]"). The latter might be attacked for failure to correspond with the facts, but not the former: we cannot retort to "I promise [such and such]" with the objection "It isn't so!"

In connection with a number of similar sentences, such as "I name this ship [such and such]," "I give and bequeath [such and such]," "I bet you [such and such]," Austin says: "None of the utterances [5] cited is either true or false: I assert this as obvious and do not argue it" (p. 6). He adds that the point needs no argument, because it is just as obvious as that "Damn!" is neither true nor false. But something's being obvious has never prevented philosophers from denying it or offering arguments to the contrary. For instance, E. J. Lemmon has recently said [6] that "I promise [such and such]" is "verifiable by its use" [7] and is satisfied to call it a "proposition" that is "true." From his comparison with "I am speaking now," [8] he seems to be thinking of a promise as if it were a

some language is now purely descriptive, language was not in origin so, and much of it is still not so" ("Other Minds," p. 174). See also the brief reference to the fallacy at p. 3 of the lectures, where the label "descriptive" is now criticized and rejected.

[5] By "utterance" Austin usually means a sentence or, occasionally, an expression, together with the circumstances of some specified use of the words (cf. p. 5 for examples, also p. 6 and especially n. 2 on that page). Statements, *i.e.* sentences used to make a truth-claim, are a sub-class of "utterances."

[6] "On Sentences Verifiable by Their Use," *Analysis,* 22 (March, 1962), 86–89.

[7] *Ibid.,* p. 89.     [8] *Ibid.,* p. 88.

self-referential statement, i.e., as if it were a remark about itself that would be both necessarily and trivially true. But it is hardly plausible to suppose that a promise-maker is telling his hearer that he is uttering the very words that he is uttering—for what would be the point of *that?* This way of looking at the speech episode looks willfully perverse: candid consideration of what happens in such episodes should establish beyond any controversy that the point of the promise, its whole *raison d'être,* is not to inform the hearer about itself, or about anything else, but to serve primarily as a way of binding the speaker to a subsequent performance (on pain of the familiar penalties of being thought fickle, irresponsible, dishonorable, etc.). Of course, the promise serves also to "inform the hearer" (Austin's phrase), as moving a pawn informs the opponent that it has been moved, but it would be impossible for that to happen unless there was something to be informed about, *viz.,* that the speaker was promising: promising is constituted by, not described by, utterance of the promise-formula. Perhaps all of this is too obvious, after all, to need further belaboring.

Let us follow Austin in calling "I promise [such and such]" a *performance utterance* or a *performative* for short.[9] Though one might think it easy to say what we mean by that label, this proves to be exasperatingly difficult: a great part of Austin's exposition is in effect devoted to this task of definition.

Austin says: "The name ['performative'] is derived, of course, from 'perform,' the usual verb with the noun 'action'; it indicates that the issuing of the utterance is the performance of an action—it is not usually thought of as just saying something" (pp. 6–7).[10] Here it seems to me of the first importance to bear clearly in mind that "saying something" has to be construed as "saying something *true or false,*" if Aus-

---

[9] The label is introduced at p. 6.

[10] This is the closest that Austin comes to giving a formal definition. Cf. conditions A. and B. on p. 5, where almost exactly the same language is used.

tin's explanation is not to be altogether useless. For a man who makes a promise is certainly "usually thought of as saying something," viz., the very words that he pronounces ("I promise [such and such]"): the point is that what he is saying is not rightly taken to have a *truth-value*. Similarly, "action," as it occurs in Austin's explanation, must be understood to mean at least "doing something *other than saying something true or false*," for it is certainly not wrong to think of a man who makes an assertion as doing something, viz., asserting; the point is that he is not doing something other than making a truth-claim. (The trouble is that we normally use "saying" and "doing" so loosely, and in such overlapping ways, that any explanation in terms of those words is apt to be unsatisfactory.)

Austin's explanation of "performative," cited above, suggests the following provisional definition of the notion:

(A) An utterance is said to be *performative*$_A$, when used in specified circumstances, if and only if its being so used counts as a case of the speaker's doing something other than, or something more than, saying something true or false. An utterance that is not performative is called *constative*.[11]

A few explanations may be helpful:

*Utterance:* I follow Austin in using this word to stand for the sentence or other expression used by the speaker. (Sometimes, however, Austin also uses the word to stand for the entire speech-act in question.)

*Performative*$_A$: The suffix is attached to distinguish the sense from another to be discussed immediately.

*In specified circumstances:* We are considering a classification of sentences or other expressions *as used in given settings*. Thus one and the same sentence may have to count as performative in one use and constative in another. Application of the definition will require not only specification of the circumstance of use, but in difficult cases an analysis

[11] "Constative" is Austin's useful label for an utterance having truth-value (cf. p. 3).

of what is really going on in such a type of speech episode.

*Counts as:* It is not enough that the utterance should *in fact* be a case of something other than or more than making a truth-claim; there must be a convention or rule making it wrong not to recognize that this is so. (A man who says "The bull is loose" may in *fact* be warning this hearer, but this does not make his utterance performative.)

*Something other than, or more than, saying something true or false:* Not in the way in which to walk jerkily is to do something more than just walk: the speaker must be doing something more than making a truth-claim or more than making one in a special way that is indicated by the utterance.

Some such definition as the above might seem to answer to our initial insight about the difference between "constatives" and "performatives," between a form of words used to make a truth-claim only and one that conventionally counts as being used to do something other than or more than this. Unfortunately, Austin, like other writers on the same topic, confuses the investigation by relying in effect upon another conception of the meaning of "performative" that seems to me less important and interesting. That he does so is shown by his reasons for classifying "I state" as a performative (e.g., at p. 90). (The example is of the first importance for him, because it seems to show that the intended contrast between "saying" and "doing" breaks down when its implications are followed through. The recalcitrance of "I state" and "I maintain" is one of Austin's main reasons for rejecting the original distinction between constatives and performatives as ultimately unsatisfactory.) The reason for classifying "I state" as performatory is the undeniable fact that a man who says "I state [such and such]" counts as stat*ing,* just as a man who says "I promise [such and such]," in appropriate circumstances, counts as promis*ing.*

The criterion Austin uses in connection with "I state" suggests another definition of "performative" that might be formulated as follows:

[213]

(B) An utterance of the form "I X [such and such]" is said to be performative$_B$, when used in specified circumstances, if and only if its so being used counts as a case of the speaker's thereby X-ing.

Here, both occurrences of X have to be imagined replaced by some English verb in its "first person singular present indicative active" form (p. 64).

That "performative$_A$" and "performative$_B$" are distinct notions is at once shown by the case of "I say." For anybody who says "I say" of course counts as saying something, but does not count as doing something other than or more than saying something true or false. Since it would obviously be desirable to have separate words for the two notions, I would prefer to reserve "performative" for "performative$_A$," using something like "self-labeling utterance" for the other. For what often seems to be happening in the cases of performatives$_B$ is that the utterance includes some formal marker or indicator of the character of that utterance (cf. Austin's good discussion of how the character of the performative is "made explicit," (pp. 69–70). Now this seems to be a special feature of English, not universally present in all languages, and in any case something that ought not to be confused with the more interesting contrast embodied in definition A. To identify the notion of "performative" with that of "performative$_B$" blurs the intended contrast between making a truth-claim and doing something else, or something more, by means of an utterance and focuses our attention too narrowly on a specific verbal form ("I X [such and such]"). Austin convincingly shows that there are many other types of utterances (e.g., the umpire's "Out!," the formula "You have been warned") that do not come out of the same mold. If his formidable ingenuity in trying to link such cases with a formula of the type "I X" fails in the end, as it does, I see no prospect of anybody else doing better. (The fact that he pays such close attention to utterances that do not conform to the pattern of definition B shows that Austin is not satisfied with sense B.)

[214]

I am therefore inclined to think that some such notion as that of "performative$_A$" will serve the purposes of Austin and all the philosophers who have had high hopes of the notion, and that many if not all of the difficulties that Austin encountered will be overcome by this choice.

It might be objected that definition A is too broad, e.g., because it applies to the utterances "Hello" and "I detest you." (Austin would certainly wish to exclude the latter: cf. his remark "To be a performative utterance, even in cases connected with feelings and attitudes . . . is not *merely* to be a conventional expression of feeling or attitude" [p. 81]. Cf. also his remarks on page 121 about excluding from consideration "expressive uses of language.") To this the retort might be that to say "Hello" is undoubtedly to do something other than make a truth-claim, viz., to *greet* the hearer, and that to say "I detest you" is to perform the action (?) of conventionally expressing detestation. Anybody who feels uncomfortable about using "action" in such cases should be invited to say how greeting and expressing detestation fail to qualify. Were this to be done, definition A could easily be modified accordingly, by imposing corresponding restrictions upon what is to be understood by "doing something" in the formulation of that definition given above. (The original definition might then survive as locating the class of *nonconstatives,* of which performatives in the narrower sense would then be a subclass.) Whether this can be done, and whether it is worth doing, I do not know. At any rate, definition A in its present form is no worse than the outcome of Austin's discussion: that he wants to use "action" in some narrowed sense is plain, but what that sense may be never becomes sufficiently clear.

Austin often refers to the action performed by uttering a genuine performative as "conventional" or "ritual" or "ceremonial," [12] but he does not explain how he is using these terms, so central to the understanding of his investigation. One might try to characterize such prime cases of "conven-

[12] See, for instance, pp. 19, 20, 25, 31, 36, 69, 80, 84, 102, 103, 104, 106, 108, 120, 121, 127.

tional" acts as bowing (p. 69), shaking hands, cocking a snook, challenging a man to a duel (p. 27), "picking sides" in a game (p. 28), etc., in the following way: (i) There is a set and prescribed way in which the act in question is supposed to be performed (within a certain range of permissible variation): you may not use a pseudonym for signing a check, nor may you omit the words "I swear" when preparing to testify on oath. To put the point in another way: there are valid and invalid ways of doing the act in question. (Cf. the opening of Austin's condition [A. 1] on p. 14: "There must exist an accepted conventional procedure. . . .") (ii) Provided the act in question is performed in the standard form and in the correct circumstances by a duly qualified person (where the restriction is relevant), the act counts as valid: even if the officiating clergyman deplores the marriage he is solemnizing and performs only under protest, he does marry the couple he "pronounces" to be man and wife. (iii) The mere doing of the act in accordance with the standard conditions normally makes the actor liable for certain social consequences: a man swearing to tell the truth may be sued for perjury, a man who bets on a horse can be made to pay whether he was in earnest or not. (Cf. the reference in Austin's condition [A. 1] on p. 14 to an accepted conventional procedure *having a conventional effect* [italics added].) More generally: there are a set of understandings, agreements, rules or regulations, in virtue of which the performer of the act (in the correct way) *counts* as satisfying certain demands, acquiring certain rights or privileges, becoming subject to determinable claims, etc. (iv) The act in question is taken to have a certain non-natural meaning or significance, which can usually be rendered specific by an available description (betting, marrying, pronouncing a benediction, signing a check, etc.). But this may be just another way of making point (iii) over again. To summarize, let us say that a conventional act is one that is (i) rule-governed, (ii) self-validating, (iii) claim-generating (an inadequate label), and (iv) conventionally significant. It is worth noting that some of these criteria can vary independently, so that we do not have a set of necessary and sufficient conditions. (There would be something pedantic about saying that the utterance of "Hello" confers privileges or generates liabilities; yet surely this a case of what we would want to call a "conventional" act?)

The trouble in trying to apply some such notion as I have sketched to verbal performances is that *any* correct use of words may plausibly be held to be "conventional" in the relevant sense: *speaking* is already a conventional act. Austin's practice suggests that part of the time he is really thinking of a subclass of "conventional" acts that have a close analogy to ritual or "ceremonial" acts in rather narrow senses of those words (he often has the analogy of legal "acts" in mind). But the analogy can easily be pressed too far: after all there are many ways of promising without using a set formula. At any rate, if the notion of *conventional* act can be sufficiently clarified, definition A can easily be amended by inserting the corresponding qualification.

A more serious weakness of definition A, in my judgment, is the prevalence of "mixed cases" of utterances that serve, in specified circumstances, both to make a truth-claim and to do something more. When I say "I warn you that the bull is loose," I may plausibly be said to be doing something other than making a truth-claim (cf. the alternative form "The bull is loose—that's a warning!" where the second sentence seems to perform a distinct function). But it is plausible also to say that I am at least "implying" or "contextually implying" [13] a truth-claim to the effect that the bull is loose. So, as Austin argues, considerations of truth and falsity seem to be relevant to cases such as these. (Even in the paradigm case of "I promise that I shall be there" it begins to look as if there is at least an implied assertion, "I shall be there.") One might then be led to think of the "performative"-"constative" contrast as dealing with *aspects* of utterances, rather than with mutually exclusive *classes* of utterances.

Considerations of this sort plainly played a large part in

[13] Cf. Austin's interesting discussion of "implies" at pp. 50–52.

[217]

Austin's decision "to make a fresh start on the problem" (p. 91) by introducing the doctrine of "illocutionary forces." [14] He proposes to reconsider the senses "in which to say something is to do something, or in saying something we do something, or even *by* saying something we do something" (p. 108). This is a hopeful program: one must agree that most of the troubles in handling the original performative-constative distinction arise from the fact that " 'doing something' is a very vague expression" (p. 91), and any clarification of this obscure expression may be expected to render the distinction more useful.

Austin proposes a threefold distinction between "locutionary," "illocutionary," and "perlocutionary" acts. We perform a *locutionary* act when we utter "a certain sentence with a certain sense and reference, which again is roughly equivalent to 'meaning' in the traditional sense" (p. 108). To perform a locutionary act is to say something "in the full normal sense . . . which includes the utterance of certain noises, the utterance of certain words in a certain construction, and the utterance of them with a certain 'meaning' in the favourite philosophical sense of that word, i.e., with a certain sense and with a certain reference" (p. 94). We normally report the performance of a locutionary act (or, strictly, that aspect of it, viz., meaning and referring, which constitutes what Austin calls the "rhetic act") by using indirect speech, e.g., by saying, "He said that the cat was on the mat," "He said he would go," "He said I was to go" (p. 96). (We use quotation marks normally only when the sense or reference of the original word is unclear—cf. p. 96, last paragraph.)

An *illocutionary act* is something we do *in* performing a locutionary act—e.g., informing, ordering, warning, undertaking, etc. (p. 108). In reporting the locutionary act we say what the speaker *meant*; in reporting the illocutionary act (he urged, protested, advised me to do such and such—cf. p.

[14] "I shall refer to the doctrine of the different types of function of language here in question as the doctrine of 'illocutionary forces' " (p. 99).

102 for examples) we convey the "force" of the original utterance, the "way it is (conventionally) to be taken." (Clearly the "illocutionary act" is what we are supposed to be performing when we produce a performative.)

Finally, a *perlocutionary act* is something we may do *by* producing an illocutionary act (e.g., persuading, getting somebody to do something, checking somebody, annoying him, etc.—see pp. 101–102 for these examples).

(I shall not discuss Austin's subdivision of the locutionary act into "phonetic," "phatic," and "rhetic" acts [pp. 92–93]. It seems to me somewhat crude and perversely idiosyncratic in its choice of labels; whatever its intrinsic interest, it has little bearing upon Austin's main problem.)

Austin says that his interest "is essentially to fasten on the second, illocutionary act and contrast it with the other two" (p. 103) and thinks that "It is the distinction between illocutions and perlocutions which seems likeliest to give trouble" (p. 109). For all the subleties in the uses of "in" and "by" which Austin proceeds to uncover, it seems to me that this distinction is not the likeliest to give trouble. The performance of the "illocutionary act" has to be *conventional* in the sense of being assured by the words that were in fact used: "Illocutionary acts are conventional acts: perlocutionary acts are *not* conventional" (p. 120). "A judge should be able to decide, *by hearing what was said,* what locutionary and illocutionary acts were performed, but not what perlocutionary acts were achieved" (p. 121). Suitably elaborated, this test seems to me sufficient in practice to distinguish an illocutionary act, such as threatening, from the associated perlocutionary act of intimidating with which it might sometimes be confused. (Austin's careful discussion is illuminating, however, and should be compared with what he said about related topics in his paper "A Plea for Excuses," reprinted in the *Philosophical Papers.*)

The serious troubles that threaten to render Austin's scheme of classification nugatory arise in trying to distinguish the locutionary act from the illocutionary one. Austin is himself unhappy about his use of "sense" and "reference" in the definition of the locutionary act ("I have taken the old 'sense and reference' ['distinction' omitted?] on the strength of current views" [p. 148]) and admits that the distinction between locutionary and illocutionary acts has been no more than "adumbrated" (p. 148) by him.

I find it difficult to conceive what a locutionary act (supposedly identified by giving sense and reference alone) would be like. In order to report what a speaker said "in the full sense of 'say'" (p. 92), it seems necessary to report how the speaker meant his words "to be taken" (whether as a statement, an order, a question, etc.), i.e., to include in the report an indication of the "illocutionary force," in Austin's terminology, of the original utterance. Reference to the examples of such reports of allegedly locutionary acts given by Austin (e.g., at pp. 101–102) will show that indication of the illocutionary force is indeed included in each case. Indeed, how could it be otherwise? A speaker cannot make a complete utterance merely by meaning and referring—he must assert, question, order, or do whatever else he is doing. The only proper unit for investigation seems to be what Austin has called an illocutionary act and the supposed locutionary act is at best a dubious abstraction. Austin says that "To perform a locutionary act is in general, we may say, also and *eo ipso* to perform an *illocutionary act*" (p. 98). I am urging that in order to perform a locutionary act one *must* perform an illocutionary one (and Austin seems to agree at p. 133). But then we seem to be back to the old difficulty of being unable to make the performative-constative distinction or anything that will replace it. That Austin was troubled by the outcome is clear from a note he made as late as 1958 (p. 103n.) in which he says that the distinctions he is trying to introduce are not clear and adds: "in all senses relevant . . . won't all utterances be performative?" (*ibid.*). I think the answer is Yes—at least if we agree with Austin's analysis.

In the end, one remains doubtful whether Austin's investigations have brought some interesting and profitable problems to light—or whether he has allowed himself to be diverted by an interest in what may be no more than a specific peculiarity of linguistic idiom (the use of the "first person singular present indicative"). I do not know which of these views is the sounder. I am inclined to think at present that the outcome of Austin's patient work illustrates the limitations of trying to "screw out of ordinary language" (p. 122) all that one can without trying to elaborate a plausible theoretical framework. In practice, this leads to somewhat uncritical reliance upon such questionable distinctions as that between "sense" and "reference." Appeal to ordinary language is very useful when the logical grammar of particular words and families of words is under investigation; it is likely to be less profitable when what is at stake is a general view of how language works.

# XI

# *Dewey's Philosophy of Language*

A new conception that is thorough-going always simplifies. . . .
But a new point of view also tends to oversimplify, to neglect,
ignore and thereby in effect to deny.

—John Dewey [1]

MY PURPOSE is to consider what Dewey had to say about
language and about related topics: Dewey has not left us a
systematic account of his views about language and symbolism, although he has said a good deal about them in his writings.[2] My reason for choosing the topic is the great interest
shown by many contemporary philosophers in problems connected with language. Before I end, I hope to say something
about the relations between Dewey's work on language and
contemporary studies of the same subject.

Dewey agrees with today's "analysts" and "linguistic philosophers" about the importance of language. "Language," he
says, "occupies a peculiarly significant place and exercises a
peculiarly significant function in the complex that forms the
cultural environment" (*L*, p. 45). Not merely one social institution among many, language is the indispensable condi-

---

[1] *Journal of Philosophy,* 19 (1922), 561.

[2] The chief sources for Dewey's views on language are *Experience and
Nature* (1925), especially chapter 5; *Logic: The Theory of Inquiry*
(1938); and *The Quest for Certainty* (1929). I shall refer to these
works as *EN, L,* and *QC,* respectively. The only previous study of
Dewey's philosophy of language known to me is Paul D. Wienpahl's
"Dewey's Theory of Language and Meaning" in *John Dewey: Philosopher of Science and Freedom,* Sidney Hook, ed. (New York, 1950).

tion for institutions, indeed for the very existence of a society and a culture; it is "the medium in which culture exists and through which it is transmitted" (*L*, p. 20).[3] The furniture and machinery of civil life can be used only "in social groups made possible by language" (*EN*, p. 186). So much is, of course, indisputable. Men without language would be subhuman animals.

But Dewey goes further. Language is a necessary condition, according to him, for the existence of individual consciousness: men without speech would be animals unable to think— dumb in both senses of the word. "Communication," he says, "is a condition for consciousness" (*EN*, p. 187), and all but the most primitive and inarticulate of "psychic events" have "language as one of their conditions" (*EN*, p. 169). Since language is a social product, and consciousness presupposes language, mental activity is partly a social product: "mind emerges" when conversation is transformed into soliloquy (*EN*, p. 170). The "higher" the mental process, the more complex and sophisticated it is, the more intimate is its dependence upon language: words have the function of "*creating* reflection, foresight and recollection" (*EN*, p. 169, italics inserted); language has "the special function . . . of effecting the transformation of the biological into the intellectual and the potentially logical" (*L*, p. 45). These are sweeping and challenging assertions; a decision as to their validity must be postponed until we have reached a sufficiently clear understanding of what Dewey *means* by "language."

Before we examine the details of Dewey's theory, however, we shall do well to consider what he understands by a philosophical *theory* of language. For when a scientist announces a new theory we know what kind of thing to expect, but a philosopher's conception of a satisfactory theory of a

---

[3] At this point, however, Dewey stretches the word "language" to apply to "all means of communication such as, for example, monuments, rituals and formalized arts" (*L*, p. 20). Similarly, he is prepared to speak of a tool or a machine as a "mode of language" which "*says* something, to those who understand it" (*L*, p. 46).

given subject matter is as controversial as his own conception of proper philosophical method.

We may take as a clue an interesting passage in *The Quest for Certainty* in which Dewey explains what would be required, according to him, in order to understand the structure of a given machine.

It is obvious that this structure can be understood not by sense but only by *thought* of the relations which the parts of the machine sustain to one another, in connection with the work which the machine as a whole performs (the consequences it effects). Sensibly, one is merely overwhelmed in the presence of a machine by noises and forms. Clarity and order of perceived objects are introduced when forms are judged in relation to operations, and these in turn in relation to work done. Movements may be seen in isolation, and products, goods turned out, may be perceived in isolation. The machine is *known* only when these are *thought* in connection wtih one *another*. In this thought, motion and parts are judged as *means;* they are referred intellectually to something else; to think of anything as means is to apprehend an object in *relation* (*QC,* p. 162).

It is implausible to think of language as a machine, but Dewey is in earnest in calling language an instrument or tool. Not idly or casually does he call it the "tool of tools" (*En,* pp. 168, 186). So we can imagine him saying of language, as he said of the machine in my illustrative quotation:

If you merely try to observe the perceptible details of linguistic activities, you are liable to be overwhelmed by the sheer babble and confusion of tongues. You must *think* about the relations of linguistic elements to one another, that is to say about the differential contributions they make to the work of the whole. Only when you conceive of words as means for achieving the proper ends of discourse will clarity and order appear. Only then will you really *know* what language is.

Accordingly, the key questions with regard to any given linguistic element will be, *What object does it serve?* and, again, *How does it serve this object?* The task will be to define the purposes of language and to delineate the mechanisms by which those purposes are achieved or, in cases of malfunction, are thwarted.

Now the functional approach, as we may label Dewey's procedure, is certainly one legitimate way of arriving at a synoptic and comprehensive view of a structure. Since a machine is deliberately constructed for a certain purpose, it is obviously a proper subject for functional analysis; we come to understand the machine by learning what it is supposed to do and how it does it. Again, a good case can be made for the functional approach to human physiology, in spite of the qualms some methodologists might have about the possible intrusion of teleological concepts. But the functional description is merely one among many ways of obtaining a synoptic view of a given structure. It is in the spirit of instrumentalism itself to judge the instrumentalist method by its fruits, and that is what I propose to do.

I am taking Dewey to be engaged in showing how language *works*, i.e., how the character and organization of linguistic elements and their position in a context of human activity contribute to the execution of personal and social tasks. The instrumental aspects of human speech are, of course, too obvious to have been altogether overlooked in the past. Indeed, some acknowledgment of the instrumental efficacy of language has been part of what may be called the traditional view, a conception that in one form or another has controlled the thought of nearly all writers about language in the past.[4] The force and the novelty of Dewey's theory of language can be seen by contrasting it with the older conception, from which he was consciously departing.

A clear statement of one version of the traditional view of language occurs at the beginning of the third book of Locke's *Essay*. The theme is announced in a phrase that might well have served as a motto for Dewey's own reflections: language, says Locke, is "the great instrument and common tie of so-

[4] A useful set of expressions of the traditional standpoint are quoted in G. A. de Laguna, *Speech: Its Function and Development* (New Haven, 1927), pp. 15–19.

ciety." [5] But the agreement is soon found to be superficial. What purpose does "the great instrument" serve? Locke answers, as many have done before and since: to transmit the private thoughts and feelings of the speaker to an audience— words, he says, are "the instruments whereby men communicate their conceptions, and express to one another those thoughts and imaginations they have within their own breasts" (Sec. 11). The controlling image is the attractively simple one of separate and distinct minds transforming their private thoughts into audible and public speech. What another person wishes to say to me is locked within his breast; but by clothing his thought in words he renders his thought perceptible; it remains for me to reverse the process and to receive into my own mind the naked thought. The thought is what counts, the words by which they are expressed are no more than a convenient medium of transmission.

Once the words are regarded as logically independent of the private thoughts and feelings conveyed by them, it is natural to locate the meaning of the words in the mind of the speaker. "The use, then, of words, is to be sensible marks of ideas," says Locke, "and the ideas they stand for are their proper and immediate signification" (Sec. 9). Having the natural power to frame those "articulate sounds, which we call words," we learn to associate them with ideas or "internal conceptions" so that they evoke, in others and in ourselves, the corresponding meanings. Language is a bridge between thoughts; its function is that of evoking concordant ideas; when the words I utter produce in your mind an echo of my own thought, speech has accomplished its whole and proper purpose.

This traditional conception characteristically imputes a simple relation between any word and its meaning: the word is "attached" to its meaning as a label may be attached to a material object; words are *names* for antecedently and independently existing objects; words *stand* for their meanings.

[5] John Locke, *An Essay Concerning Human Understanding* A. C. Fraser, ed. (Oxford, 1894), II, 3.

I shall have more to say about this later, when I come to criticize Dewey's own views about language.

There are three strands, then, in the traditional theory: meanings are objects of a peculiar sort, having the distinctive property of capacity for direct presence in consciousness; words *stand for* their several meanings, as personal names stand for the persons they name; the function of speech is to induce in the hearer acquaintance with the relevant meanings, or sufficiently accurate copies of such meanings. Language, in short, is a medium for reproducing the thoughts of the speaker.

This conception would not have had so persistent an influence were it not in a way obviously correct. When I succeed in speaking intelligibly to another, I am of course expressing my thought; it would be pedantic to say that when the thought evoked in my hearer is parallel to my own, speech has failed to achieve its object. Trouble begins when this familiar conception receives the emphasis characteristic of serious metaphysical thought—when it is taken too literally, as it were. It would be preposterous, for instance, to suppose that the meanings of obscure words must finally be established by entry into the mind of another, if that means more than: by understanding what he says. To think of meanings as lodged in an inaccessible realm of private consciousness is to set the stage for the agonizing doubts of the solipsist. The image of mental entities tallying with words in an exact one-to-one correspondence leads to obfuscation if taken seriously, and a disembodied thought is an idle and harmful fiction. Finally, the account of speech as terminating in an evoked thought is too banal to be useful. It is about as illuminating as saying that the function of eating is to get food down the throat: the further consequences of the act, for the sake of which it is performed, are too important to be ignored. The traditional view of language, so vehemently rejected by Dewey, is too simple-minded to be a useful model for philosophical investigation.

As might be expected from Dewey's reiterated polemic

against the "dualism" of mind and matter, he looks at language through the lenses of a behaviorist. In an important article published as late as 1922,[6] he pays his respects to the "notion of behavior"—a notion, according to him, that "is only beginning its career" (p. 561). He adds: "I believe that the identification of knowing and thinking with speech is wholly in the right direction" (*ibid.* ). But he is equally emphatic about the need to recognize "the facts which common sense and common speech independently of any theory" call by the names of "qualities, meanings, feelings, consciousness, etc." (*ibid.*). To reject a "helplessly subjective and private metaphysics," as Dewey urges, is not to deny that there *are* thoughts and feelings. Nor is it to deny that there are meanings. Dewey intends to find a place for all of these in behavior—it is no part of his design to conjure them out of existence.

This may help us to understand why Dewey, unlike some other behaviorists, makes a sharp distinction between response to a *sign* and response to what he calls a *symbol* (L, p. 51).[7] By a "symbol" Dewey means primarily a word that has meaning and is thereby equipped to combine with other words in complete statements. A symbol may also be a gesture, an image, or anything else that has meaning. A sign, however, in the technical sense intended, is any event regularly conjoined with some other event, in such a way that the occurrence of the first can arouse expectation of the second. The occurrence of a sign gives us reason to expect the occurrence of its significate; the sign has *signification*. But the occurrence of a word that is not functioning as a one-word statement is usually not the sign of anything; the word does not signify, but *means,* and its meaning is not that some contingent event will occur. A sign acts as a preparatory stimulus

6 "Knowledge and Speech Reaction," *Journal of Philosophy,* 19 (1922), 561–570.

7 A similar distinction is effectively made in Susanne K. Langer's *Philosophy in a New Key,* 3d ed. (Cambridge, Mass., 1957). See, for instance, page 31 of that book.

upon the organism receiving it and trained to respond: Pavlov's dog, hearing the dinner bell, salivates in anticipation, or a patient in the dentist's chair shrinks from the prospective pain. But it would be irrational to salivate on hearing the word "dinner" (when this is not being used as a one-word statement) or to cringe at the sound of the word "drill." The words have meaning, they do not signify. There is all the difference between responding to verbal or other stimuli and using words to *talk about* things.

Dewey often calls attention to the important fact that signs function in relative independence of other signs, while a word (a symbol, in Dewey's terminology) is necessarily part of a system: "Any word or phrase has the meaning which it has only as a member of a constellation of related meanings. Words as representatives are part of an inclusive code" (*L*, p. 49). The importance of this for Dewey is that the existence of a pattern of implications among the meanings of words composing a language system makes "reasoning or ordered discourse" (*L*, p. 54) possible. We use signs to *infer* the existence of the corresponding significates; but we perform another and more sophisticated intellectual operation when we see that one statement *implies* another.

How is intelligent response to signs (i.e., response to them as signs of their significates) to be explained on behaviorist principles? I have not been able to find a discussion of this point by Dewey. Others have thought it sufficient to rely upon the mechanism of the conditioned reflex. But there are difficulties here. Suppose an organism initially makes some standard response to a kind of stimulus, $A$, is then repeatedly exposed to an $A$-stimulus accompanied by another stimulus of kind $B$, and so at last is found to have been "conditioned" to respond to a stimulus of kind $B$ alone. When this occurs, the response to a $B$-stimulus, say $R_B$, will always differ from the original response to the $A$-stimulus, say $R_A$: the dog is conditioned to salivate at the sound of a bell, but he does not try to eat it. A behaviorist analysis of sign-using behavior must therefore specify the relation between $R_B$ and $R_A$ in virtue of which the former will count as a case of treating *B* as a sign of *A*. So far as I know, this has not yet been satisfactorily accomplished. No doubt, attempts will continue to be made to fill this large gap in behaviorist theories of sign-using behavior.[8]

Relatively primitive animals can use signs, but only men can talk. Let us now consider how Dewey envisages the emergence of the distinctively human activity of speaking—or, in his terminology, of using "symbols." Dewey's main point can be stated very simply: words and other symbols come into existence through cooperative action for a common purpose. It is the human need to join with others in accomplishing social tasks that makes possible and requires the emergence of symbols.

What this theory intends can be made plainer by a simple illustration, modeled upon an example given by Dewey himself (*EN*, p. 178). Suppose a mother teaches her child to hand her a ball when she says "ball," while looking or pointing at the plaything. If the child merely responds automatically to the total gesture (i.e., if he makes a conditioned response to it), he is responding to a sign that may signify the reward that follows. So much a circus animal can be trained to do. As the child's intelligence develops—so the theory runs—he learns to respond to the ball "from the mother's standpoint": he comes to perceive the ball as something that *she* wants, something that *she* can handle and grasp. In handing it to her, he is first satisfying her demand and only indirectly his own desire for approval and reward. When the episode moves to its successful climax, with smiles and chuckles on both sides, the two actors, mother and child, have "come to agreement in action" (*EN*, p. 179). When this level of cooperation has been attained, the child's acts are determined not by the sight of the ball alone (as would be the case if he merely reached for it), nor simply by his mother's words and gestures acting as simple stimuli; his acts are determined at this stage

[8] For a recent attempt of this sort, see Charles E. Osgood, *The Measurement of Meaning* (Urbana, Ill., 1957), pp. 5–9.

[230]

by the more complex anticipation of the successful "consummation of a transaction in which both participate" (*ibid.*). In plain English, the child does not want the ball for himself, but wants mother to have the ball, because that is what *she* wants and because he wants the approval that will come when he does what she wants him to do. Mother and child have now managed to communicate with one another, because they have succeeded in cooperating "in an activity in which there are partners, and in which the activity of each is modified and regulated by partnership" (*ibid.*). The essence of communication, according to Dewey, is the "making of something common" (*L*, p. 46) by means of a "concerted action" (*EN*, p. 184) that satisfies each participant by virtue of fulfilling a group purpose. To communicate is to act together for a common purpose, and to understand is to respond adequately to the demands of a situation in which "mutual assistance and direction" (*EN*, p. 176) are evoked. "To understand is to anticipate together, it is to make a cross-reference which, when acted upon, brings about a partaking in a common, inclusive, undertaking" (*EN*, pp. 178–179). To understand we might say, is to *act for* another; it is a concordant interplay of bodies, rather than a "meeting" of disembodied minds.

It is easy to anticipate where this conception of meaning as grounded in social activity will lead us. For example, the exercise of speech will now be held to *create* meanings: the "release and amplification" of human energies in social interaction *confers* upon human actions "the added quality of meaning" (*EN*, p. 174). Meanings are not to be regarded as evanescent private ideas, nor as "ideal essences" (*EN*, p. 172) in a timeless realm, awaiting designation by some articulate Adam; it is human actions that have the quality of meaning. As might be expected, the emphasis throughout is upon *action*: "communication . . . (is) . . . an activity" (*EN*, p. 179), "the word . . . (is) . . . a mode of social action" (*ibid.*) and "meaning is a method of action" (*EN*, p. 187). Even soliloquy is conversation muted and transposed: in the not so silent sessions of sweet thought, a man speaks to himself as if he were another—"If we had not talked with others and they with us, we should never talk to and with ourselves" (*EN*, p. 170). Hence, "it is heresy to conceive meanings to be private, a property of ghostly psychic existences" (*EN*, p. 189). Meaning is "objective" (*EN*, p. 188), and the "meaning which a conventional symbol has is not itself conventional" (*L*, p. 47), because it is a "possible interaction" (*EN*, p. 189)[9] revealed in and by means of a mutual activity. As usual with Dewey, a practical moral follows closely. If speech activity is parochial or disjoined, insulated from the wider concerns of society, the transmitted meanings are correspondingly impoverished. Our social purposes are stunted by the existence of a "multiplicity of meaning constellations . . . (which) is the real Babel of communication" (*L*, p. 50).

Dewey's view of communication is basically the same as that elaborated by George Herbert Mead in his celebrated Chicago lectures on social psychology (published posthumously under the title *Mind, Self, and Society*). The central ideas of the emergence of meaning through cooperative activity and the importance of "taking the standpoint of the other" appear again and again in the lecture notes of Mead's course. To be sure, a number of Mead's distinctive ideas are slurred over or altogether omitted by Dewey: notably the crucial role, according to Mead, of the "vocal gesture" in arousing in the speaker the same attitude as in the hearer (e.g., pp. 46, 62, 67) and the importance of the standpoint which he calls that of the "generalised other" (p. 90). But the main ideas are there—Dewey's theory of communication is a diluted version of Mead's thoughts on the same subject.

What are we to say about this Mead-Dewey theory? Its charm is undeniable. There is something very attractive in this story of mutuality and common purpose, the alternating roles of speaker and hearer, the shared meaning arising from

---

[9] An ampler discussion of Dewey's view of language would require an examination of the important part played by the notion of possibility.

the shared labor, as it could not from the solitary contempla-
tion of the isolated individual. Communication is presented
to us here as a lively and an edifying spectacle. But is the
theory true? Does it help us to see linguistic activity as a coherent and intelligible pattern? We must admit this persuasive story to the drab routine of criticism.

Let us ask, first, whether Dewey intends his account to be
read as history or as analysis. Is he telling us how the sons of
men learn to speak—or is he explaining *what it is* to speak?
As an outline of the genesis of infant speech, Dewey's account
is not so much plausible as truistic. Given the dependence of
the human child upon adults, we can hardly conceive of children learning to speak except in a social context. But we
should also remember observed facts of child behavior that do
not fit readily into the conception of speech as a factor in
shared activity—I mean such things as babbling behavior,
solitary naming of objects, and so on. If the child is from
the start a member of social groups, he is also a slowly developing individual, and a faithful empirical account of the
development of his capacity to speak and to think must take
account of both dimensions—the individual no less than the
social. But on the whole, the only criticism to be made of
Dewey's account, considered as a chronicle of child development, is its schematic character. Right as it may be in its
main outlines, it omits the details, often surprising, that we
look for in a faithful account of the aetiology of infant
speech.

I think Dewey was trying to do something more than provide a partly speculative reconstruction of how language
comes into existence. He was trying to make plain *what communication is*—to analyze it in its full development. And
whether he was consciously practicing analysis of this sort or
not, this is the aspect of his teaching that is now of most interest. The full story of how children learn to speak can be
left to the child psychologists to discover. Our present hope
is to get a clear understanding of what communication is.

Dewey's sustained emphasis upon the *context* in which

[233]

words are used seems to me wholly admirable. Only it may be doubted whether Dewey's simple paradigm of response to the expressed wishes of another will take us very far. When mother wants baby to show how clever he is by reaching for the ball, the situation is clear enough. But there is an enormous gap between this and, say, the familiar linguistic performance of telling somebody the time. What is *here* the "common purpose"? To say that it is the purpose of informing and being informed about the correct time is trivial and unilluminating. For what is in question is just what kind of a thing telling the time is. Of course, we already know the answer, in a fashion that could hardly be bettered by verbal description; we know *how to* "tell the time" and could enumerate the details of the procedure at tiresome length. But what is added to our common-sense understanding of this kind of situation if we are told that it is an instance of cooperative action, of a shared common purpose, and so on? At this point the philosophical formula of meaning as social activity threatens to degenerate into an automatic gloss. Consider a more complex case, say that of giving a promise. Here, emphasis upon cooperation, shared purposes, and the like may deflect our attention from aspects of the promise-giving situation that are worth noticing—I mean such things as the existence of a background institution, the relevance of shared presuppositions, the connection of the act of promising with subsequent consequences in the way of blame, excuse, and so on. Attention to these factors can lead us to a clearer view of what promising amounts to; and in such a case, I suspect Dewey's framework might be a hindrance.

I am convinced, however, that Mead's insistence upon the importance of "taking the role of the other" is a valuable clue to understanding all kinds of linguistic transactions. The difficulty here is to attach a literal and nonmetaphorical meaning to the key expression. For example, what is it precisely to "take the standpoint of the other" while promising? Is more implied than this: that a man who is able to *give* a promise must also be able to *receive* one, i.e., must know what claims and expectations he would be entitled to in such a case? Or is it being said that in order to give a promise, in full knowledge of what he is doing, a man must know what the "other" is entitled to expect? Or does the formula mean, less plausibly, that the promise maker must somehow "identify" himself with the promise receiver? The notion of "taking the role of the other" obviously needs further clarification.

Here is another difficulty: I have taken Dewey's theory to be an account of the use of *speech* in communication. But all that we have so far found him to be saying would apply equally well to any kind of cooperation or concerted activity, whether involving the use of words or not. Consider, for instance, the case of two men moving some heavy piece of furniture. Here it is plausible to say that the acts of each man are modified by the acts of the other, each taking account of his partner's position, difficulties, and intentions; and certainly each man has in view the successful completion of a common task, the final placing of the armchair, or whatever the object may be. Yet in all this not a word may pass; all the criteria offered by Dewey are present, yet no verbal communication has occurred. It may be retorted that the various gestures made by the furniture movers in the course of their labor have meaning for each of them. But if so, something more is needed to explain how words function as *words*. For this we must now turn to Dewey's account of the individual meanings of individual words. For so far we have been told only what it is for a word—or, for that matter, a gesture—to be meaningful. But Dewey holds, as we shall immediately see, that it is necessary also to explain what the individual meanings are.

What is the meaning of a word, or symbol, according to Dewey? We may notice, first, that he repeatedly equates a meaning with an "idea": any number of phrases can be found in which the two words are plainly treated as synonyms. Thus Dewey will speak of a "meaning or idea" (*L*, pp. 109, 112), of an "idea or conceptual meaning" (*L*, p. 118), and of "embodied meanings or ideas" (*L*, p. 110), to take only three examples. Another approximate synonym for "meaning," in Dewey's usage, is "essence." Typical locutions are "meaning or essence" (*EN*, p. 191), "meaning, fixed as essence" (*EN*, p. 194), and "meaning or essence embodied in a symbol" (*EN*, p. 201). No doubt, Dewey wanted to rescue the word "essence" from the grasp of his philosophical adversaries and hoped to give it a new career by changing its meaning. But the word is redolent of implications quite unsuitable for Dewey's purposes, and I shall avoid using it. On the other hand, we shall not go wrong if we assume that for Dewey the meaning of a word or a verbal expression is an idea, in something like the common-sense meaning of "idea." We are entitled to apply to meanings many of the remarks he makes about ideas.

Dewey provides an extraordinary variety of lapidary formulas for meaning. For example, he says that "meanings are rules for using and interpreting things" (*EN*, p. 188) and tells us soon after that a rule is "the standardized habit of social interaction" (*EN*, p. 190). So, according to him, the meaning of a given word must be a standardized habit of social interaction. He discusses at some length the case of a traffic policeman holding up his hand to stop traffic. What is the relevant rule, and what is the relevant habit of social interaction? I suppose the rule is "When a traffic policeman raises his hand, stop!" and the social habit is that of stopping when the hand is raised. We notice that the rule and the habit are quite different kinds of things, so that there would be a logical absurdity in identifying the two; hence the meaning of the policeman's gesture cannot be *both* rule and habit. But can it reasonably be said to be either? I think not. There would be a patent absurdity in saying that the gesture means "When a traffic policeman raises his hand, stop." The gesture does not *refer to* policemen in general, or even to the particular officer who is making the gesture. It would be better to say that the gesture simply means "Stop!" But then we are simply equating one imperative symbol with another, without saying *what* the meaning is of either. If the meaning of the gesture were the corresponding habit, then we would also have to say that the meaning of 'Stop!' was the habit people have of stopping when they hear the word "stop." This would be a violation of the logical grammar of "meaning."

If we try out Dewey's formulas on a nonimperative expression, such as "one meter in length" we get even stranger consequences. Think of how odd it would be to say that "X is one meter long" means the same as "Call anything one meter long when a standard meter rod is congruent with it"—or, alternatively, that it means the same as "People are in the habit of calling anything one meter long when it is congruent with a meter rod." The attempt to equate the meaning of an expression with a rule or a habit simply will not do.

A more sympathetic reading of Dewey's intentions would be to regard him as saying something like this: To discover what a gesture or a set of spoken words means, consider the context in which it is used and the relevant background of rule-governed behavior. This reminds us of Wittgenstein's formula: Don't ask for the meaning, look for the use. But this formula will not tell us, and was not intended to tell us, what *the* meaning, or *the* use of a word is. Wittgenstein was trying to rid us of the compulsion to ask the question, "What is *the* meaning of X?"; Dewey, however, often gives us an answer, though not the same answer every time.

Here are some of the other answers he gives. "A meaning," he says, "is a method of action" (*EN*, p. 187) or, again a "method of procedure" (*EN*, p. 200). The "proximate meaning" of a symbol "is a coordination of the movements of persons" (*EN*, p. 191) with each other and with the objects of the immediate environment; while the "ultimate meaning" is a sum total of shared human consequences (*ibid.*). Again, "ideas are anticipated consequences (forecasts) of what will happen when certain operations are executed under and with respect to observed conditions" (*L*, p. 109). On the other hand, an "idea or conceptual meaning" is also an "attitude"

(*L*, p. 185) of discriminating attention and anticipation. On one page we read that ideas "are statements not of what is or has been but of acts to be performed" (*QC*, p. 138), but the preceding page contains the contradictory claim that "our conceptions and ideas are designations of operations to be performed *or already* performed" (*QC*, p. 137, italics added). We are also told that ideas are "plans of operations to be performed" (*QC*, p. 138); they are "anticipatory plans and designs" (*QC*, p. 166). No doubt, other formulas having some kind of vague reference to active verification would be found without much trouble; for I have the impression that Dewey uses these various formulations interchangeably, as if they differed only by negligible shades of meaning. But the differences are not negligible. If we are to speak with a respectable degree of precision, we must choose between the rules, habits, methods, coordinations, forecasts, attitudes, plans, and designs that Dewey bundles together. Otherwise, we shall be left with nothing more than a blurred idea of meanings as having *something* to do with future consequences, with operations, plans, and so on.

I believe it will be found that none of Dewey's formulas will sustain a literal interpretation. It is sufficient to apply any one of these formulas to a particular example to reveal the violation of grammar and logic that results. Take the case of the word "sweet," used by Dewey himself as an illustration (*QC*, p. 160), and consider the suggestion that its "ultimate meaning" is the sum total of all possible human consequences of its use. I suppose a description of this set of consequences would run somewhat as follows: "If something is called 'sweet,' it is expected to taste sweet, will be desired by those who like sweet things, will be sold by those who hope to profit from peoples' desire for sweets, and so on *ad lib.*" The exact form taken by this catalogue of consequences is unimportant, since any attempt to replace the word "sweet" by such a list must fail. Or take the simpler formula employed by Dewey when he says that "The idea of the sweetness of, say, sugar, is an indication of the consequences of a possible operation of tasting as distinct from a directly experienced quality" (*ibid.*). This may amount to saying that "X is sweet" means that if X is tasted, X will taste sweet. But what then of the expression "tastes sweet" that occurs in the *definiens?* Does that in turn mean that if something is done, something else will result? If so, we are caught in an infinite regress. It would seem that words standing for characters of immediate experience ought to be excluded from the scope of Dewey's instrumentalist analysis of meaning.

The origin of this stress upon plans, designs, methods, and procedures is plain enough. Working in the pragmatist tradition, Dewey nevertheless wants to avoid any taint of subjectivity.[10] We are to think of meaning always in terms of public *consequences,* not in terms of some private image or transcendental essence. The program is full of promise, but I fear the promise is unfulfilled.

It seems to me that Dewey's theory of meaning is marred by two large mistakes. First, it is disconcerting to realize, as one follows his discussions, that he treats the meanings of words and the meanings of sentences as if the two belonged to the same logical category. When he speaks of "the ultimate meaning of the noise made by the traffic officer" (*EN,* p. 191), he is referring to the equivalent of a full utterance; yet in the very same paragraph he talks about "the ultimate meaning, or essence, denominated fire" (*ibid.*), i.e., about the meaning of a sentence component. To suppose that the same formula of "the total consequent system of social behavior" (*ibid.*) applies equally to a statement and to a word is to overlook, in a way that is bound to lead to trouble, the radical difference in logical type between the two. Obviously, all sorts of assertions that can be made of the one generate nonsense when made of the other: it is absurd to speak of verifying or refuting a word—or, for that matter, of its

10 See, in this connection, Dewey's illuminating essay, "The Development of American Pragmatism," reprinted in his *Philosophy and Civilization* (New York, 1931), pp. 13–35.

social consequences. To put the matter in another way, a statement is not properly to be regarded as a complex word —any more than a house is properly to be regarded as a complex brick—or a brick as a rudimentary house. Hence, any account of meaning that is presented as applying indifferently to statements and to their components is bound to be at least systematically ambiguous. Recognition of the relevant difference of type would have led Dewey to see that he was using such key words as "idea" in at least two different senses.

The other mistake is this. I suggested earlier that Dewey's theory could be usefully regarded as a revolt against the traditional theory exemplified in Locke's theory of language. But revolutionaries often unconsciously accept the basic assumptions of the positions they are attacking. Dewey consciously rejected an identification of meaning with psychic events or transcendent essences; but he seems to have been unaware of still conceiving of meaning as a *nonverbal counterpart* of a symbol. He still accepted the mistaken principle that the distinctive meaning of a given symbol can be independently designated. Anybody accepting this principle will think that a question of the form "What is the meaning of $S$?" can be answered by a statement of the form "The meaning of $S$ is $M$," in which the letter "$M$" is replaced by some *designation* of a meaning. Thus, when Dewey says, "The meaning of 'sweet' is a certain plan of action," he seems to be referring to something, a plan of action, that exists independently of the symbol whose meaning it is alleged to be. This might be called the *dogma of substantive meaning*. Dewey said that there is "no one-to-one correspondence of names with existential objects" (*L*, p. 53). He should have taken the further step of denying one-to-one correspondence with any objects whatsoever. He rightly objects to "the classic hypostatizing of essence" (*EN*, p. 207), but himself succumbs to a more subtle variety of the same error.

There are, of course, commonplace and harmless uses of expressions of the form, "the meaning of something," as there are harmless and philosophically neutral uses of expressions of the form, "the value of something." But it is not always legitimate to press the further question, "What, then, *is* that meaning?" There is no more need for the meaning of a word to be something that can be named or described than there is for the same to be true of the economic value of a commodity. (The commodity has at least an identifiable price or market value, but there is no universal medium of exchange for meaning.) It would have been in the spirit of Dewey's general view of language as an instrument for effecting human purposes for him to have been satisfied to show how linguistic components contribute to the work of statements. It was unnecessary for him to search for counterparts of the several components. In order to understand how the gears of an automobile contribute to the work of the whole machine it is unnecessary to postulate something literally identifiable as *"the* work done by the gears." And similarly for the work that is done by words.

Were there sufficient time, it would be appropriate to say something at this point about what Dewey calls the "liberation" of meanings (*L,* p. 52). For this topic provides a convenient pragmatic test of the usefulness of his own theory as an instrument for bringing perceptible organization into the complex web of linguistic activities. I shall have to confine myself to a few remarks about this important topic. A symbol, says Dewey, can be "detached from its own context . . . and by being placed in a context of other meanings . . . it is liberated from the contingencies of its prior use" (*EN,* p. 193). In the process of such liberation (or "abstraction," as Dewey also calls it), words serve as "agencies of fixation" (*Essays in Experimental Logic,* p. 51). They help to free us from the insistent demands of the immediate context, so that we can consider means and consequences in the ampler and less hurried context of deliberation. Such thought, in abstraction from immediate consequences, is the germ of scientific inquiry, and finds its most sophisticated expression in mathematics. No student of Dewey's writings needs to be told how central for his philosophy is this conception of thought that is intelligent because of its relative detachment from immediate practical concerns, or how misleading the vulgar stereotype is that thinks of him as interested in only the narrowest kind of practical consequences.

How do symbols contribute to the work of abstract thought? The basic idea invoked by Dewey is that of a *symbolic operation*. We must recognize, he says, "a distinction between operations overtly performed (or imagined to be performed) and operations *symbolically* executed" (*QC*, p. 150). But what is it for an operation to be "symbolically executed"? Dewey says that "by means of symbols . . . we act without acting. That is, we perform experiments by means of symbols which have results which are themselves only symbolized, and which do not therefore commit us to actual or existential consequences" (*QC*, p. 151). Abstract liberated thought, "rehearses the act" (*ibid*). But I wonder whether this attractive talk about experimentation in thought and rehearsal of action is more than a metaphor for thinking. To rehearse a stage part is to speak the lines in the absence of an audience; but thinking is not an informal performance in an informal setting—to think of going for a walk is not to rehearse the act. Again, the point of an experiment is that we must actually do something in order to discover in the light of what actually happens whether an antecedent hypothesis was correct, but when I think about the consequences of setting my dog at my neighbor's cat, I do not perform the trial. Nor do I experiment with words when I utter them aloud or silently. At this point, Dewey's vocabulary spins in the void.

I would now like to say something about the relation of Dewey's theory of language to contemporary philosophical interest in the same subject. Let us consider, first, the so-called "ordinary language philosophers." Some philosophers today regard a certain kind of appeal to the ordinary uses of words as being, if not the end-all of philosophy, at least the "begin-all," in Professor Austin's phrase.[11] They do so in the

[11] See J. L. Austin, "A Plea for Excuses," *Proceedings of the Aristotelian Society*, 57 (1956–57), 1–30.

conviction that the only practicable way to describe a concept is to observe the uses of the words by which that concept is expressed. With so much Dewey might cordially agree. Applied to the philosophy of language, the "ordinary language" approach would require a detailed examination of the ways in which such words as "sign," "symbol," "meaning," "communication," and their cognates are used by laymen. This would be expected to make plain to us what we in fact mean by these words, prior to philosophical theorizing about them, but it would not prejudice the philosopher's privilege of modifying the relevant concepts or of inventing new ones. It is much to be regretted that so little has yet been done to apply the "ordinary language" techniques to this important group of words. While it would be illegitimate to anticipate the detailed outcomes of these missing researches, a few plausible guesses can be made. For instance, it would be most surprising if these semantical concepts, as we may call them, were to prove relatively simple in their structures and mutual affiliations. Given the notorious variability of "meaning" and its cognates, the inquiry must be expected to be intricate, prolonged, and laborious. The cartographer of semantical concepts must anticipate convoluted outlines and uncertain contours in his conceptual maps. The odds against a simple and compendious description of the concept of meaning are as great as those against a corresponding summary of the shape of the American continent. But we can become familiar with that shape, given enough acquaintance with a map of suitable precision, and the same may be hoped for after the bounds of the concept of meaning have been beaten. The "ordinary language philosopher" may seek simplicity of analysis, but is skeptical of its existence. He would be astounded to find any of Dewey's brief formulas adequately representing the conceptual webs of the semantical concepts; and his skepticism is based on what is now a considerable experience of inquiry into comparable families of concepts.

The attitude to philosophical problems that I have been alluding to is, of course, quite alien to Dewey's conception of philosophical method. He never had much respect for "ordinary language" or patience with it, and he would probably regard the "ordinary language philosopher" as a frivolous splitter of nonexistent hairs. Certainly the appeal to ordinary language runs the risks of pedantry, academicism, and irrelevance; yet a good case can be made, in my opinion, for the claim that the "ordinary language approach," for all its patent dangers, is more genuinely empirical than Dewey's picturesque forays. Minute philosophy will inevitably repel certain bold philosophical temperaments, but habitual and persistent neglect of "minute particulars" is no more defensible in philosophy than in science, and bold views will never be a substitute for close and patient attention to facts.

I will add, finally, some brief comparisons with the work of the later Wittgenstein. Between certain aspects of Dewey's and Wittgenstein's views of language there is at any rate a strong superficial resemblance. An important basis for agreement between the two is their common warfare against what I have been calling the traditional view of language.[12] In Wittgenstein's case, there is the added passion of a man repudiating his past errors, for a variant of the classical view is integral to the doctrine of the *Tractatus*. Certainly, the early Wittgenstein never identified meanings with images or Lockean ideas, but the "objects" (*Gegenstände*) of the *Tractatus* are suspiciously like timeless essences. Whether this interpretation is justified or not, it is certain that the *Tractatus* identifies the meaning of a word with what Wittgenstein later called its "bearer," i.e., with some correlated object supposedly having independent existence. The *Philosophical Investigations* begin with a powerful and convincing attack on the dogma of substantive meaning; here, I think, Wittgenstein made a contribution of lasting importance to the philosophy of language.

In Wittgenstein's repeated injunctions to view language in its full context, to consider words as they are used in a "way

[12] Cf. Paul Feyerabend, "Wittgenstein's *Philosophical Investigations*," *Philosophical Review*, 64 (1955), 449–483.

of life," and in his insistence upon looking for the "use" rather than for the meaning in the traditional sense, there is much that a follower of Dewey should find congenial. The same can also be said of Wittgenstein's rejection of a "private language" and of his polemic against the idea of a special mental realm. Common ground might even be found for faithful Deweyites and loyal Wittgensteinians in the somewhat skeptical attitude of both parties toward certain exaggerated claims made on behalf of formal logic. But behind these accords there is a profound disagreement. Wittgenstein preached the end of all metaphysics, and had less sympathy for a metaphysics that aspired to be empirical than for one that was avowedly transcendental or mystical. And he reserved some of his sharpest stings for those who thought the method of science apt for the purposes of philosophical investigation. Now Dewey, if I have not altogether misunderstood him, thought there was no basic distinction in method between science and philosophy; and for better or worse, he must be viewed as a metaphysician in the grand manner.

The last impression that remains with me after a laborious examination of much of what Dewey wrote about language and related topics is that he did not approach the subject as an inquiring empiricist, eager to discover what was antecedently unknown, but rather as an investigator whose broad philosophical position was already so firmly established in his own mind that he sought illustrations rather than material for new conclusions. In place of a fresh examination of the use of speech in its social setting, we find examples and formulas that serve only to fortify opinions antecedently crystallized. That metaphysical principles shed little light upon the distinctive features of language is no objection to those principles. My aim has not been to pass judgment upon Dewey's metaphysics, but rather to watch a thinker of extraordinary energy and tireless industry at work in a field which, for various reasons, I hold to be of central importance to philosophy.

# XII

## *Wittgenstein's Views about Language*

A perspicuous representation produces just that
understanding which consists in "seeing connexions"
(*Philosophical Investigations*, § 122, p. 49).

1

WHERE should we start in trying to get a "perspicuous
view" of Wittgenstein's conception of language? Perhaps with
the theme that runs strongly through all his teaching: the
seduction of thought by language. Or, rather: by inadequate
theories *about* language. For prejudices about language are
a prime source of metaphysical confusion.

In the *Tractatus,* Wittgenstein said: "All philosophy is 'cri-
tique of language' " (4.0031) and, more explicitly: "Most
philosophical questions and answers arise from our not understanding the logic of our language" (4.003). At this early
stage, Wittgenstein conceived of the perfidiousness of language somewhat in Russell's way—as a disparity between apparent and authentic logical form.

In *The Blue Book,* when Wittgenstein had already dis-
carded many of the dominant ideas of the earlier book, he
could still say: "Philosophy, as we use the word, is a fight
against the fascination which forms of expression exert upon
us" (p. 27). And near the end of his life, in the *Investigations,*
he holds the same thought steadfastly: "Philosophy is a battle
against the bewitchment of our understanding by means of
language" (§ 109, p. 47).

The root of this "fascination," this "bewitchment," might

be called *grammatical sclerosis*. Easily misled by the superficial simplicities of syntax, we petrify a linguistic analogy
into a metaphysical dogma: we project a caricature of language into "the world." We are guilty of conceptual impatience: "When words in our ordinary language have *prima
facie* analogous grammars we are inclined to try to interpret
them analogously; i.e. we try to make the analogy hold
throughout" (*The Blue Book*, p. 7). Our thought is perversely rigid: " . . . we aren't able to rid ourselves of the
implications of our symbolism" (*The Brown Book*, p. 108).
Above all, we are prone to make illegitimate inferences from
language to ontology: "We predicate of the thing that which
lies in the method of representation. Impressed by the possibility of a comparison, we think we are perceiving a state of
affairs of the highest generality" (*Phil. Inv.*, § 104, p. 46). We
misread linguistic analogy as identity of essence.

The penalty for such faults is mystification. If a savage
thinks that an automobile must have a horse concealed inside
it, he is bound to endow the horse with magical properties.
If you take Bohr's model of the atom literally, you will have
to accept particles that instantaneously jump from one orbit
to another. If Frege's dichotomy between "objects" and "functions" seems inescapable, you will find yourself driven to
recognizing such queer "objects" as The True and The False.

2

Each metaphysical theory has its distinctive style and plot,
but all of them alike are apt to be sustained by *a priori* preconceptions concerning language and its supposedly necessary relations to thought and reality. We wander all the
more readily into the wrong path because we trust a distorted
map of the entire region.

It is ironical that the *Tractatus*, for all its warnings against
conceptual rigidity, itself turned out to be—as its author
later recognized—an example of dogmatic metaphysical distortion. It is easy to recognize in that book the faults of

oversimplification, ("conceptual impatience"), obsessive attachment to a monolithic conception of language, and illegitimate ontological inference. But the pattern that emerges in the *Tractatus* is very persuasive. Wittgenstein had to rid himself of the "picture" that held him "captive" before he could reach the enlightenment of the *Philosophical Investigations* (§ 115, p. 48). That is why he said, in the Foreword, that his new ideas could "be seen in the right light only in contrast with and against the background of my old ways of thinking" (p. x).

3

When Wittgenstein first speaks of "the author of the *Tractatus*" in the *Investigations* (end of § 23, p. 12) he implies that he was a "logician." (Significantly, he chides his early self and "logicians" generally for ignoring "the multiplicity of the implements of language.") The *Tractatus* is, indeed, a book written by a logician with strong metaphysical interests.

Now modern logic was deliberately created in the image of pure mathematics, itself typically regarded as a science of the relations between timeless entities. (This is no longer true: mathematical logicians are now more apt to profess "nominalism" or "formalism" or some combination of such toughminded philosophies.) Thus the objects of logical investigation—whether "propositions," "terms," "functions," "sets" "proofs," or the like—are deliberately removed from any contingent relations to men and their purposes. The autonomy of logic and its absolute divorce from psychology or sociology have been take for granted ever since the polemical onslaughts by Husserl and Frege against "psychologism." So it is that Wittgenstein, in the *Tractatus*, explicitly contrasts philosophy with psychology (4.1121) and warns his reader against getting "entangled" in "inessential psychological investigations" (*ibid.*). That reference to the "inessential" is arresting: if you approach language in the spirit of a mathematical logician (like Russell or Frege—Wittgenstein's principal influences), you will naturally search for its "essence" —some abstract design that necessarily lurks behind the untidy surface of actual discourse. You will be interested, as it were, in the *lingua abscondita* that is partially, but only partially, revealed in ordinary language (cf. 4.0002 on how language "disguises" thought).

In the *Tractatus,* Wittgenstein deliberately turns his back upon all that, in the modern idiom, is "pragmatic" about language, and tries to ignore the complex network of conventions, habits, expectations, purposes, that go into the making of language *as we know it.* For ordinary language is "enormously complicated " (4.0002), while the logician's goal is the ideal simplicity of a unified, coherent, exact design. This is what lies behind Wittgenstein's favorite expression, "the logic of language": only much later did he turn from "logic" to "natural history" (a recurrent expression in the *Investigations*) and look with freshened vision at just those "details" of the human employment of words that once seemed to him "inessential." However, even in the *Tractatus* the policy of ignoring the *users* of language cannot be followed with full rigor: the connection between names and the objects they stand for is established only by their "employment" (3.262), and the sense of propositional signs is constituted by the "thought" that "projects" them on to the world (3.12). But such references to human activity remain unelaborated in the *Tractatus.*

### 4

In the *Tractatus,* then, language is conceived, in abstraction from its users, as a system of interconnected symbols, controlled by rules of combination—its "logic." Unlike other systems of symbols—such as games—language has the *essential* property of referring to "the world." Propositions must necessarily have truth-value—can be true or false, and must be one or the other. So Wittgenstein's great question in the *Tractatus* becomes "How is this possible?" (The

Kantian echoes have been noticed by more than one commentator.) What is it about Language (with a capital L) that makes it possible for it to "reach up to" reality?

Wittgenstein answers: The connection is made by means of "elementary propositions," composed of authentic names, each standing for a logical simple (a *"Gegenstand,"* an "object") and so combined as to reflect the "logical form" of the state-of-affairs whose existence is asserted by the proposition. What we call names or nouns in ordinary language are not, from a logical standpoint, genuine names—not what Russell called "logically proper names"—for they have meanings explicable by means of other words. And so the propositions in which such apparent names occur must be capable of analysis into simpler propositions and those, in their turn, into others. But this process of logical analysis *must* come to an end, if our language is ultimately to point beyond the network of linguistic connections to real things in the "world." We can mean something about reality, however indirectly, only because there are, and must be, propositions in *direct* contact with reality—and all the propositions of ordinary language or science mean what they do, as Wittgenstein puts it, *via* the postulated "elementary" propositions. In these, the logically simple names stand *directly* for their bearers and so no further explication or analysis is possible. *How* we learn to use such names or manage to agree with the usage of others is no concern of logic. But an aggregate of names is not a language: indeed *the* function of "names" is to combine, without intermediaries, in elementary propositions (so that to know what a name stands for is to know how to use it, in association with others, to make elementary propositions). If we could penetrate to the last level of analysis, at which the elementary propositions emerge intact, unmodified by superimposed logical operations, we would find their liberties of association restrained by rules of "logical syntax." Thus the elementary propositions have "logical forms" (manifested in the rules of logical syntax governing their components, the simple names). And this logical form is *the very same* as the logical

[250]

form of the atomic states-of-affairs represented by the elementary propositions. The rules of "logical syntax" are therefore not arbitrary or conventional: if certain "names" can or cannot combine to produce sensible elementary propositions, that is because their bearers, the "objects" for which they stand, have the corresponding objective liberties or restraints in their power to combine into facts. This is why Wittgenstein insists that "logic must take care of itself" (5.473) and adds, in the *Notebooks*, "all we have to do is to look and see how it does it" (p. 11). It is only a step from this to saying that *language* takes care of itself (cf. *Notebooks*, p. 43, entry dated 26/4/15), for the investigation is concerned precisely with the logic—but the *hidden* logic— of language. Behind the bewildering irregularity and complexity of the propositions we use in ordinary life (a kind of shorthand for the ideally perspicuous ideography in which logical form would shine forth beyond any possibility of misinterpretation) everything is in "complete logical order" (5.5563).

The "picture theory," which I have here merely sketched, must be fully elaborated before its formidable persuasiveness can be felt. One thing is clear, that it is an *a priori* conception, imposed upon the language we know for what seemed conclusive metaphysical reasons. The propositions we use in ordinary life do not much resemble "logical pictures," necessarily reflecting the logical form of reality. If we insist that they are so, nevertheless, that is because—from the standpoint of logical atomism—it looks as if they *must* be so. That there are genuine names, objects for which they stand, elementary propositions in direct contact with reality—all of this is the outcome of what might be called "transcendental" inference. We cannot lay our hands upon a single elementary proposition, nor could we recognize one if *per impossible* it came into our possession. So the desire to achieve clarity about "the logic of our language" necessarily involves us in a baffling search for the *hidden logic,* the ultimate but everlastingly concealed semantical connections that underlie the "accidents" of ordinary language. Our enforced ignorance of the ultimate logical form of the bedrock of language, the elementary propositions, is partly responsible, I surmise, for the abortive outcome of Wittgenstein's efforts in the *Tractatus* to analyze, at least in outline, the logical form of nonelementary propositions. That all of them must be extensional truth-functions of elementary propositions seems only a dogma, and an unproductive one at that.

An integral aspect of this approach to the "logic of language" is, as Wittgenstein later emphasized in the *Investigations,* a singularly "sublime" conception of that logic. Anybody who thinks, like Frege, of reality as timeless and unified can hardly be expected to admit of any objective vagueness or imprecision. If the essence of language reflects the essence of reality, it seemed to Wittgenstein in his youth, there must be in both a perfect unity, simplicity, order. This must be judged to be still another preconception imposed upon the vagaries of experience. As he said in retrospect: ". . . this order, it seems, must be *utterly simple.* It is *prior* to all experience, must run through all experience; no empirical cloudiness or uncertainty can be allowed to affect it—it must rather be of the purest crystal" (*Investigations,* § 97, p. 44).

Those who have no taste for metaphysical speculation in the grand style will find it easy enough to reject this conception of language as preposterous. But when Wittgenstein rejected it, in later life, he never condemned it as foolish. Nor is it. On the contrary, with all its incidental blemishes (the scrawls of a draftsman who had an irritable inability to fuss with details) it remains a grandiose and admirable construction, embodying, with unequaled boldness, ideas about the necessary character of language that have been obsessively attractive to many who have thought deeply about the problems that the young Wittgenstein raised.

## 5

Between the *Tractatus* and the *Investigations* there are dramatic shifts in mood, style, purpose. Turning from the earlier book to the later is like leaving the ruins of a Greek temple for a Baroque church. Or, to invert a remark of Conrad's (in his preface to *The Secret Agent*) one feels as if walking out of a plain into a forest—there may not be much light at first, but there is plenty to see. It would hardly be an exaggeration to say that the primary topic, still labeled "language," has undergone a drastic change. In the *Tractatus,* as we have seen, the search was for the unitary *essence* of language, the crystalline logical form that ordinary forms of expression conceal; but in the *Investigations* the emphasis is always upon what lies clearly in view (cf. § 92, p. 43), upon "perspicuously" arranging what is overlooked precisely because it lies in full sight. The author of the *Tractatus* fancied he could extort the hidden essence of language and the world by pure thought, so all his "conclusions" seemed fraught with inescapable necessity. But this was an illusion. We must *observe* language—as it is and how it actually works: "One cannot guess how a word functions. One has to *look at* its use and learn from that" (§ 340, p. 109). Wittgenstein now demands metaphysical innocence: he wants us to *look,* not to "think" (§ 66, p. 31).

So we are to search for particular kinds of description, obtained by unprejudiced observation, and not to be anticipated by *a priori* reflection. Characteristically, then, the earlier expression *"logic* of our language" is displaced in favor of "natural history." And in the "natural history" of linguistic behavior there will be no necessity—at least of the logical or metaphysical varieties. One might convert the earlier slogan, "Language takes care of itself" into the counter-slogan *"We* must take care of language."

But the "descriptions" in the *Investigations* are of a special sort. We need to remember Wittgenstein's own warning that "What we call 'descriptions' are instruments for particular uses" (§ 291, p. 99). The immediate "uses" of his own descriptions of language were to combat the "picture theory" of the *Tractatus.* More generally, he aimed at a distinctive type of philosophical clarification, by emphasizing those aspects of language whose neglect tends to generate metaphysical distortion. So there can be no question of completeness or of "scientific truth" in Wittgenstein's later description of language. Wittgenstein is no linguist in search of "linguistic invariants," or empirical generalizations of maximal scope; nor is he a philosophical "analyst" seeking to reconstruct language, or parts of it, into some tidier and "formalized" structure. He offers us, as he says, another "picture"—and even a good picture selects and omits, offers us "one out of many possible arrangements [*Ordnungen*], not *the* arrangement" (§ 132, p. 51). To use the description properly, we must treat it as it is intended—"as an object of comparison—as, so to speak, a measuring rod; not as a preconceived idea to which reality *must* correspond," (§ 131, p. 51).

6

What *do* we see, if we open our eyes to language as it is, and not as we thought it must be?

Above all, replies Wittgenstein, a congeries of public *activities*. An utterance is a social act, performed against a background that is partly verbal, partly not, and having, by convention, further social consequences. Utterances typically demand verbal responses and appropriately conformable actions. Integral to this approach is an initial emphasis upon what is directly observable: our attention is directed to such bodily responses as fetching objects, making drawings, and speaking. Imagining, hoping, wishing, expecting—whatever tends to be conceived as something "internal" does not count as an "activity." Wittgenstein is fighting the powerful inclination to locate meaning "in the mind" as some occult feature that breathes life into "mere words." From this standpoint, the use of words is no less, but also no more, mysterious than any other human behavior, and it is subject to the same kind of description or explanation: speaking and responding to speech is part of the "natural history" of man.

Words are not used in isolation—the apparent exception of one-word sentences notwithstanding. They are detachable components, like the cog wheels of a mechanism, designed for use in joint association: the simplest verbal act employs a full sentence—is articulated. But even a sentence is an abstracted feature of the situation in which it is used: its full meaning depends upon its verbal context (the discourse that precedes it), upon the inanimate setting (what speaker and hearer see, or think that they see), and upon the purposes, intentions, and understandings of the speech partners. So, after all, supposedly "inner" factors still remain crucially important. Contrary to popular misinterpretation, Wittgenstein is not a simple-minded behaviorist. Living, breathing human beings, banished to the wings by the logical purism of the *Tractatus,* are back in the center of the stage.

Wittgenstein typically admonishes his reader: "Ask yourself: On what occasion, for what purpose, do we say this? What kind of actions accompany these words? (Think of a greeting.) In what scenes will they be used; and what for?" (§ 489, p. 137). And he obeys his own admonition. When the need arises to make a distinction, to provide an explanation, or to frame a definition, he characteristically and helpfully asks, What *particular* misunderstanding is to be removed? (cf. e.g., § 87, p. 41) and What *specific* purpose is to be served? Or, What will satisfy you? In this way he brings the language of philosophical discussion down to earth, in renewed relation to those human problems that lend it interest and point. One might say that, in a certain sense, he takes philosophical problems more seriously than those classical philosophers who sometimes seem to be addressing a disembodied intelligence.

Wittgenstein's celebrated stress upon "use" rather than "meaning" is consonant with this enlarged and liberalized conception of the dependence of the utterance upon its animate and inanimate setting. The maxim of some of his followers: "Don't look for the meaning, look for the use," might usefully be regarded as a generalization of the Verification Principle (with which Wittgenstein flirted at one time). When a proposition is conceived as adequately expressed by some sentence, or symbolic formula, that is context-independent, an assumption that sometimes calls for radical manipulation of ordinary language, it is plausible enough to locate its meaning in some set of "truth-conditions." But anybody who thinks first, with the later Wittgenstein, of the sentence as tied to particular surroundings and contexts will find it more natural to think of the *role* played by it in relation to its users: the preferred analogy will not be that of a "picture" (a logical "representation") but a *tool.* (In any concordance of the *Investigations,* entries under "tool," "implement," "instrument," would be very numerous.)

Of course, Wittgenstein's maxims about searching for uses were never intended as panaceas: indeed, the notion of some automatic "decision procedure" for settling questions about meaning or use would have been in jarring discord with the tentativeness of his approach. His own statement is carefully guarded: "For a *large* class of cases—though not for all [notice that qualification]—in which we employ the word "meaning" it can be defined thus: the meaning of a word is its use in the language" (§ 43, p. 20). To describe the "use" of a word is, in some ways, still harder than to find a conventional definition of its meaning—if only because the entire background and setting must be brought into the description. To explain Hamlet you must talk about the play.

## 7

We have now arrived at the conception of an utterance as a distinctive feature of what might be called a speech *transaction,* in which words uttered in a determinate order and mode of combination, and perhaps accompanied by characteristic gestures and facial expression, are directed towards an identifiable receiver, in a definite setting, partly verbal, partly not, that partially determines the character, significance, and point of the total act.

But our notion of the "setting" is still too narrow, too

much focused upon the immediately observable. If we are to "see" all that is fully operative in the speech transaction, we must look beyond the immediate agents to the *speech community* to which they belong. Behind the directly observable speech episode, and powerfully affecting it, stands a *linguistic practice,* a system of conventional rules—a "grammar" in a broad sense of that word—specifying what may be said, and how, and when. Only because speaker and hearer know this "grammar," this system of received understandings, and know that both know it, can they communicate at a level of sophistication beyond that of sign language. The compelling analogy that immediately springs to mind, is that of some conventional game, such as chess, in which the significance of a particular "move," the specific act performed by a given player at some point in an actual game, derives from the system of rules that constitute the game. From a myopic perspective, what the chess player is "really" doing is shifting a lump of wood from one place to another: if that counts as "checking the King" the reason is that both players know and have accepted the system of conventions that qualifies what they are doing as "playing chess." Similarly, for such other human practices as conducting a trial, answering an examination, giving a promise—above all, in the supremely important practice of using language. If what I say to you, when I speak in a recognizable language, counts as more than mere sound, that is because both of us have been trained to treat such sounds as conforming to and exemplifying a certain "grammar," a system of rules of use—and trained to have the associated expectations. This "grammar" is supra-individual, inherited not invented, beyond the power of its users to change at will. Explicit or covert deviations are permissible, but that is a story for another occasion.

Wittgenstein's repeated reference to "language-games," when he might as well have spoken of "linguistic practices," is perhaps unfortunate as suggesting a more conventionalistic standpoint than he really held. The term "language-game" he says, "is meant to bring into prominence the fact that the *speaking* of language is part of an activity, or of a form of life" (§ 23, p. 11). Here "activity" no longer stands for particular actions in a speech situation, but rather for a type, or way, or mode of acting. In practice, the term "language game" also strongly suggests, as it was intended to do, the *systematic* character of speech and the dependence of the linguistic act upon the invisible context of the enveloping speech community. Questions about the proximate use of words in the immediate context send us back to the constitutive rules of the supporting *practice*. (But these rules are usually not "exact": language is seldom as clear-cut as chess.) This is why Wittgenstein says "To understand a sentence means to understand a language" (§ 199, p. 81).

## 8

But why does Wittgenstein immediately add "To understand a language means to be master of a technique" (*ibid.*)? The answer is that if we trace back the chain of reasons for its being correct to talk in a certain way (in a given language-game), we shall find at last only a certain general training or indoctrination, concerning which no further philosophical questions can be raised. A chain of verbal definitions has to end in words or constructions that are taught "ostensively," i.e., by precept and exhortation. There is not, and cannot be, anything in such basic linguistic training that "compels" the learner to generalize correctly—to "go on" as the teacher intends. He must, as it were, "pick up" what is required of him without further instructions. One might speak here of a "linguistic leap" as philosophers speak of an "inductive leap." Indeed learning how to use words lacking complete verbal definitions has much in common with inductive inference.

To take an example of the kind that Wittgenstein used to illustrate this fundamental point: Suppose a child who was taught arithmetic in the conventional fashion refused to "recognize" any number greater than a million—i.e., refused to write or read the corresponding numerals. Wittgenstein would insist that, in the face of such abnormal response to the training, there is, beyond a point, nothing to be done. Or, rather: there is no rational procedure to turn the arithmetical heretic into a conformist. You cannot prove that he is acting "wrongly." No matter how large, or how varied, the stock of paradigmatic instances used in the training, there are always infinitely many language games that could be played without inconsistency.

This being the case, the general agreement among human beings that in fact makes it possible for them to play the same language games—to speak the same language *on the whole*—is a remarkable fact, by no means to be "taken as a matter of course." That men constantly misunderstand, and not always willfully, is obvious enough; what is easily overlooked—in moments of pessimism, at least—is the extent of *de facto* agreement that makes the very existence of a shared language possible. Human beings do, on the whole "agree in the *language* they use. That is not agreement in opinions but in form of life" (§ 241, p. 88). Stress upon "forms of life" (*Lebensformen*) constantly reappears in the *Investigations*: the *Lebensform*, as manifested in the corresponding "language-game," must simply be taken as "given." It is a mistake to look for a further explanation (§ 654, p. 167): the language-game can only be noted, recorded (§ 655).

It seems to follow that to the extent that such fundamental "agreement" in judgment and action is absent—as say, in a conflict between a religious man and an equally sincere atheist—further rational *argument* is excluded. We can try to work upon the other by persuasion or intimidation, or we can practice an irenic tolerance, but we cannot talk to him, cannot make ourself fully understood. What makes sense to us will be nonsense in his language-game and vice versa. The limits of "agreement" are the limits of our languages: whereof one must radically disagree, thereof one must be silent. "What has to be accepted, the given, is—so one could say—*forms of life*" (*Phil. Inv.*, p. 226, italics in the original).

[259]

9

So much by way of summary of Wittgenstein's later views on language, inadequate as it must be as a substitute for the rich convolutions of Wittgenstein's own exposition. Any précis of Wittgenstein's later views must inevitably do violence to his method, with its insistence upon the value of the releasing, *"erlösende,"* example. Now for some critical comment.

Considered as a model of language, the account contained in the *Investigations* must be judged to be immensely superior to the "picture-theory" of the *Tractatus.* Where the earlier conception is rigid, dogmatic, even obscurantist, the later one is supple, adaptable, and, on the whole, admirably tentative. Wittgenstein's new model is—or ought to be—an effective prophylactic against *a priori* metaphysical prejudice: it has the extraordinary merit of facilitating further philosophical investigation. If Wittgenstein had lived longer, we can be certain that he would have modified many things found in the posthumous text of the *Investigations:* like Goya, he had the right to say at the end of his life "I am still learning." But certain features of the texts he has left us can easily arouse disquiet or misunderstanding.

I have reminded the reader of Wittgenstein's repeated emphasis in the *Investigations* upon the "public activity" that is intertwined with speech. Now this stress upon the directly observable is plainly appropriate for cases in which speech, to use an older terminology, has a mainly "practical" function of inducing an overt response. Wittgenstein's examples of language-games nearly always require actions conforming to *orders* or *questions.* See the many examples of such games in *The Brown Book.* Such attention to "activities" is however less immediately illuminating when applied to situations in which language is used in primarily "theoretical" ways, e.g., to argue hypothetically about alternative explanations of some anomalous phenomenon.

[260]

Consider the following case. There is a kind of game sometimes played by beginners at arithmetic which begins with the order "Think of a number"—and may then continue with supplementary orders such as "Double it, add 6, etc., etc." Now although "thinking of a number" is a language-game—or part of one—in Wittgenstein's sense, it does not fit smoothly into his model. To be sure, his usual insistence upon the purpose to be served by such "imagining" (i.e., the further moves in the game—cf. his remarks on naming as a mere preliminary to further activities) is well-taken. Yet it is hard to conceive of "thinking of a number" as a *public* act. We might imagine a still more primitive game consisting *only* of imagining numbers—perhaps for the sake of trying to avoid duplicating the choice of the other player. Would Wittgenstein say that the *announcement* of the imagined number was an essential feature of the game? Perhaps.

Or again: in the well-known and much discussed linguistic practice of *formally promising,* the promise-maker is required, by the accepted rules of the practice, to "be in earnest," to *intend* to keep his promise. To utter a promise-formula with a silent reservation is clearly not to play the promising game in the standard way. If a child did not understand this, he would not yet understand what it is to make a formal promise. Yet it would be perverse to assimilate intention and good faith to "activities"—nor would Wittgenstein have wished to do so.

In general, Wittgenstein's primary picture of an act of speech as a miniature drama in which overt actions are triggered by some utterance (a move in the relevant language-game) fails to fit, without distortion, many cases that come readily to mind: silent reading of a weather-report, composing a poem in one's head, and so on. This might have been expected. Every "object of comparison," and Wittgenstein's model of language is intended to be no more, will fail to work in *some* situations. This may be said about any instruments: the better for some uses, the more unfit for others. There are no universal tools and no universal models of

[261]

language. If this is overlooked, there is a danger of Wittgenstein's insights hardening into a new dogmatism. He himself said (on ending a course of lectures in 1939): "The seed I am most likely to sow is a certain jargon."

10

I have previously reminded the reader of Wittgenstein's insistence upon the diversity (the *"Buntheit,"* motley) of linguistic practices. In this he goes too far, perhaps. Reacting to the monolithic conception of language that dominated his early thought, he sometimes emphasizes the autonomy and independence of his exemplary language-games to an implausible degree. For instance, I cannot accept his suggestion that a primitive "language-game" designed for getting a builder's mate to fetch bricks and slabs (§ 2, p. 3) might be "the whole language of a tribe" (§ 6, p. 4). Wittgenstein says "we could imagine this": but I find that I cannot. It is hard enough to imagine, contrary to all that we know, a "tribe" lacking a full-blown language; harder still to imagine such a tribe with a vocabulary designed exclusively for giving orders to builders' assistants. What a queer "way of life" *that* would be. This is no better than trying to imagine chess played without a King—e.g., with pawns alone. As Wittgenstein himself said elsewhere (although in another connection): "There is not enough regularity for us to call it 'language' " (§ 207, p. 82).

A closely connected point, and a puzzling one, is Wittgenstein's admonition to treat his language-games as "complete" (§ 18, p. 8). In context, this is intelligible as a warning against imposing upon linguistic phenomena some *a priori* conception of what language *must* be like: but it cannot be treated as a general license for *any* kind of deviation from our given standards of "completeness," and hence also of correctness. Wittgenstein's challenge to his reader to consider what he means by "completeness" is not necessarily unanswerable.

Consider the following example, in the spirit of the exotic

"arithmetics" that Wittgenstein often invented in his later writings. We discover a "tribe" apparently possessing an arithmetic like our own, except in the disconcerting respect that its members seem to have no word or symbol answering to our numeral "7." If the reader will try to pursue this fantasy into its detailed implications, he will find the imagined situation surprisingly hard to describe—which is itself significant. If these eccentric arithmeticians fall silent upon being asked for the sum of 4 and 3, one is tempted to say that they must recognize the forbidden number in order *not* to name it—just as a subject under hypnosis, forbidden to see the ace of spades, must still be able to see it, in order not to "see" it.

Playing the game of arithmetic without the 7 would clamor for explanation—no matter how much we were admonished to take "ways of life" as "given." An intelligible explanation might invoke some superstitions or religious taboo, forbidding the *utterance* of the sacred name—so that 7 would be like the unpronounceable tetragrammaton of the Hebrews (which is, however, *written*). If this failed to work, because the evidence suggested that our tribesmen did not know what to say—even in the privacy of their own thoughts —in cases where we should say "7," we would be at a loss. This is how the fantasy breaks down when elaborated. It is easy enough to invent a fairy tale that introduces a man with an empty space between his head and trunk—but the details are apt to be troublesome. To say that the tribesmen had a mental "blind spot" for 7 would be to rephrase the puzzle without solving it.

It would be wrong, it seems to me (although strongly suggested by some of Wittgenstein's remarks), to rely on the formula "Well, that is just their language-game—that game is played!" On the contrary, I think we should be justified in saying: "We know that 4 and 3 make 7—and if these people fail to recognize it, so much the worse for them." This is neither dogmatic, nor an arbitrary expression of prejudice, because we can, after all, *prove* that 7 is the right answer. Of course, we need definitions and principles of inference, that the others might reject. But then we would either have to regard those "others" as stupid—or be utterly puzzled. A "way of life" that involves "violation" of principles of logic makes no sense, because we cannot attach any interesting sense to such a "violation."

Here is a point where the helpful analogy between language practices and games threatens to become sclerotic. A variation upon chess (say, without the Bishops) may or may not be called "chess" at our pleasure: since chess is wholly conventional, there really can be no question of its being uniquely correct vis-a-vis its possible variations. But our notion of arithmetic is different: here the notion of a correct answer—in a sense not simply analogous to the notion of a "legal move" in chess—is part of the practice. The concept of arithmetic, *as we have it,* does not permit the drastic variation envisaged in my foregoing example of the "arithmetic" lacking the 7. "Alternative arithmetic" does not make sense, in the way that "alternative geometry" does. Why should not the uniqueness of arithmetic be *part* of our idea of arithmetic? And how could such an idea be convicted of error?

I have not scrupled to use such normative words as "correct" and "right" in speaking about arithmetic, because they play essential roles in our use of arithmetical language. Similarly, it is an essential feature of logical language, in whose use our mastery of logical concepts is manifested, that certain modes of inference or transformation *count as* "valid," with corresponding normative implications. It is, however, a general weakness of Wittgenstein's conception of language—in the *Investigations* no less than in the *Tractatus*—that it overlooks the normative, appraisive, and evaluative aspects of discourse. I do not know whether this is a hangover from Wittgenstein's early flirtations with positivism and his lifelong preference for a non-naturalistic, "transcendental" ethics. Whatever the reasons, his omission to admit such words as "right" and "wrong," "correct" and "incorrect," into his survey of language impoverishes his vision. The language that we actually use—in Wittgenstein's phrase, the "language-games" that we do in fact play—sometimes have built-in standards of criticism that must be applied to imaginable variations of that language. This restricts our freedom to imagine "alternative" languages and prevents us from falling into the facile conventionalism which superficial reading of Wittgenstein's later work sometimes encourages.

## 11

Not *all* linguistic practices are acceptable: some can and should be criticized and rejected. One way in which such criticism becomes relevant is in connection with the background of presupposed beliefs and judgments which, as Wittgenstein usefully emphasizes, is integral to a given linguistic practice. "The common behaviour of mankind is the system of reference by means of which we interpret an unknown language" (§ 206, p. 82). Unless the behavior of the imagined "tribesmen" in our *Gedankenexperiment* sufficiently resembled our own, we could not recognize them as human and could not interpret their uttered noises as *language*. But we can understand them, sometimes, without accepting their prejudices and myths: If the system of beliefs incorporated into their language is provably erroneous, we may have good reasons for *rejecting* the language. I have heard a philosopher of neo-Wittgensteinan persuasion argue that the language of the Azande, who believe in the prevalence and efficacy of witchcraft, must simply be "accepted" because "that language game is played." He proceeded to assert that there was (could be?) "nothing wrong with their language"—indeed that questions of right and wrong "simply could not arise." To speak the language of the Azande is already to be committed, by the rules of that language, to belief in witches: so, if we wish to persuade them by rational

means, that is to say by using the only language they understand, we ourselves must believe—or at least speak as if we
believed—in witchcraft. This preposterous argument, this
facile and sweeping relativism, is not implicated by Wittgenstein's insights and must be regarded as a parody of his
intentions.

Yet Wittgenstein's own discussion of specific philosophical
perplexities sometimes encourages such a misinterpretation.
Consider, for instance, his elaborate examination of mathematical generalization—or, as he might say, the "grammar"
of the expression "and so on." We show a child the beginning of the series 1, 4, 9, 16, . . . , say, and ask him to "go
on." Well, says Wittgenstein, at some point he continues the
series independently—or else he does not (§ 145, p. 57). One
might get the impression that this is the end of the matter—
so that if, for instance, the learner chose to continue the
series with 16, 16, 16 . . . *ad nauseam* we would have no
recourse but to "accept" his performance as some kind of
inconvenient mutation from the intended routine. I doubt
whether Wittgenstein intended this: he was contending with
a strong inclination (one of the main sources of philosophical
mystification) to suppose that "being able to go on" *must*
consist in the occurrence of some occult mental event. As
directed against this model of understanding, his resourceful
parade of the multiplicity of relevant criteria for understanding how to "go on" does indeed have the desired "releasing"
effect. But it is one thing to be reminded of the complexity
of the concept of "understanding how to continue" and quite
another to deny that there is, or can be, such a thing as
understanding. (A hasty reader of Wittgenstein's later writing
is repeatedly liable to confuse analyzing with analyzing away:
that is one reason why Wittgenstein has been mistaken for a
behaviorist.) If a pupil is unable to prolong our series with
25, 36, 49, etc., he has so far failed to *understand* the plan
of construction of the series and can properly be condemned
as stupid. If it helps, we can supply him with the formula $n^2$
as a concise expression of the relevant plan. "But could he

not fail to understand that formula—and every further explanation that you might supply?" No doubt. It is important, however truistic, that "explanations must come to an end"—that, eventually, if the learner does not understand, there is nothing more to be *said*. But this does not imply that the fool is justified in his folly—or that we need feel abashed in censuring him, just because there may be, in the end, no way of explaining to him his mistake. It is a sign of folly not to be able to recognize folly as such.

12

If Wittgenstein's later theory of philosophical activity seems to reject the propriety of evaluation, his actual practice seems to be in flagrant conflict.

He says: "Philosophy may in no way interfere with the actual use of language; it can in the end only describe it. . . . It leaves everything as it is" (§ 124, p. 49). Yet in fact he is far from being as tolerant or as detached as this remark would suggest: When he exhibits an example of the metaphysical use of language (and after all metaphysicians have played *their* language-games for a long time) he does not leave it "as it is." Quite the contrary: the practice is stigmatized as "nonsense" in a pejorative sense, as language "running idly" and the like. It is ironic to contrast Wittgenstein's attitude towards "nonsense" with his tolerance of logical contradiction. Towards contradiction he does practice a degree of tolerance that logicians and mathematicians, whose practice he officially claims to be no more than "describing," emphatically reject. He chides them for attaching excessive importance to the logical paradoxes and recommends the use of systems in which inconsistencies are unimportant because we normally avoid stumbling upon them. Then why is he not equally complaisant about "nonsense"? Why does he want us to bump our heads on "plain nonsense" (§ 119, p. 48) in order to mend our ways? It will not do to say that nonsense is a more serious and insidious matter than contradiction: the one has its uses like the other—if only to reveal the limiting constraints of our grammatical rules. Wittgenstein will not accept the language games of his philosophical predecessors as a form of life that is simply "given"—he has his own language game, and a better one. But then the *critical* function of philosophical activity needs to be brought into the open—and not concealed behind a curtain of allegedly descriptive neutrality.

### 13

I have been arguing that the model of language presented in the *Investigations,* although a vast improvement upon the "picture-theory" of the *Tractatus,* still has serious limitations. And these limitations encourage misinterpretations of Wittgenstein's important insights. His over-emphasis upon speech as activity, in a narrowed sense of that word, permits some readers to label him as a behaviorist. In his desire to stress the complexity of what we mean by "understanding how to generalize" (or "knowing how to continue") he sometimes sounds like a dogmatic conventionalist. His almost willful neglect of the appraisive and evaluative functions of language provide a handle for the attribution to him of positivism. But Wittgenstein was neither a behaviorist, a conventionalist, nor a positivist, and his methods of investigation elude all such summary classifications. One of the great merits of his view of language is that it contained the means for its own supplementation.

# *Additional Notes and References*

## I. REASONING WITH LOOSE CONCEPTS

Originally published in *Dialogue,* 2 (1963), 1–12. For an earlier and more extensive treatment, see "Vagueness: An Exercise in Logical Analysis" in *Language and Philosophy* (Ithaca, N.Y.: Cornell University Press, 1949), pp. 23–58. For a recent criticism of my position, see Douglas Odegard, "Excluding the Middle from Loose Concepts," *Theoria,* 31 (1965), 138–144.

Formal investigation of the logic of loose concepts is now receiving a fair amount of attention. See, for instance, L. A. Zadeh, "Fuzzy Sets," *Information and Control,* 8 (1965), 338–353, and J. A. Goguen, "L-fuzzy Sets," *Journal of Mathematical Analysis and Applications,* 18 (1967), 145–174.

## II. THE JUSTIFICATION OF LOGICAL AXIOMS

A contribution to an international colloquium held in Warsaw, September 18–23, 1961. First published in the proceedings: Kazimierz Ajdukiewicz, ed., *The Foundation of Statements and Decisions* (Warsaw: Polish Scientific Publishers, 1965), pp. 65–71.

## III. THE GAP BETWEEN "IS" AND "SHOULD"

On its first appearance in the *Philosophical Reveiw,* 73 (1964), 165–181, this essay provoked a good deal of discussion.

J. R. Searle argued to conclusions consonant with my own in "How to Derive 'ought' from 'is,'" *Philosophical Review,* 73 (1964), 43–58. See also the more extended discussion in chapter 8 of his *Speech Acts* (Cambridge: Cambridge University Press, 1969).

## IV. RULES AND ROUTINES

A revised version of an address originally delivered at the Hebrew University, Jerusalem, December 8, 1965. First published in R. S. Peters, ed., *The Concept of Education* (London: Routledge & Kegan Paul, 1967), pp. 92–104. For further background, see my essay "The Analysis of Rules," in *Models and Metaphors* (Ithaca, N.Y.: Cornell University Press, 1962), pp. 95–139.

## V. INDUCTION

Originally published in Paul Edwards, *The Encyclopedia of Philosophy* (New York: Macmillan, 1967) IV, 169–181. © The Macmillan Company 1967. An extensive bibliography has been omitted.

## VI. PROBABILITY

This essay, which complements the preceding one, also appeared in the same *Encyclopedia,* VI, 464–479. © The Macmillan Company 1967. The bibliography has not been included here.

## VII. SOME HALF-BAKED THOUGHTS ABOUT INDUCTION

Originally prepared "as a birthday card in affectionate tribute to Ernest Nagel" for Sidney Morgenbesser, Patrick Suppes, and Morton White, eds., *Philosophy, Science and Method* (New York: St. Martin's Press, 1969), pp. 144–149.

## VIII. THE *RAISON D'ETRE* OF INDUCTIVE ARGUMENT

Reprinted from the *British Journal for Philosophy of Science,* 17 (1966), 177–204.

## IX. NOTES ON THE "PARADOXES OF CONFIRMATION"

First published in J. Hintikka and P. Suppes, *Aspects of Inductive Logic* (Amsterdam: North-Holland Publishing Co., 1966), pp. 175–197.

## X. AUSTIN ON PERFORMATIVES

From *Philosophy,* 38 (1963), 217–226. An important recent contribution to the growing volume of discussion of Austin's work is John R. Searle, *Speech Acts* (Cambridge: Cambridge University Press, 1969).

## XI. DEWEY'S PHILOSOPHY OF LANGUAGE

This was delivered as an address at Brandeis University on March 17, 1959, and published in the *Journal of Philosophy,* 59 (1962), 505–523.

## XII. WITTGENSTEIN'S VIEWS ABOUT LANGUAGE

An address to the Israel Academy, Jerusalem, on January 23, 1966, published in *Iyyun* (Jerusalem, Israel), 17 (1966), 1–16, 61–64 (in Hebrew, with English summary).

# Index

[273]